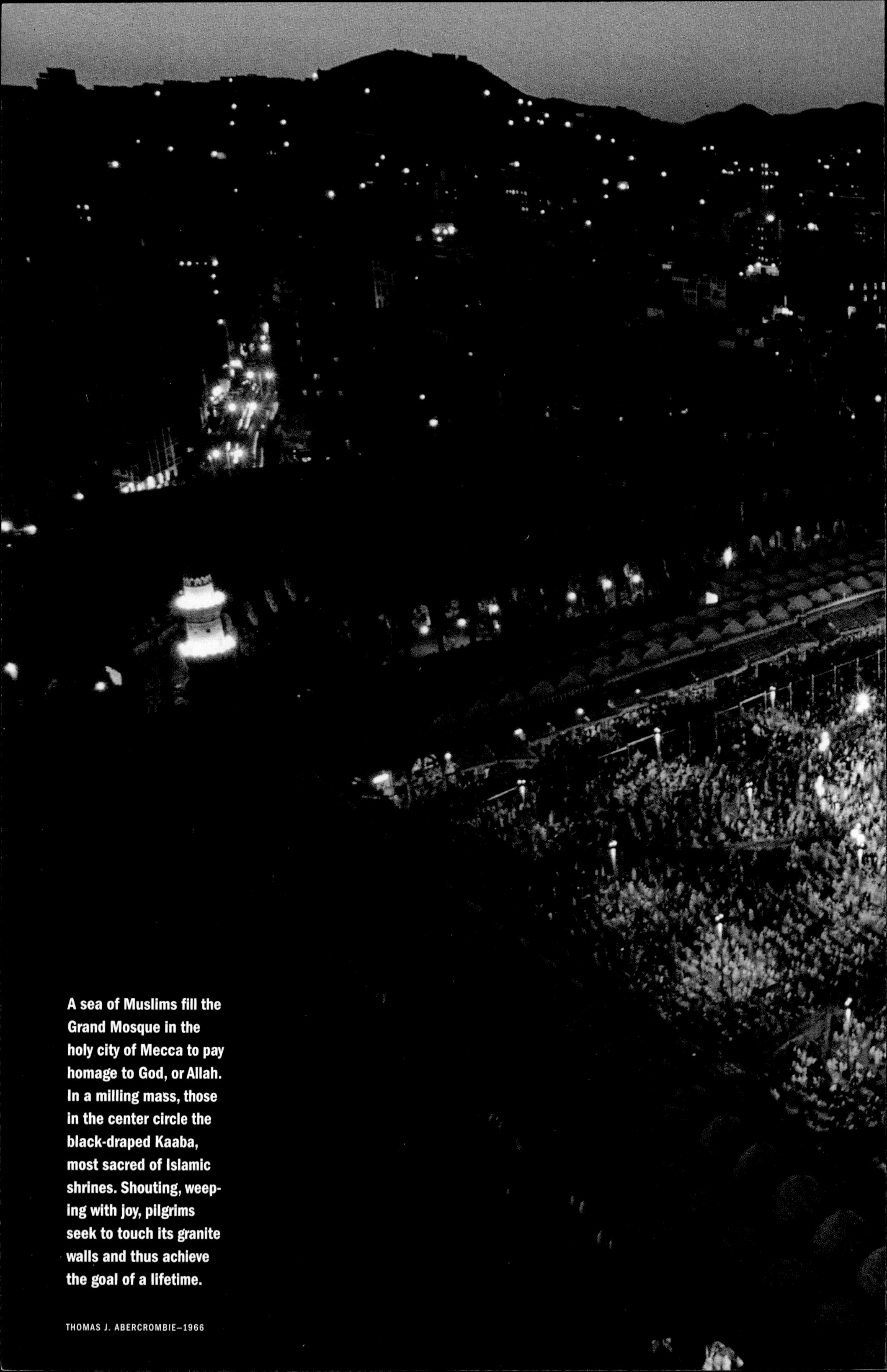

A sea of Muslims fill the Grand Mosque in the holy city of Mecca to pay homage to God, or Allah. In a milling mass, those in the center circle the black-draped Kaaba, most sacred of Islamic shrines. Shouting, weeping with joy, pilgrims seek to touch its granite walls and thus achieve the goal of a lifetime.

THOMAS J. ABERCROMBIE–1966

The
World
of
Islam

EDITED BY DON BELT

THE SACRED KAABA IN MECCA, PHOTOGRAPHER UNKNOWN—1917

NATIONAL GEOGRAPHIC

WASHINGTON, D.C.

CONTENTS

STEVE McCURRY–1991

Royal ornaments beyond price bedeck the Shah of Iran in 1967 at his self-coronation, where he appears face to face with a Muslim cleric. Twelve years later, another Muslim religious leader, the Ayatollah Khomeini, would overthrow the Shah.

A camel boy marches his charges past a Palestinian refugee camp near Nablus in what was then Jordan, and is now the West Bank. Following the creation of Israel in 1948, thousands of jobless Arab refugees lived in tented cities supported by the U.N.

Palestinian security
forces in Gaza raid the
house of a suspected
member of Hamas,
the Islamic Resistance
Movement. But all they
found here were the
woman of the house
and three empty
beds, still warm from
being slept in.

ALEXANDRA AVAKIAN—1996

Enemies join forces in Afghanistan's national army, as bearded *mujahidin*, holy warriors, train with clean-shaven Afghan communists, whose government lasted until April 1992. Soviet troops withdrew in 1989 after a decade of war killed 15,000 Soviets and more than 1.5 million Afghans.

FOREWORD

From the sands of the Sahara to the mountains of Afghanistan to the Pacific islands of Indonesia, *National Geographic* magazine has covered the world of Islam for more than a century.

Few Americans in 1914 had any knowledge of innermost Iraq when Frederick Simpich journeyed to the dusty pilgrimage town of Nedjef—only to be cursed as an infidel by an angry mob and chased out of town. But he took our readers along for the experience.

When Junius B. Wood motored from Jerusalem to Amman in 1923, the territory of Transjordania was brand new. Created by treaty makers in distant Paris—and many years before it would become Jordan—its boundaries were so fresh that "few persons more than 500 miles from its borders know where or what the kingdom is," Wood reported. And fewer cared. "Every man carries a long black-barreled rifle sticking up back of his ears— camel-drivers, peasants working in the little fields, and even the boys watching the herds of goats on the hills. Transjordania is of the desert, where everybody is his own policeman."

These were the days when our writers and photographers were literally the eyes of the Western world, revealing distant places and ways of life. Consider Simpich's chilling portrait of blood-soaked religious fanatics in Iraq in 1914 (a Shiite rite, during Muharram, that Fen Montaigne reports on in his 1999 story about Iran). Or the spectacle of thousands of pilgrims circling the holy Kaaba in Mecca in 1917. Or the adventurers of the Citroën-Haardt Trans-Asiatic Expedition driving past the troops in Afghanistan.

In later years our photographers continued to document pivotal moments in time: the Shah of Iran on the peacock throne in 1968; panicked spectators in the grandstands after the killing of Anwar Sadat in 1981; Afghan resistance leader Ahmad Shah Massoud praying in the shadow of a tank in 2000—all images brought to the world by *National Geographic*.

Looking back on some of our earlier articles, I was struck by how many of the observations by our earliest correspondents would be considered impolitic today. When they headed off on an assignment, our writers took with them not only the gear of their craft but also the baggage of their time and culture. Describing her visit to a Baghdad harem in 1914, Margaret Simpich admits feeling disappointed to find most of the women "absolutely commonplace; some of them even stupid-looking." I doubt if we would be that blunt today. More embarrassing are the patronizing attitudes and racial insensitivities that sometimes crept into print. Rather than delete these passages, we've chosen to leave them in, giving modern readers insights into the times in which these accounts were set down—and the men and women who wrote them.

As part of our coverage of the peoples of cultures of the Muslim world, we also offered glimpses of the inner life of Islamic devotion. Taking his family on the annual *hajj*, or pilgrimage, to Mecca, Muhammad Abdul-

Rauf describes the ecstasy of seeing the Kaaba for the first time: "I became suddenly dazed. My wife clung to my arm, trembling and sobbing. This time my daughter shuddered as if an electric current had shot through her, and my son was speechless. He later told me he was struck by deep feelings of sweet tranquillity." Hypnotized by the scene, Rauf focuses on "the humble man behind this spiritual fervor, whose teaching has molded the daily lives of these multitudes, giving them spiritual and moral guidance, certainty, and comfort and drawing them here from all corners of the globe."

Retracing the footsteps of the Prophet Muhammad for a July 1972 article, staff writer Tom Abercrombie, also a Muslim, fulfilled a personal dream of traversing that empire—"more far-flung at its zenith than ancient Rome's." Following Islam's historic armies and scholars, Tom found "a remarkable modern legacy of their power and learning. For the blood of desert-born conquerors still flows in the veins not only of sheiks and sultans, but of matadors and nuns and Bolsheviks as well."

What a tragedy, then, that Islam's message of achievement and peace could be so distorted by terrorists, as writer Edward Girardet reminded us recently, after traveling to Afghanistan for the story excerpted in these pages from the December 2001 issue. Confronted years ago by a tall bearded Arab who called him a *kafir*, or infidel, Ed got into a heated argument. The Arab, "haughty, self-righteous, and utterly sure of himself," proceeded to lambaste the West for its "feebleness and lack of moral conviction," finishing by threatening to kill Ed if he ever saw him again. Later Ed learned the stranger's name: Osama bin Laden.

The articles excerpted in this volume are a tribute to the toughness and insight of the writers and photographers of *National Geographic*, who had the grit to get behind the headlines to reveal larger truths. As eyewitness accounts, their words and photographs still possess a direct relevance to understanding the world of Islam today, a world our magazine will continue to explore with passion and curiosity for many years to come—even if it means getting chased out of town every now and then.

ANNIE GRIFFITHS BELT—1998

National Geographic **Editor Bill Allen, at left, and Don Belt, right, compare notes with a Bedouin friend at the mosque marking the tomb of Haroun—Aaron in the Bible—in Jordan.**

William L. Allen
Editor in Chief, *National Geographic*

INTRODUCTION

Borne aloft five times a day, from Shanghai to Chicago, Jakarta to Timbuktu, the music of Islam's call to prayer stirs the soul of devout Muslims everywhere. Whether cast from metal loudspeakers over teeming city streets or lifted as the murmured song of camel drivers kneeling in the sand, it begins with the same Arabic phrase Muslims have used for nearly 1,400 years, Islam's melodic paean to the Creator.

"*Allah . . . u akbar,*" the faithful sing out.

"*Allahhhhh . . . u akbar!*—God is great!"

Some 1.3 billion human beings—one person in five—heed Islam's call in the modern world, embracing the religion at a rate that makes it the fastest growing on Earth, with 80 percent of believers now outside the Arab world. For these people Islam is an intimate personal connection to the same God worshiped by Jews and Christians, a source of strength and hope in a troubled world.

The term itself, Islam, is an Arabic word meaning "submission to God," with its etymological roots firmly planted in *salam*, or peace. That may come as a surprise to many non-Muslims, whose perceptions have been skewed by terrorists, many from the Middle East, whose unspeakable acts in the name of Islam have been condemned by leaders everywhere.

"Peace is the essence of Islam," says Prince El Hassan bin Talal of Jordan, brother of the late King Hussein and a descendant of the Prophet Muhammad. Prince El Hassan helps lead the World Conference on Religion and Peace and spends much of his energy building bridges of understanding between the Muslim world and the West. "Respecting the sanctity of life is the cornerstone of our faith," he says, "and of all great faiths."

Like Judaism and Christianity, Islam traces its lineage to the prophet Ibrahim (Abraham), a wandering Bronze Age shepherd with whom God (*Allah* in Arabic) made covenants that became the foundation of the three faiths. Muslims revere the Hebrew prophets, including Moses, and regard the Old and New Testaments as an integral part of their tradition. They disagree with Christians about the divinity of Jesus but honor him as an especially esteemed messenger from God. The ultimate messenger for Muslims is the Prophet Muhammad.

Born about A.D. 570 at Mecca in present-day Saudi Arabia, Muhammad was an orphan raised by his grandfather and uncle. He grew up to be a modest and respected businessman who rejected the widespread polytheism of his day and turned to the one God worshiped by the region's Christian and Jewish communities.

At about age 40 Muhammad retreated to a cave in the mountains outside Mecca to meditate. There, Muslims believe, he was visited by the archangel Gabriel, who began reciting to him the Word of God. Until his death 23 years later, Muhammad passed along these revelations to a growing band of followers, including many who wrote down the words or committed them to memory. These verses, compiled soon after Muhammad's death, became the Koran, or "recitation," considered by Muslims the literal Word of God and a refinement of the Jewish and Christian scriptures.

The Koran consists of 114 suras, or chapters, and covers everything from the nature of God (compassionate and merciful) to laws governing the mundane affairs of men. Do not usurp one another's property by unjust means, it commands. Kill no game while on pilgrimage.

Its underlying message is "a prescription for harmony in everyday life," says Sheikh Anwar al-Awlaki, the *imam*, or spiritual leader, of the Dar al-Hijara Mosque just outside Washington, D.C. "In the Koran, God commands us to be merciful with one another, to live an ethical life. These concepts are not new, of course; the Koran confirms many of the teachings already laid down in the Bible. In many ways God's message in the Koran boils down to 'treat others better than they treat you.'"

For Muslims the Koran is also a poetic touchstone, a source of the pure Arabic language memorized by Muslim school-children and recited by Muslim adults on every important occasion—weddings, funerals, holidays. In a religion that forbids statuary and icons, this book is the physical manifestation of the faith, and small, tattered copies of it are found tucked into the pockets of every shop-keeper in the Muslim world.

SARAH LEEN—2001

Tracing out a prayer, a traditional healer in Mali consecrates dirt from the floor of the Great Mosque in Djénné so that it can be worn in an amulet.

Just as verses of the Bible can be pulled out of context and made to march to a zealot's cause, so is the Koran subject to distortion. A verse that counsels women to adopt modest dress and behavior is widely read as good practical advice; other interpretations supply the Taliban with a rationale to imprison Afghan women in their homes. Verses prescribing *jihad*, or struggle, against the enemies of God are usually taken to mean the internal striving of each individual for spiritual purity and enlightenment. Others describe Muhammad's armed struggle against his enemies and give the radicals of today a pretext, however twisted, for waging a holy war against nonbelievers.

Such interpretations cannot be overruled, because Islam is a faith without an established hierarchy; there is no Muslim pope, no excommunication of heretics. So while an imam can offer his congregants guidance and scholarship, in the end Islam's authority resides in its scripture, freeing individuals to interpret the Word of God in their own way. The Koran itself acknowledges this dilemma in Sura III:7: "Some . . . verses are precise in meaning—they are the foundation of the Book—and others ambiguous. Those whose hearts are infected with disbelief follow the ambiguous part, so as to create dissension . . . no one knows its meaning except God."

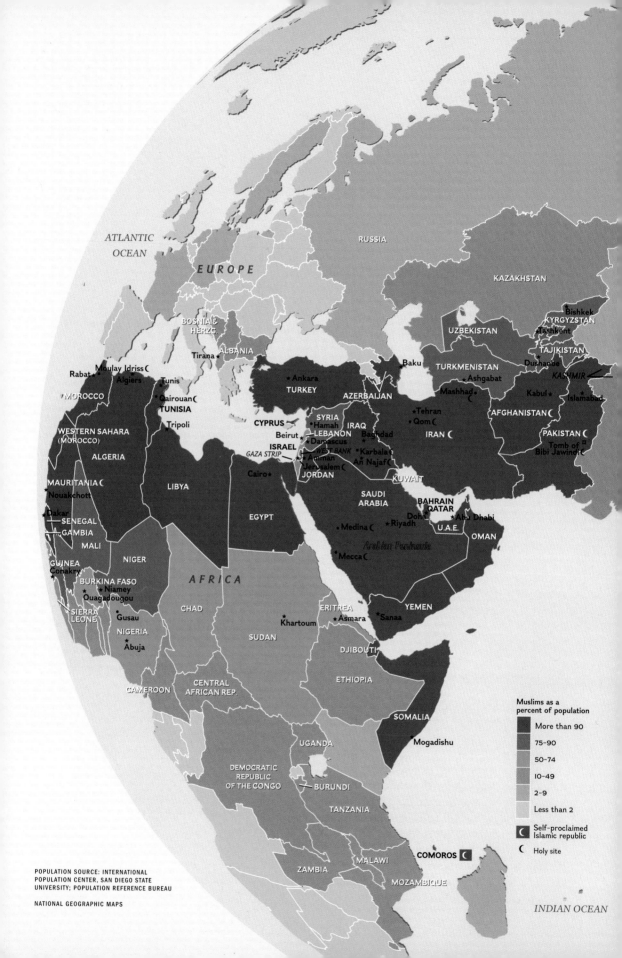

ATLANTIC
OCEAN

EUROPE

RUSSIA

KAZAKHSTAN

BOSNIA &
HERZG.

Tirana ★

ALBANIA

Baku

UZBEKISTAN

Bishkek
KYRGYZSTAN

Tashkent

TAJIKISTAN

Dushanbe

Rabat ★
Moulay Idriss ☾
Algiers ★

Tunis ★

TURKMENISTAN

Ashgabat ★

KASHMIR

MOROCCO

Qairouan ☾

TUNISIA

CYPRUS

★ Ankara

TURKEY

AZERBAIJAN

Mashhad ☾

Tehran ★

Qom ☾

Kabul ★

AFGHANISTAN

Islamabad

Tripoli ★

SYRIA
Hamah ★

IRAQ

Beirut ● LEBANON

Damascus ★

Baghdad ★

IRAN ☾

PAKISTAN ☾

WESTERN SAHARA
(MOROCCO)

ISRAEL

WEST BANK

Karbala ★

An Najaf ★

Tomb of
Bibi Jawindi

ALGERIA

GAZA STRIP

Amman ★
Jerusalem ●

JORDAN

KUWAIT

Cairo ★

MAURITANIA ☾

LIBYA

Nouakchott ★

EGYPT

SAUDI
ARABIA

BAHRAIN
QATAR

Doha ★

★ Abu Dhabi

Dakar ★

Medina ☾

★ Riyadh

U.A.E.

OMAN

SENEGAL

GAMBIA

MALI

Arabian Peninsula

Mecca ★

GUINEA
Conakry ★

NIGER

AFRICA

SIERRA
LEONE

Gusau ★

BURKINA FASO

Niamey ★

Ouagadougou ★

CHAD

ERITREA

Asmara ★

Sanaa ★

YEMEN

NIGERIA

Abuja ★

Khartoum ★

CAMEROON

CENTRAL
AFRICAN REP.

SUDAN

DJIBOUTI

ETHIOPIA

Muslims as a
percent of population

More than 90

75-90

50-74

10-49

SOMALIA

2-9

Less than 2

UGANDA

Mogadishu ★

DEMOCRATIC
REPUBLIC
OF THE CONGO

BURUNDI

☾ Self-proclaimed
Islamic republic

TANZANIA

☾ Holy site

COMOROS ☾

POPULATION SOURCE: INTERNATIONAL
POPULATION CENTER, SAN DIEGO STATE
UNIVERSITY; POPULATION REFERENCE BUREAU

ZAMBIA

MALAWI

NATIONAL GEOGRAPHIC MAPS

MOZAMBIQUE

INDIAN OCEAN

BY THE NUMBERS Some 40 percent of Muslims live in South and Southeast Asia, where Islam was carried by soldiers and traders. Thirty percent live in Africa, whose north became part of the Muslim world within a century of the death of Muhammad.

NUMBERS IN MILLIONS

Country	Muslims (millions)
INDONESIA	181
PAKISTAN	141
INDIA	124
BANGLADESH	111
TURKEY	66
EGYPT	66
IRAN	65
NIGERIA	63
CHINA	38
ALGERIA	31
ETHIOPIA	29
MOROCCO	29
AFGHANISTAN	27
IRAQ	23
SUDAN	22
UZBEKISTAN	22
SAUDI ARABIA	21
YEMEN	18
SYRIA	15
TANZANIA	13
RUSSIA	12
MALAYSIA	12
MALI	10
TUNISIA	10
SENEGAL	9
NIGER	8
AZERBAIJAN	8
SOMALIA	7
KAZAKHSTAN	7
GUINEA	6
BURKINA FASO	6
UNITED STATES	6
TAJIKISTAN	5
CONGO, DEM. REP.	5
LIBYA	5
TURKMENISTAN	5
JORDAN	5
CÔTE D'IVOIRE	4
CHAD	4
CAMEROON	4

The World of Islam

More than a fifth of humanity—1.3 billion people—follows Islam, which has become the world's fastest growing religion. Today Arabs represent only about 20 percent of the world's Muslims, with the largest populations found in Indonesia, Pakistan, India, and Bangladesh. In the western hemisphere most Muslims live in the United States, where they represent roughly two percent of the population.

God forbade religious coercion but directed Muhammad to declare his new faith among the people of his region—no small task, given the vicious tribal warfare and idol worship rampant in seventh-century Mecca, much of it focused on the Kaaba. This cube-shaped shrine was used for pagan rituals to honor a pantheon of deities. Muhammad and his followers were ridiculed and violently attacked for their belief in a single, unseen God.

After a decade of persecution Muhammad and his followers migrated to Medina, a city some 200 miles from Mecca, where the Prophet won more converts and eventually came to govern the town. After several years he and a small army of the faithful returned to Mecca, took the city, destroyed the idols of the Kaaba, and rededicated it to the God of Abraham. From that time to this, pilgrims have revered the Kaaba as the holiest shrine in Islam, reenacting the Prophet's journey to Mecca in the annual *hajj*, or pilgrimage, which draws as many as 2.5 million Muslims from all over the world to circle the Kaaba in the footsteps of Abraham and Muhammad.

"Islam gave me something that was lacking in my life . . . for the first time in my life I'm at peace."

One of the Five Pillars of Islam (along with fasting in the holy month of Ramadan, prayer, charity, and profession of faith), the hajj is required of all who can manage it at least once in a lifetime.

By the time the Prophet died in A.D. 632, Islam was established throughout the Arabian Peninsula, bringing peace and unity to the tribes for the first time in memory. Within a century of his death the armies of Islam, empowered by faith, had conquered a vast swath of territory stretching from India to the Atlantic coasts of Spain and Portugal, including North Africa and the Middle East.

This Islamic world built on the intellectual achievements of the Roman and Persian cultures it usurped, sponsoring an explosion of learning unparalleled until the Renaissance. According to historian Bernard Lewis of Princeton University, Islam's unsung heroes included its translators, who preserved the classics of the ancient world in "epoch-making" Arabic versions of Greek texts on "mathematics and astronomy, physics and chemistry, medicine and pharmacology, geography and agronomy, and a wide range of other subjects including, notably, philosophy." At a time when Europe was languishing in the early Middle Ages, Muslim scholars and thinkers were giving the world a great center of Islamic learning (Al-Azhar in Cairo) and refining everything from architecture to the use of numbers. At the same time, seagoing Muslim traders were spreading the faith to southern Asia, China, and the east coast of Africa.

As Europe rose to glory during the Renaissance, the Islamic world coalesced around the Ottoman Empire in the 14th century. This powerful state fell at the end of World War I, resulting in the subdivision of its mostly Muslim lands into the Middle Eastern countries we know today.

Although a few Muslim nations are wealthy from oil resources, most are poor and increasingly demoralized by their position in the world. Few Muslim societies enjoy the range of civil liberties that Western nations take for granted, such as freedom of expression and the right to vote in a fair election. And their populations are booming: Four people out of ten in Muslim countries are under the age of 15.

Disaffected and disenfranchised, many people in these societies are turning to Islam, and to Islamic political movements, to assert their identity and reclaim power over their own lives. In addition many Muslims, especially in the Arab world, are angry at the United States for its support of Israel, its military presence in Saudi Arabia, land of Muslim holy places, and its continuing economic sanctions against Iraq, which are widely perceived to have spared Saddam Hussein but hit the people of Iraq—fellow Muslims—right between the eyes. Muslim societies also have a long-standing love-hate relationship with U.S. popular culture, and these days those intense feelings may be closer to revulsion than respect.

"To many Muslims, especially in traditional societies, American pop culture looks like old-fashioned paganism, a cult that worships money and sex," says Imam Anwar al-Awlaki. "For such people, Islam is an oasis of old-fashioned family values."

Some Muslim nations, like Iran and Saudi Arabia, today base their governments on *sharia*, or Koranic laws and teachings, which are themselves subject to debate and interpretation. Others, like Malaysia and Jordan, combine these traditional principles of justice with more modern, secular forms of government and society. But for most of the world's 1.3 billion Muslims, Islam is not a political system. It's a way of life, a discipline based on looking at the world through the eyes of faith.

CHARLES O'REAR–1989

Raising Allah's name on high, a factory worker in Indonesia hoists a stylized ornament in Arabic script onto a spire built for a mosque.

"Islam gave me something that was lacking in my life," says Jennifer Calvo of Washington, D.C. Calvo, 28, was raised Catholic and works as a registered nurse.

"I used to get so depressed trying to conform to our crazy culture and its image of what a woman should be," she said, "the emphasis we put on looking good—the hair, the makeup, the clothes—and our hunger for material wealth. It left me feeling empty all the time."

Two years ago, as people have done for 1,400 years, Jennifer became a Muslim by simply declaring the words: "*La ilaha illa Allah, Muhammad rasul Allah*—There is no god but God, and Muhammad is his Messenger."

"Everything is so much simpler now," she said. "It's just me and God. For the first time in my life I'm at peace."

For Calvo and most Muslims on Earth, that is what Islam's call to prayer represents. Kneeling to God five times a day, in unison, facing Mecca from wherever they happen to be, they find peace in an act of surrender.

Don Belt
Senior Editor, *National Geographic*

Residents strike a relaxed pose inside a house in Qairowan, Tunisia. One of Islam's sacred cities, Qairowan in 1911 boasted 85 mosques and 90 religious schools.

PART ONE

FIRST IMPRESSIONS

1888-1922

Peering through the lens of Western culture, *National Geographic* explores the starkly unfamiliar: the world of Islam, in the twilight of the Ottoman Empire.

"Club life in Meso-
potamia," the caption
read in the April 1922
issue. "The outdoor
coffee-house is the club
of every town. Here the
men exchange opinions
on politics and trade."

ERIC KEAST BURKE—1922

A stream of horse-and-buggies fills a road in 1919 Palestine. During the Crusades, a Muslim force led by Saladin defeated a Christian army in the hills known as the Horns of Hattin, seen in the background.

According to legend, the minaret of the mosque at Mosul, Iraq, bowed its head to the Prophet as he passed—and was unable to regain its equilibrium.

Catching the Shah of Iran off balance, Muslim revolutionists (opposite) demanded the establishment of a national parliament in 1906.

Persia and Its Women

BY ELLA C. SYKES

■ **Editor's note**
*Ella C. Sykes was not
one to pull punches.
An Oxford-educated
traveler who came to
Persia with her diplo-
mat brother (Sir Percy
Sykes, who negotiated
the secret Sykes-Picot
Agreement of World
War I), Sykes gives the
Shiites of Persia a cool
appraisal in the Octo-
ber 1910 issue. To
prove her point, she
dishes up tart, closely
observed details in
the lives of the Persians
she encounters.
Though writing from
a "modern" European
perspective, Sykes does
succeed in penetrating
the veiled despair of
Persian women—and
bringing their world
to life.*

Ella C. Sykes, "A Talk About Persia
and Its Women,"
Oct. 1910, pp. 847-866

P ersia is one of the oldest empires in existence. It
has been a kingdom for 25 centuries—ever since
Cyrus the Great, about 550 B.C., conquered
Media and united that country to his under the name of
Persia. It has had many glorious episodes in its long
history; has produced the great teacher Zoroaster; such
world-famous poets as Firdawsi, Omar Khayyam, Saadi,
and Hafiz, and such great soldiers and rulers as Darius I,
Shapur I, and Shah Abbas.

Again and again the empire has been a prey to anarchy;
again and again conquering hosts have swept through the
country, Alexander the Great having many a successor, the
most destructive conqueror being Chinghiz Khan with his
hordes of savage Mongols—a leader who boasted that he
had slain thirteen millions of his fellow-creatures! At the
present day, though shorn of its former dimensions, Persia is more than
three times the size of France, yet it has only nine and a half millions of
inhabitants—15 to a square mile. As the population of the whole country is not equal to that of London, New York, and Paris combined, none
will be astonished to learn that it is possible to travel for days at a time
without coming across a village or even a human being.

In order to understand Persian domestic life at the present day, we
must carry ourselves back to patriarchal times. The Persian is lord and
master of his house much as was Abraham or Jacob. He has enormous
power over the persons of his wives, children, and dependants, all of

M. SEVRAGUINE

Author Sykes decried the disparity between males and females in Persian society, fixed at birth in families like this one, in Tehran.

whom he can treat much as he pleases.

When a woman is handed over to her husband with her dowry, he regards her far more as a chattel than as a wife. She may never show her face to any man save her husband and near relatives, and, owing to the extreme seclusion in which she lives, it is most difficult for her to get justice should she be ill-treated. There are certain laws for her benefit in such cases as that of divorce, but these are only enforced when a man divorces his wife.

If the case be reversed and the woman carries her slipper to the judge and demands separation from her husband, the latter is not obliged to refund the dowry that he received with her.

Brutal husbands who wish to be rid of their wives and yet retain their dowry sometimes ill-use them in order to force them to sue for a divorce themselves.

If a man is angered with his wife and says three times, "I divorce you!" he has legally severed himself from her, and, should he desire to have her back again, she will be obliged to marry and then be divorced by another man.

The happiness and position of a Persian woman usually depends upon her children. Her great wish is to present her lord with sons. "He that has no son has no light in his eyes" is a well-known saying, and a man feels that he is disgraced if he has no heir to carry on his name. When a child is about to come into the world two cradles and two little suits of clothing are in readiness. If a boy makes his appearance he is placed in a silken bed and clad in beautifully embroidered garments; but if a girl should arrive, to her falls the cotton cradle and the common attire. Her nurse goes in fear and trembling to break the news to the father, who may, in his anger, order the luckless woman to be bastinadoed instead of giving her the gift that would have been her due had she announced the birth of a son. From the moment of his entrance into the world, throughout his entire life and even in the hereafter, the Persian man has decidedly the best of everything and the woman the worst.

The man of well-to-do parents receives his education from a *mulla*, or priest, who teaches him to read and write, and to recite the Koran in Arabic, probably without understanding a word of the Mohammedan bible. At about eight years of age he is more or less separated from the women, and now practically lives with his father and with the latter's men friends, being in the charge of servants who teach him to ride and to shoot. His dress is that of his father's in miniature—the brimless astrakhan hat, the European trousers, the frock coat much kilted at the waist, the vest of Kerman shawl, and often the elastic-sided boots. He will accompany his father when visiting, and soon learns the elaborate code of Persian etiquette, being careful to address royalties, officials, church dignitaries, merchants, and so on by their proper titles, and deal out to each the right amount of courtly phrase.

H.R. SYKES

The author reports that a typical Persian woman, fearing unspeakable punishments in the afterlife, kept sins to a minimum and tried to make a pilgrimage to the holy shrine of the Imam Reza, in Meshed, at least once in her life.

He will be told to speak of himself as the *baudeh* or slave of any superior, but will be warned that it is considered sarcasm if he gives to any man more compliment than is his due.

The "strenuous life" finds no favor in Persia, the ideal of a young Persian being to act as a hanger-on at court, or to be included in the suite of some governor of a province or high official, such sinecures being spoken of as "doing service." The Persian, however, is a fearless rider and a keen sportsman. He loves to gallop his horse at its fullest speed, digging the points of his shovel-shaped stirrups into its ribs to urge it to yet greater efforts; and then he will pull it up suddenly with the severe Persian bit.

H.R. SYKES

Or he will take part in a gazelle hunt, making one of a large circle of horsemen, who gradually hem in a small herd of these shy animals, drawing closer and closer until the terrified *ahu* attempt to break through the ring. Then the sportsmen fire at their quarry, Persians being so reckless in moments of excitement that sometimes the riders get shot instead of the game.

The well-to-do Persian is roused before sunrise by the call of the *muezzin* summoning all men to prayer. He throws aside the padded quilts that form his bed, hastily dons his garments, and exchanges the felt skull-cap in which he sleeps for the black lamb's-wool hat.

His servant then pours water over his hands, and he washes his face, arms, and feet before prostrating himself on his prayer-carpet, which is turned in the direction of Mecca.

When a Persian reaches manhood his parents busy themselves in arranging a suitable marriage for him. As he has never looked upon the face of any lady, unless she be a near relative, he has absolutely no choice in the matter.

His mother selects his fiancée and he is not supposed to meet her until the public betrothal by a priest takes place. If he then dislikes what he sees of a face that is almost disguised with rouge and powder, he can draw back, but he has to hand over to the girl's parents half the value of the dowry that he would have received with her, and, moreover, he is socially disgraced. Marriage is, however, by no means such a serious matter as it is in some countries. The Prophet permits his followers to have four wives apiece and as many temporary connections as they please, and we have already explained how easy it is for a man to rid himself of an uncongenial helpmate.

Moreover, many Persians have no home life in the usual sense of the word. A Persian house is divided into the *birooni*, or men's apartments, and the *anderoon*, or part consecrated to the women. A strong door, set in a high blank wall, gives entrance to a narrow passage that leads into a square court-yard on which open several rooms. Here the men live, and here they usually feed and entertain their friends, while their women dwell in rooms set round an inner courtyard, the only entrance to which is through the birooni.

As a Persian is instructed from earliest youth that a woman's advice is of no account—in fact, the priests tell him that he had better do the exact opposite of what a woman counsels—it can be understood that as a rule he has no exalted opinion of his wife or wives, and seldom turns to them for companionship.

And now I will ask the reader to turn to the life of the Persian woman and contrast it with that of her lord and master.

Often she comes into the world unwanted and meets with no welcome, and through life she is usually neglected and made of little account. Sometimes she is educated with her brothers up to the age of eight, but after that she is separated more or less from them and is relegated to the anderoon.

In Persia it is rare to find a woman who reads or writes, and a girl will employ her time in embroidery, in making sweetmeats and sherbets, and in much gossip with her women friends and servants.

Her indoor dress in summer is a gauze jacket, and very full, short trousers that do not reach to the knee, this latter garment being introduced by Nasr-ed-Din Shah, who was greatly fascinated with the costume of the Paris ballet girls.

A Persian lady cuts her hair in a straight fringe across the forehead and

Turning their backs to the camera, two women on a street in Persia contrast sharply with a boldly staring man. When Sykes wrote this story in 1910, Persian men and women led separate lives, right down to their living quarters.

mixes her tresses, if not abundant, with horsehair; but she always covers her head with the chargat, a handkerchief of fine muslin that she wears by day and night, and which it would be the height of impropriety to remove.

In appearance she has fine eyes and good features, small hands and feet, and a figure usually too stout for European taste, while, owing to her secluded life, she often looks dull and unintelligent. Her fondness for cosmetics leads her to rouge and powder her face most inartistically, and she uses *kohl* to impart a languishing look to her eyes and to double the width of her eyebrows, making them sometimes meet at the bridge of her nose.

When a woman wishes to leave the anderoon her dress is a complete disguise. She draws up to her waist a garment, socks and trousers in one, and over this she drapes the *chadar*, a large black wrap covering her from head to foot. Hiding her features is a white silk or cotton cloth with just a strip of lace-work across the eyes, and death would be the penalty were a man rash enough to raise that face-cloth. Heel-less, flapping slippers complete a costume which is almost suffocating in the summer heat, and which at any time makes its wearer look like a waddling bundle.

The public bath is the Persian woman's chief dissipation. Here she meets her friends and spends many hours in the hot, steamy atmosphere, while her servants dye her hair with henna and indigo and tint her nails and the tips of her fingers and toes with the scarlet juice of the former plant.

Perhaps she will go to the mosque on Friday, but if she does so she will be confined in a closely latticed enclosure from which she can see and hear but little of the proceedings.

Of course marriage is the great crisis in a girl's life, but in this, as in every thing else, she has no choice. Her parents often have no idea of consulting the tastes of their daughter, and girls are sometimes handed over to men old enough to be their fathers or even grandfathers; there is also much marriage among cousins in order to keep the property of a family together.

Once married, the young wife's strongest wish is to become the mother of a son, for she knows that her husband's affection, and, in fact, her entire position, depends on this. If no son is born to a man he will take to himself a second wife, or perhaps divorce the first, and it may easily be imagined what jealousy and heart-burning are roused if there are rival wives in the same establishment.

In any case a wife cannot be a real companion to her husband. It is not etiquette for him to be seen with her in public; he may not salute her should he recognize her in the street; her secluded life prevents her from knowing what is going on in the world, and she is not acquainted with any of his friends, nor can he meet any of hers. Consequently he spends his days apart from her and usually eats with his men friends, the women of the household finishing what he may leave.

A woman's great consolation lies in her children, there being much filial piety in Persia, though the son's love for his mother has apparently no influence on his behavior toward his wife.

When a woman becomes old her thoughts turn often to the other world, and she makes up her mind to go on a pilgrimage. The Prophet, it is related, when permitted a glance into hell, found that the great majority of the victims writhing in torment were women. As lions with 7,000 teeth and vipers with 7,000 fangs mingle with fiends, all working away with a will to torture the luckless inmates of the infernal regions, most women would count no effort too great to escape from such a doom. Only by a life of unremitting virtue can they attain to a paradise into which apparently any man may enter with comparative ease.

A woman knows, however, that a pilgrimage to Mecca, Kerbela, or Meshed will save her from the terrible Mohammedan hell, and she cajoles what money she can from her husband, sells her jewels, and starts off with a party of friends and servants. Meshed, being in her own country, is probably the goal of her journey, and what a journey it is for a woman well advanced in years and unaccustomed to exertion! If she cannot afford the swaying takht-i-ravan, or litter, she must sit cramped up in a *kajaveh*, or pannier, strapped on one side of a mule, or else ride astride on a rough pack-saddle. However hot may be the weather, she must keep her face covered up and her figure shrouded in the all-enveloping black cloak.

At sunset she will arrive at some caravansary; her servant will sweep out a recess for her, will hang a carpet before the opening, and spread out her *resais*, or cotton quilts, and all night long she will hear the noise of mules and the talk of the muleteers, and will probably be troubled by the insect life which is very active in these rest-houses.

Day after day her mule jolts her over great plains destitute of a single tree and with only veitch or camel's-thorn sprinkled on the gravelly soil. She will cross the ranges by passes that lead into other plains, the replica of those which she has traversed; her food will probably be insufficient, and she will be forced to drink water often brackish and sometimes absolutely foul, for she has no filter with which to purify it.

At last, coming to the crest of a hill, she sees the glint of a gilded dome and knows that the goal of her journey, the sacred shrine of the Imam Reza, is not far off, and that from henceforth she will bear the proud title of *Meshedi*.

When a Persian woman dies the hired mourners arrive to weep and lament; all water in the house is thrown away lest the inmates be afflicted with colic; a priest recites the Koran, and the corpse is placed in the coffin with a stick under each armpit.

This is for the purpose of enabling the deceased woman to raise herself when the blue-eyed angels come to question her as to her orthodoxy. If she can answer to their satisfaction her coffin will expand to the size of a room, but if they are not pleased with her, her last resting-place will close in upon her, all animals being able to hear her shrieks of agony as she is thus tormented. Even if all goes well, she has to pass the Bridge of Sirat, "finer than a hair and sharper than a sword," which spans the fires of hell, and only a minority of women can tread this in safety and enter into the regions of the blessed.

Here apparently the Prophet did not contemplate that husbands and wives should meet one another again, and we find that the women are relegated to a paradise of their own with angel attendants. In fact, this glimpse of the life of a Persian woman assuredly bears out my contention that she has the worst of it in every way, from the moment of her birth even to her life in the world beyond the grave. □

The Persian man has decidedly the best of everything, and the woman the worst.

■ *"Here was old Arabia in original bindings,"* observes Frederick Simpich at one point in *"Mystic Nedjef, the Shia Mecca."* By the time his night in the holy city was over, he'd been taken for a Christian and chased out of town by a mob, but not before he'd gotten a good long look at the place, so as to render the sights and sounds and smells (especially the smells) for his readers. Early field men like Simpich were tough old birds; they carried their biases with them and didn't hesitate to commit them to paper. But rather than reedit these old stories for modern tastes, we chose to present them as they are—frayed around the edges, perhaps, but still in their original bindings.

Frederick Simpich, "Mystic Nedjef, the Shia Mecca," Dec. 1914, pp. 589-598

Journey to Shia Mecca

TEXT AND PHOTOGRAPHS BY FREDERICK SIMPICH

F ew white men of any race have made the pilgrimage to mystic Nedjef, the Mecca of Shia Mohammedans and one of the marvels of inner Arabia. It is five days by mule or camel caravan from Baghdad to Nedjef, and in the eventful centuries since the Shias founded Nedjef—on the spot where a nephew of the Prophet Mohammed was slain—it is estimated that over 25,000,000 Moslems have made the pilgrimage to this mysterious desert city of golden domes, fabulous treasures, and weird rites.

"Furious fanatics" is how Simpich describes this bloody scene at Nedjef. In annual rites of self-laceration, Shiites grieve for Husayn, the Prophet's grandson, who was martyred nearby in A.D. 680.

Thousands of devotees from the Shia hordes of India, Persia, and South Russia flock through Baghdad each year, bringing with them their mummified dead—salted and dried—for burial in the holy ground about the mystic city. By camel caravan and winding mule train the patient pilgrims make the long march; many from distant Turkestan are a whole year making the round trip. To help handle the throng that pours through each spring and autumn, enterprising Baghdad Jews have established an *arabanah*, or stage line, from Baghdad to Kerbela, the half-way town on the desert route to Nedjef. And for a taste of stage-riding in Arabia, I started my journey by arabanah, a four-wheeled coach drawn by four mules harnessed abreast.

It was 2 o'clock on a starlit morning when I walked over the rude bridge of boats that spans the Tigris at Baghdad, ready for an early start from the west bank. Soon the jolting, noisy coach was in motion, the Arab driver cursing the religion of his four mules and plying his long whip of rhinoceros hide as we whirled away through the still empty streets. Only a few watchmen, shouting occasionally to keep up their courage, and the eternal vagabond dogs of Baghdad were astir.

Through the outlying Sunni cemetery we rolled past the beautiful tomb of Zobeida, favorite wife of Harun-al-Rashid, past the white tents of sleeping Turkish troops, through a gap in the ruined wall, and out onto the gray desert. The mules galloped evenly on, the wheels hummed, and we seemed to float over a sea of haze that lay on the desert, bathed in starlight.

Halfway to Kerbela, and scattered for a mile along the route, we passed a caravan taking corpses for burial at the holy city of Nedjef. Among the dead was the body of a Persian nobleman. Three hundred paid mourners, who had come all the way from Teheran, sent up their weird chant as we passed.

Strict as are the Turkish quarantine regulations, badly "cured" bodies or bones are often smuggled in from Persia, and on a hot day the wise traveler will stay at a discreet distance from these death caravans. The odor, when noticeable, is peculiarly penetrating and sickening.

It is a month's marching from Teheran to Kerbela, and these dismal persons had wept all the way.

All about us lay the flat, empty world. Not a tree, a shrub, a plant, or a bird—not an object, dead or alive—broke the vast stretch of sun, sand, and silence. Only the muffled footfalls of the plodding mules, or the soft, slopping sound of water splashing in the goatskins, came to our ears. At times we rode up and down over billows of gray sand, stretching away to the right and left in endless swells like giant furrows.

The day was well spent when we came upon the mean, mud-walled *khan* built at the wells marking the half-way resting place. Already others who traversed the desert had reached the friendly spot. They proved a caravan from the busy Euphrates town of Kuffa, and were on their way to the stronghold of the Amir of Nejd. Rumors of fighting between Arab clans on their direct route had sent them on this roundabout course. Half a hundred pack-camels laden with bales of Manchester "piece-goods," bags of rice, and Marseilles sugar in blue cones, lay about, chewing contentedly, or nosing among the meager clumps of camel's-thorn which grew about the camp.

The rough, half-clad camel drivers rested on their haunches, talking volubly and plying my servant with questions as to my nationality, destination, wealth, family relations, etc. Off to themselves, the two *zaptiehs*

Near this mosque outside Kerbela, author Simpich passed a caravan bearing the body of a Persian nobleman to be buried at Nedjef. Three hundred paid mourners had accompanied it during the month's march from Tehran, he reports, weeping all the way.

ate, smoked long Baghdad cigarettes, and talked in low, droning voices.

Sleep is sweet in the pure air of the Arab desert, and soon I lay dreaming. Only once I was awakened, when a restless camel came sniffing near. Overhead burned the planets, big and steady in their glare, like nearby arc lights. About rose the snores of tired, sleeping Arabs; the bulk of herded camels loomed large, and I heard the low crunching of their rolling cuds. The glow of the night watch's cigarette came to me from one side; in Bedouin camps no one knows the hour when desert thieves may come.

The next day we followed our course, as on the day previous, through seas of sand. Toward noon we met hundreds of Persians returning from the pilgrimage. All the men could now dye their beards red and enjoy the title of *Hahji*—one who has made the *Hahj*, or pilgrimage. Soon I, too, would become a Hahji, for Nedjef was now near at hand.

The sun was nearly down, sliding like a fire ball from the copperish sky, when we caught the first glimpse of holy Nedjef. First the great gold dome of its mosque, burning in the sun rays; then, as we drew nearer, the high, frowning walls that surround the sacred city came into view. It was a gorgeous spectacle, mirage-like vision, as of a mighty city floating in the air. The high, sharp walls shut it off abruptly from the desert, and it seemed a mighty thing apart from the surrounding sea of sand. In a few moments we were passing through the acres of graves outside the walls and soon arrived at the city gate.

We spent the night in a fairly comfortable khan, sleeping on its flat mud-roof, Moorish fashion. From the house tops about came the dull rattle of tom toms and the sound of Arab women's voices, singing to the accompaniment of their jangling tambourines. Two captive desert lions, caged on a roof near the khan, roared at intervals during the night, and each time they roared I awakened, startled by the unusual sound.

Nedjef is a freak city. Not a green thing—a plant, shrub, or tree—lives within its dry, hot limits. It is built on a high plain of soft sandstone. The narrow, crooked streets, in many places mere passages three or four feet wide, wind about like jungle paths. But for the four zaptiehs sent with me as a guard by the friendly Kaimakam, I must soon have lost my way when I set forth to see Nedjef.

Turning from the native quarter, we came to the long straight bazaar leading to the mosque. I was struck with the difference in the looks of the Nedjef people and the crowds at Kerbela. Few Persians were about; the folk seemed all Arabs. Many uncouth, swaggering desert men were among them, their long hair, faded dress, and camel sticks, or oversupply of guns and side-arms, marking them as from the wild places. There was a spirit of crude, barbaric primitiveness in the crowd that surged past. The little touches of outside influence one sees at Baghdad, like an occasional European hat or an imported overcoat, were all lacking at Nedjef. Here was old Arabia in original bindings.

The mosque we came on suddenly, for the crowded bazaar street ends in an open plaza before this dazzling structure. In amazement I gazed on its wonderful facade; golden tiles and fancy silver work rise above and about the great portal, and across the wide entrance is hung a giant chain of brass, worn smooth and shiny from contact with the millions of turbans, *tarbooshes*, and *keffeyehs* which have brushed under it in centuries gone by. This chain is so hung that all who enter the mosque must bow.

Through this open gate, from where we stood, some 20 yards back, I could see the base of the great mosque itself. To my profound surprise, the great gold tiles which cover the dome also run to the very base of the mosque! And on the inside of the walls about the court were more gold tiles. Above the outer portal, too, on the outside, were sprawling Arabic characters 20 inches high, seemingly cut from sheets of gold!

Lost in admiration of the splendid structure before me, I had failed to note the gathering crowd of Shias who now packed the plaza about us. It was the anxious voice of the zaptieh urging that I move away that finally roused me. In an instant, it seemed, fully 200 people had gathered in the small square before the mosque and were glaring at me and asking why and whence I had come.

One zaptieh, feeling my dignity assailed, foolishly struck or pushed a Shia who had cursed my religion and spat at me. A serious disturbance seemed about to break out, but we managed to slip away through a narrow side passage and thus avoid the crowd. As it was, a hundred or more men and boys followed, nor left off until we passed through the south gate of Nedjef and out onto the desert for safety.

More human bodies are buried in the plain outside the walls of Nedjef, it is said, than in any other one spot on Earth.

Myriads of fancy tombs, terminating at the top in little blue-tiled domes, rise from the plain. I asked how many might be buried there. "Allah knows all their names," said a zaptieh, simply. And all the millions of pilgrims who have come in ages past with corpses for burial have also brought money to spend. The richer the man who brings the body, the greater the toll taken. Twenty thousand dollars was spent on one funeral.

Burial sites within view of the great mosque bring a high price. The Turks put a tax on every corpse imported from India, Persia, etc. Many bodies are smuggled in. It is told of one astute Persian pilgrim that he divided his grandfather's skeleton and sent it in separate parcels by mail to save freight and tax.

When a death caravan reaches the outskirts of Nedjef, they unpack their gruesome baggage and prepare the various bodies for burial. The crude methods of embalming or mummifying would expose Nedjef to disease were it not for the dry desert air. The very few folk of Nedjef who work for a living make money manufacturing fancy shrouds, stamped with Koranic sentiments, for the burial of corpses brought in by the pilgrims.

As crooks prey on the crowds that throng our "world's fairs," so a large criminal element thrives in Nedjef, living off the timid pilgrims. Gamblers, thieves, and sharpers abound, and few pilgrims leave Nedjef with money. Many fall by the wayside and eke out the life of beggars on the streets of Kerbela, Baghdad, etc.

In all of this unnatural city I saw not a tree or shrub; not even a potted plant. It is a dry, prison-like place of somber gray stones and mud-plastered walls. Remove its mosque, its one priceless possession, and Nedjef, with its horde who live on those that come to pray, would perish from the Earth. In the 1,200 years of its eventful life, not one useful article has been manufactured within its fanatical precincts.

Yet in all Islam, Shias turn to Nedjef to say their prayers. To Nedjef every good man must make the pilgrimage once in his life, and at Nedjef he hopes to be buried when he dies. ▯

Lost in admiration of the splendid structure before me, I had failed to note the gathering crowd of Shias who now packed the plaza about us . . .

Inside a Baghdad Harem

BY MARGARET SIMPICH

■ *Any reader of the* Arabian Nights *has a vivid mental picture of what life in a Middle Eastern harem would be like. But as Margaret Simpich makes clear in this account, her romantic visions soon gave way to a surprisingly drab, though keenly observed, reality.* This is National Geographic's *first report from inside the harems of the Muslim world—but it wouldn't be the last.*

Frederick and Margaret Simpich, "Where Adam and Eve Lived," Dec. 1914, pp. 546-588

From the first day at Baghdad I felt the subtle charm of the East—that mystic spell that seizes on the souls of those who trespass on its ancient places—and here every law of the life we know seems changed. Between us—women of the West—and these daughters of the desert is a gulf, impassable and not of our own making; it is a barrier of religion—a religion that allows one man to have four wives at once.

In Baghdad I went to an Arab harem and visited with the *hareem*, as the women are called. It was not an ordinary, ill-kept harem of a common trader or desert sheik that I saw. It was the ornate domestic establishment of a rich and influential person—a former government official and a man of prominence in the days of Abdul Hamid.

I went one Sunday morning in spring. The Pasha's imposing home—a Moorish house of high walls, few windows, and a flat roof with parapets—stands near the Bab-ul-Moazzam in Baghdad. Scores of tall date palms grace the garden about the *Kasr*—palace. In a compound beside the palace pure Arab horses stood hobbled, and a pack of desert hounds called *slugeys*, used for coursing gazelle, leaped up at my approach.

The dignified old Pasha himself escorted me through his domain. Clad in shining silk, turban, flowing *abba*, and red shoes with turned-up toes, he looked as if he might have just emerged from the dressing-room of some leading man in a

"The road to Baghdad is devious and long," the author notes. En route to her experience in the harem, Simpich passes **"peculiar double-decked horse-cars."**

modern musical comedy. His make-up was common enough for Baghdad, but to me he seemed positively "stagey;" but he was all affability, talking brightly in very fair French. He showed me a remarkable falcon—a hawk only three years old, with over 200 gazelles to its credit. In a cage near the palace door were two lean, gray lions, trapped in the jungle marshes along the Tigris. Finally we entered the corridor leading to the *bab-el-haremlik*, or gate to the harem.

During all the talk about horses, dogs, and lions I had been consumed with curiosity to say something about the human harem pets of the old Pasha; but in Arab eyes it is a gross impertinence to ask after the women in a man's family. Like as not he would reply that the "wretched creatures are barely keeping alive." So I had to wait till the Pasha himself spoke of his harem and asked me to come and see its beauties.

As we walked toward the doorway of the walled, windowless structure, wherein the women were imprisoned, my fancy rioted with visions of languorous Eastern beauties in baggy bloomers and gilt slippers. I thought of all the insipid, maudlin rot slung from the false pens of space-writers whose paths never led to this maltreated East. I thought of marble baths, wherein olive-skinned beauties lolled, as in the toilet-soap advertisements. I thought of precious perfumes and beveled mirrors 30 feet high, of priceless jewels blazing on beautiful breasts, and of bronze eunuchs waving peacock fans, while sinuous serving maids gently brushed the soft tresses of some harem favorite; but these dreams did not last long.

Almost before I knew it we had passed the great bolt-studded gate, stepped from behind a tall screen of hideous Persian tapestry, and were within the sacred precincts of the harem itself. The interior was a great square court, surrounded on three sides by small rooms—the individual rooms of the Pasha wives and women folk. On the tiled floor of the court was strewn a variegated lot of cheap Oriental rugs and *passats*. A few red, plush-covered chairs and divans completed the meager furnishings.

Scarcely were we within when my host called out, and women began pouring from the tiny rooms. Fourteen females, of various size, shape, hue, and dress, emerged—each from her own little room. I looked at their faces—and their clothes—and I knew suddenly that all my life I had been deceived; it came over me that an amazing amount of rubbish has been written around the hidden life of harem women. And before I left that strange institution I felt that even Pierre Loti had juggled lightly with the truth in his harem romance, "Disenchanted."

The women before me were not beautiful—at least they were not to be compared with any type of feminine face and figure commonly thought attractive by men in our Western world. Two or three were exceptions; light of complexion, large-eyed, and not too fat, they resembled very much the Circassian maids—and possibly they were. Anyone familiar with Turkey knows to what extent these girls—often very beautiful—have figured in the harem life, especially about the Bosphorus. Most of all women who stood before me in that Baghdad harem, however, were absolutely commonplace; some of them even stupid-looking.

A few wore bright-colored scarves about their necks, with more or less jewelry on their ankles and wrists. The popular item of dress seemed a shapeless sort of baggy "mother-hubbard" like garment, worn over yellow trousers. Gilt or beaded slippers adorned the feet of the younger and better-

On the flat plain outside Baghdad, dapper Turkish officers, drilled in German military schools, train Arab recruits, teaching them to fence and to do the German "goose step." By the time this photo appeared, Ottoman Turkey and Germany were allies in World War I, fighting Britain, Russia, and France.

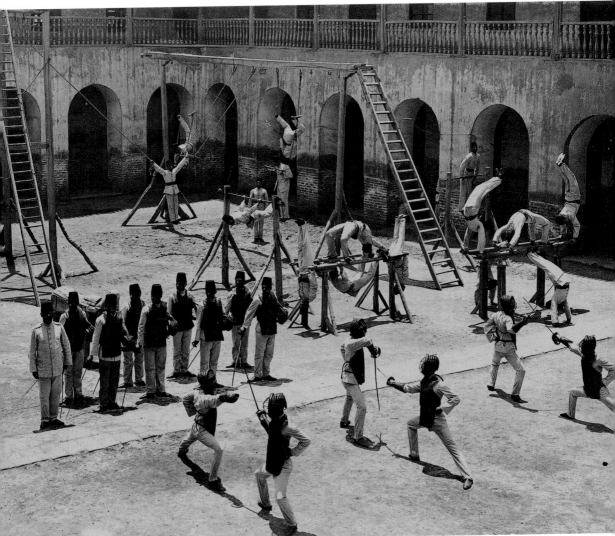

looking women; the older ones were barefooted. None of them seemed
to have made much of an effort at hair-dressing; two or three wore their hair
loose, hanging in tangled wisps about their faces. However, the old Pasha
beamed with pride as he looked them over; and after all, if he was pleased,
nothing else mattered. He introduced me all around and bowed himself
out, leaving me alone with the fourteen. Two girlish youngsters—in their
early 'teens—he had told me were his daughters; but to this day I do not
know which of the several wives shared their ownership with him.

Hardly had the old Pasha withdrawn when the women were up and
about me. And such chattering, giggling, exclaiming, pulling, and pushing
as followed! It was a great day—a day long to be remembered—in that
Baghdad harem. So far as I could learn, I was the first woman from the
Western world who had ever visited there; I was the first white woman that
some of the inmates had ever seen. Think what a sensation would ensue
in any American sitting-room if an Arab woman, her nails, lips, and eye-
lashes dyed, her limbs tattooed, rings in her nose, and anklets jangling,
might suddenly appear—silk bloomers and all—in the midst of a crowd of

Yankee women! Our own composure and self-restraint might not be any greater than that showed by these Arab women at Baghdad when I, an American girl in street clothes, appeared among them. They crowded about, feeling my hands and face, getting down on their knees to admire my high-heel shoes, stroking the skirt of my blue tailored suit, behaving like excited children with a new toy. My hat-pins were a source of great wonder, and my tight-fitting coat brought forth many a fervent "All-a-a-h!"

They asked me, too, how many children I had; how old I was; if there were many women in "Amerique," and inquired eagerly how many wives my husband had, and wanted to know how I had managed to get out of the harem alone.

When I told them I was a Christian—a *Kaffir*, they call it—and that in my country men have but one wife, and that she may go and come as she likes, they spoke aloud their disappointment and pity for me; for these women do not wish to leave the harem. It would shock them to walk alone, unveiled, in the street. These women will not even expose themselves to the chance sight of passers-by in looking from the latticed windows—if there happen to be any windows—in the houses where they live. They count it immoral to be seen by other men than their husband.

"America must be a poor country," said one, "if your husband can keep but one wife; a Bedouin keeps but one woman—and all the Bedouins are poor, because they live on the barren desert." From their viewpoint, the multitude of a man's wives, slaves, and retainers is the measure of his greatness.

Love, except that of the mother for her child, is undoubtedly an emotion absolutely unknown to these women; whence it follows that jealousy, too, must be but an infrequent disease.

Yet, poor in mind as these imprisoned women seemed, and painfully inquisitive as they were, kindness cloaked all their curiosity, and their every act displayed a friendly feeling for the strange woman—the heretic—in their midst. They brought in a great tray of dried fruits, baked gourds, toasted pumpkin seeds, and fresh pomegranates; they brought me wine, too, made from the juice of dates. They offered me long Arab cigarettes, called "Bagdaddies," when the repast was finished; and when I declined to smoke they found new cause for wonder, for I lied for my country and told them that American women never smoke. It was a great day for me, reared in the normal quiet of an old Missouri town. If only my knowledge of Arabic had been better, or some of the women had known more French, this story would be much longer.

When I finally rose to go, I asked them, though I knew they would not comply, to come and visit me. In this part of the Moslem world upper-class women go about but little. In Constantinople, where reform germs are working, the women have begun to clamor for permission to attend public entertainments, theaters, etc. But it's 30 days by caravan from Baghdad to Constantinople, and the modern spirit of the capital is felt not at all in the secluded harems of the old home of Harun-al-Rashid.

The sudden reappearance of the old Pasha, as he came to conduct me to my carriage, threw the whole fourteen into a noisy panic of giggles. One of the younger women, dropping to all fours, hid her face behind her arms and accidentally burned a hole in the rug with her fallen cigarette. Think of a high-spirited American girl kneeling or hiding her face just because a mere man entered the room! ☐

One of many oddities encountered by the Simpichs in their travels, a gufah, shown here, carried the adventurers from steamer to shore. Woven from willows, about six feet in diameter, the vessel is perfectly circular and basket-shaped, and coated with bitumen. Simpich writes: "Some say Moses was cut adrift in one of these craft."

Published in the twilight of the Great Game—the 19th-century struggle between Britain and Russia for dominance in Central Asia—parts of this story, which ran in 1921, might have been reported yesterday, give or take a few names and affiliations and the type of weapons at hand. In keeping with this era of intrigue, Simpich based the article on the observations of "Haji Mirza Hussein," a European traveler who disguised himself as a Muslim pilgrim.

Frederick Simpich and "Haji Mirza Hussein," "Every-Day Life in Afghanistan," Jan. 1921, pp. 85-110

Everyday Life in Afghanistan

BY FREDERICK SIMPICH

A company of Afghan infantry stand at attention, having returned to Kabul after a punitive expedition against the emir's rebel subjects.

The buffer state of Afghanistan, historic shock-absorber between Great Britain and Russia in middle Asia, years ago put up a "Keep Out" sign, a "This Means You" warning, to all white men and Christians. The land is "posted"—to use a poacher's phrase—posted against trade and concession hunters, against missionaries, and against all military and political hunters in particular.

Time and again the British have pushed up from India to invade this high, rough region hard by the "roof of the world." More than once their envoys have been massacred or driven back, or imprisoned, with their wives and children, in the frowning, gloomy citadel of Kabul; and once a retreating white army "shot it out" almost to a man, scattering its bones all the way from Kabul back to the Indian frontier.

In sheer drama, in swift, startling action, in amazing, smashing climax, no chapter in all the tales of the romantic East is more absorbing than this story of Britain's wars with the Afghans. And Russians, too, in the splendid glittering days of the Tsars, waged their fierce campaigns from the North, over the steppes of Turkestan, with wild Cossack pitted against wary Afghans.

NG MAPS

An iron man-cage (right) near the summit of Lata-bund Pass, was used during the reign of Abdur Rahman. In it a thief was raised to the top of the pole so that friends could not pass food or poison to him. He was then left in the cage to die.

But the "Keep Out" sign is still up. Today the foreigner is no more welcome in Afghanistan than he was a hundred years ago. Forbidden Lhasa itself is no more exclusive than brooding, suspicious Kabul, the capital of this isolate, unfriendly realm of fanatic tribes, of rocks, deserts, irrigated valleys, and towering unsurveyed ranges.

No railways or telegraph lines cross this hermit country or run into it, and its six or seven million people are hardly on speaking terms with any other nation.

Night and day, from stone watchtowers and hidden nooks along the ancient caravan trails that lead in from India, from Persia and Russia—trails used long ago by Alexander and Jenghiz Khan—squads of bearded, turbaned Afghans, with imported field glasses and long rifles, are keeping watch against trespassers from without.

For reasons of foreign policy, the Amir has long felt the necessity of secluding his little-known land to the greatest possible extent from the outside world. Only a few Europeans, mostly British, but occasionally also an American and now and then a few Russians or Germans, have had permission to come into this country and to sojourn for a while in its curious capital. But even on such rare occasions as when a foreign engineer, or a doctor whose services are badly needed, is admitted by the grace of the Amir, the visitor is subject to a surveillance that amounts almost to imprisonment.

No ambassadors or ministers, not even missionaries, are permitted to reside in this forbidden Moslem land. "Splendid isolation" is a sort of Afghan tradition, a conviction that the coming of the foreigner will spell the end of the Amir and his unique, absolute rule.

P.O. CRAWFORD

Today no other monarch anywhere wields such undisputed authority or is in closer touch with the everyday life of his subjects. He personally runs his country's religion, its foreign affairs, and he even supervises much of its commerce. He also owns and censors the only newspaper printed in all Afghanistan. Incidentally, he keeps 58 automobiles, and he *never* walks. Even from one palace to another, he goes by motor over short pieces of road built especially for his pleasure.

From the World War, though he took no active part in it, the Amir emerged with singular profits. His old and once rival neighbors, Great Britain and Russia, drawn together as allies in the world conflict, left him a free hand, and in 1919 Great Britain officially recognized the political independence of this much-buffeted buffer state, to whose rulers she had so long paid a fat annuity.

With an area of 245,000 square miles, Afghanistan is, next to Tibet, the largest country in the world that is practically closed to the citizens of other nations. But political life at wary, alert Kabul is in sharp contrast to the meditative seclusion and classic aloofness of the pious lamas at Lhasa.

Amir Amanullah Khan, through his agents in India and elsewhere, is in close touch with the world's current events; and, as the last remaining independent ruler of a Moslem country, now that the flower of the Caliph at Stamboul is broken, he wields a far-reaching influence throughout the Mohammedan world; also, because his land happens to lie just as it does on the map of the world, it is plain that for a long time to come he will be an active force in the political destinies of middle Asia. Like Menelik of Abyssinia, Queen Lil of the Hawaiian Islands, or the last of the Fiji kings, this Amir, remote and obscure as his kingdom is, stands out in his time as a picturesque world figure.

The Amir's word, his veriest whim, is law to his millions of subjects. He is, in truth, the last of the despots, a sort of modern Oriental patriarch on a grand scale. His judgments are, of course, based primarily on the Koran, or on the common law of the land; for there is no statute book, no penal code, and no court.

The emir's palace in Kabul looks fortress-like in this view from an airplane, a rarity at the time in Afghanistan. During the Third Anglo-Afghan War in 1919, the author writes, British planes flew up from India to drop "a few persuasive bombs" in the vicinity.

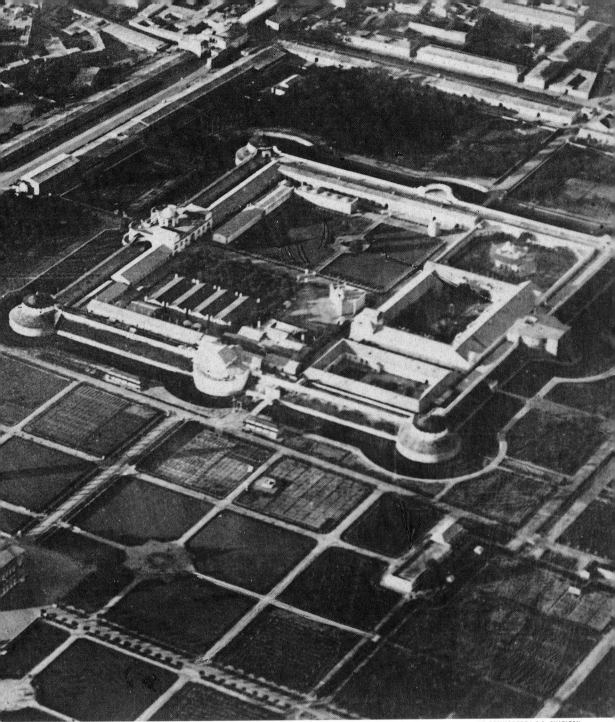

AIR COMMODORE L.E.O. CHARLTON

To keep the wires of politics, of military and economic control, in his own hands, the Amir vests subordinate authority only in his relatives and close friends; and woe betide the incautious underling who dares think for himself or act contrary to the Amir's wishes; for in this primitive, secluded region there still survive many unique and startling methods of "rendering a culprit innocuous."

The Amir reserves to himself the right of passing death sentences. The cruel Afghan forms of punishment, such as shooting a prisoner from the cannon's muzzle, sabering off his head, stoning him to death, burying him alive, cutting off his hands and feet or putting out his eyes, are seldom employed nowadays; yet often the criminal himself will choose a quick though violent exodus to paradise rather than suffer long imprisonment in a filthy iron cage, perhaps to die eventually of starvation.

The way of the transgressor in Afghanistan continues to be uncommonly hard, however. Time and again, in the recorded history of this land, deposed amirs, troublesome relatives, and political enemies have been deliberately blinded, there being a tradition here that no man with any physical affliction may hold a public office of honor or profit.

From the Persians the Afghans got the idea of marrying more than one wife; but, like the Persians, too, they have found, to their dismay, that polygamy is nowadays more expensive than exciting.

Sometimes, when the Amir wants to favor his faithful officials with presents, or perhaps to play practical jokes in certain cases, he distributes women among them; but these "gifts" often prove so troublesome that no great degree of gratitude is apparent among the recipients.

Amir Habibullah Khan (who was assassinated in 1919) had a harem of over one hundred women, and among these, strangely enough, were a few Europeans. The present Amir, Amanullah Khan, has but one wife.

The trade of Afghanistan is moved entirely by caravans and is largely in the hands of Hindus and Tadjiks. The chief route lies through the famous Khyber Pass, the great gateway from India, which has been fortified by the British Government. This pass is open every week, on Tuesdays and Fridays, except in very hot weather, when it is available to trade only on Fridays. A most rigid scrutiny is exercised by the Amir's agents on all who come and go. As soon as caravans from India enter the country, their Indian leaders are turned back and heavily armed Afghan guides take their places.

Some of these Afghan caravans, organized with military precision, number thousands of camels and a proportionate number of guides and camel-drivers. In the morning the Khyber Pass is open for caravans coming into Afghanistan, and in the afternoon for those routed in the opposite direction. The pass is absolutely closed between sundown and sun-up.

Camels leaving the country are usually loaded with wool, skins, dried fruits and vegetables, assorted gums, and spices. Thousands of horses are also driven along for sale in India as cavalry and polo mounts.

Supplying the wants of the Amir and his court is an interesting undertaking and is usually accomplished by his own agents, who reside in the cities of India. All goods consigned to him come in duty free; he buys anything that strikes his fancy, and often amuses himself by studying the pictures in mail-order catalogues.

The Yankee fountain pen and cheap watch are popular in Kabul. Most imports, however, come from India and China. Of late much Japanese merchandise is finding its way into the country. Either directly or through reshipping, India supplies Afghanistan with cotton goods, hardware, sugar and tea, dye materials, and silver bars for the coining of money. Gun running and the smuggling of ammunition, which flourished for many years, have recently been restricted by British supervision of the Indian frontiers. Though camels and packhorses, *yabus,* are mostly used for transport, it is not at all uncommon to see elephants, and even wheelbarrows, on the Afghan trails.

Owing to the aggressive pursuit and harsh punishment meted out by the Amir's troops, the once famous robbers of the Afghan hills have almost

Absolute monarch: Amanullah Khan, emir of Afghanistan, alone had the power to pronounce death sentences. He also ran his country's trade, religion, and politics—and edited its only newspaper.

"HAJI MIRZA HUSSEIN"

disappeared, so that caravans, even in the desert districts, can now travel in safety; but in some provinces near the borders constant quarrels and raids are going on among hostile tribes.

In military matters, Turkish influence is noticeable, and Turkish officers are used as instructors. In all Asia no fighting force is more picturesque or presents a more astonishing mixture of ancient and modern fighting methods than does the army of the Amir. Most of his troops are mounted, either on horses or camels, and a few of his better regiments of cavalry are organized somewhat after the Anglo-Indian style. The regulars are recruited mostly from among the town-dwelling Tadjiks.

The Malkis, or territorials, are organized and used in the various provinces as a sort of home guard. Some of them use flintlocks, and many depend on the spear and the long, curved sword for dispatching an enemy at close quarters. This army is about 70,000 strong. Save a few field howitzers and mountain guns it has no artillery.

Afghanistan's willful isolation of herself has, of course, affected the life of her people. Even among the different tribes within the country, jealousies and ethnological differences are conspicuous. The high mountains and frequent deserts so separate the cultivated and inhabited districts that tribal

Guarding the eastern entrance to the Khyber Pass, Fort Jamrud was built by the British, who fought three wars against Afghanistan between 1838 and 1919.

customs and habits, tongues, and religious differences are found here in sharper contrast than in most other countries of the East.

The Amir keeps at Peshawar a political agent, who occasionally pays a visit to the Viceroy of India; and, since Afghanistan's formal independence of 1919, envoys have been sent to Persia and one is perhaps now in Soviet Russia.

But because of the Afghan's chronic aversion to all foreigners, and the clever exclusion policy of the Amir, aided by nature's own barriers of sand wastes and almost inaccessible mountain ranges, it is likely that for a long time to come foreign influence will spread but slowly in this isolated land.

Yet the Amir and his military aristocracy follow intently all big events in the turbulent outside world. America is spoken of with sympathy and admiration, and, despite the prevailing illiteracy, many Afghans display an amazing knowledge of geography and current history. During the World War even the nomads on the steppes had fairly accurate news of great battles, and they had heard of air raids and submarines.

Today all Islam is in ominous ferment. Though the World War is officially ended, fights and disputes are still sweeping over Asia. Eventually and inevitably Afghanistan must again become the object of rivalry among big powers that rub shoulders in the East. □

■ *When staff writer Frederick Simpich roamed the banks of the Nile for this October 1922 story, Egypt was newly independent from Britain, and not at all sure yet what that meant. Perhaps a bit jaded by now (he'd been traveling the Middle East since 1914), Simpich presents an unvarnished account of post-colonial Egypt in transition.*

Frederick Simpich, "Along the Nile Through Egypt and the Sudan," Oct. 1922, pp. 379-410

Following the Nile

BY FREDERICK SIMPICH

Many of us know Egypt as tourists know any other country. You will all recall the old fakir at the "Continental," in Port Said, who rolls an egg between his palms till it turns to a live chick, while his assistant inhales a tired snake or plucks a fat toad from the beard of a scandalized Scotchman.

Some of you, too, have bought "real Egyptian antiques" and "scarabs" made in Naples; and you have marveled over mummies 3,000 years old (fitted with teeth, for verisimilitude, bought from an advertising dentist in London). And every year enough ancient coins are "found" to meet all demands! In other words, we know superficial Egypt—the donkey boys, the beggars whining for *bakshish*, the smirking guides; we have seen the tawdry *café chantant*, and Shepheard's, and we have been photographed astride a blasé, flea-bitten old camel standing on the sands before the Sphinx.

But we Westerners, what do any of us really know of the *Egyptian?*

I remember a night at Kantara. Standing where the pontoon bridge now is, and where the ancient caravan route from Egypt crosses the Suez on its way to Syria, in the red blaze of desert dusk, I saw a woman, an erect, slim-limbed woman of the Nile, barefooted, in all the unconscious dignity of her ancient race. On her head she carried a water-jar—gracefully and easily, like Rebekah on her way to the well. About her lithe form flowed the black folds of the loose, primitive robe that marks the Moslem woman.

Casually, without interest, from over the rim of her *yashmak* she glanced at us; but with what

In Old Cairo, pedestrians pass by the Aksunkor Mosque, called *al-Azrak*, the blue, for the color of its tiles.

eyes! Lustrous, long-lashed, unlike the eyes of any other women any where—
eyes set under heavy, straight brows, the odd eyebrows of old Egypt.

"A woman of the pyramids," whispered my companion, "young and a
good looker, yet 6,000 years old in face and form!" Handsome she was,
indeed; yet astonishingly like the crude pictures of the women of ancient
times, as we see them carved on the temple walls.

These strange people, isolated here for ages, have developed and main-
tained certain distinct physical and racial characteristics. When you see
the modern *fellah* at work with mallet and chisel, or scratching the sun-
baked plain with his crude hoe, or dipping his clumsy fish net into the
Nile, he is, in face and physique, startlingly like the pictured Egyptians of
the Pharaohs' times.

Since prehistoric days this race, a vast farming colony, has lived along
the Nile and in that great delta which ages of floods have built out into the
Mediterranean. Though the Persian conquest, about 521 B.C., ended the period of native rule, the mental and physical aspects of the modern fellah
are, so far as we can judge, exactly like those of his early ancestor who
sweated under the Pharaohs—and this notwithstanding centuries of submission to Persian, Macedonian, Roman, Arab, Mameluke, Turk, and Briton.

Four-fifths of all Egypt's population, or something near nine millions,
belong to this ancient race.

Culturally, the fellah has been Arabized; he speaks a form of Arabic and
turns to Mecca in his prayers. Otherwise he is the same silent, melancholy,
inscrutable person who doggedly dragged granite blocks for hundreds
of miles to build the pyramids, who blindly bent to the big sweeps of the
early Egyptian galleys, or who conceived and began to dig the Suez Canal
centuries before de Lesseps was born.

ELMENDORF, FROM GALLOWAY

Towering palm trees tilt in a sandstorm at the town of Beni-Hassan, on the banks of the Nile.

Hard work is his lot from the cradle to the grave. Riding through the great delta region, you will see a boy or girl of eight leading the ox in the fields, while the father holds the rude plow. The children herd goats, too, and aid in cotton-picking.

And though "Egypt is the gift of the Nile" it is a gift with a string to it, whose name is *mud*. Keeping the canals free of silt and keeping the water going has, figuratively, broken the tired backs of millions.

Many power pumps are in use, of course, especially on the larger estates; but today gasoline is scarce and expensive, and the average small farmer must water his little patch of land with the *shadâûf*, a primitive balancing apparatus wherein a long pole with a rock weight on one end and a pail on the other is used to lift water from the canals.

Two other awkward but ancient irrigating machines are the "water snake," or "Archimedean screw," and the *tâbût*; these wooden water wheels are used to lift water from the canals and pour it onto higher levels.

The thousands of miles of canals serve not only for irrigation, but also to distribute drinking water and as channels of traffic. Sailboats on these ditches, seen from a distance, seem to be running on the ground over the flat country.

The Mahmûdîveh Canal connects Alexandria with the Nile, and the Ishmael Canal takes off from the Nile near Cairo and carries water to Suez. Nile mud alone no longer is adequate to enrich the fields, and today the fellah must buy much high-priced imported fertilizer.

The renter usually leases a piece of land for two or three years; the owner furnishes seed and work animals, and takes his share of the crop. Cotton, sugar cane, corn, wheat, and rice are staples. Egypt grew corn for export to feed Rome in ancient times.

Water buffalo, oxen, and camels are the chief work animals on the farms; most of the horses and donkeys in Egypt are owned by the townspeople.

While the milk of goats, cows, and camels is used, the fellah depends mostly on the water buffalo for his milk supply. This ugly, awkward beast requires less food and gives more milk than the cow and is less susceptible to diseases.

Few animals are raised for slaughter, probably because of the unfavorable climatic conditions. Turkeys and chickens are numerous, but domestic ducks and geese are rare. Around the margins of the lagoons, however, and in the Nile Delta waterfowl, snipe, and other shore birds are abundant; snipe are trapped in great numbers—in so wasteful a manner that police regulations now seek to protect these birds. And you who know the Suez trip will remember the amazing number of flamingoes that rise and fly about as your steamer passes through the Bitter Lakes.

Nile fish are fat and unsavory; along the seacoast Arabs catch fish enough for the hotels in the larger Egyptian cities.

In the daily home life of the country *fellaheen*, the influence of Arab culture is uppermost. "Marry what you like of women, by twos and fours," says the Koran; so polygamy exists; but it is too expensive for the average fellah.

Every village has its coffee shop, where water pipes are for rent. Here, too, is the ever-present professional storyteller, the letter-writer, the snake charmer, the fakir, and the dancing girl.

From our viewpoint, such a life is hopelessly dull. The Egyptian monologue artist has told the story of Sultan Baibar and the adventures of Abu-Zed, without variation, for probably a thousand years; every member of the coffee-house crowd knows the yarn by heart: also, the tune that is played on the "Aüd" lute, the "Nai" flute, and the "Kamenge" fiddle, for it is always the same. So is the Egyptian dance—not a new step or movement since the days of Rameses!

Amusements are more varied in the larger towns. Here American moving pictures are shown, shabby one-ring traveling circuses are met, and the rising generation is beginning to go in for games and sports.

Plainly, a new era is dawning in Egypt, and it is admitted through all the East that far-reaching economic and cultural changes are sweeping over the country. But it probably will take many years of progress to transform the slow-moving, fatalistic fellah of the lower rural class. He still sticks to his humble mud hut, scantly furnished with earthen pots, tin cans, and straw mats, and to the habits of life and work that long centuries have drilled into him.

The economic and political future of the Sudan is closely linked up with that of Egypt.

Since that day in January 1885, when the madmen of the Mahdi killed General Gordon with their spears, many a stirring scene in the drama of civilization has been staged in the Sudan. Like Baghdad, Afghanistan, and the Forbidden City, the Sudan is one of those picturesque places whence adventure and romance seem always to spring.

Because of our own growing cotton shortage, the Sudan holds new interest for us, as it is called the greatest potential cotton land in the British Empire. In area it covers about a million square miles.

No count has ever been made of its people, but they are estimated at three and a half million. A few British officials (about one to every 10,000 square miles), with the help of minor Sudan and Egyptian assistants, administer the government.

On the whole, it is a thinly peopled land of amazing distances. You can go south from the Egyptian frontier 6 hundred miles by rail before you get to Khartum. From there south you can go another thousand miles on a flat-bottomed, paddle-wheel Nile steamer before you reach the southern boundary of the Sudan, which is almost on the edge of the great lakes and a third of the way to the Cape of Good Hope.

The White Nile splits the Sudan for nearly 2,000 miles from south to north and is navigable the year round above Khartum.

The Blue Nile runs down from the Abyssinian hills and joins the main river at Khartum, forming an apex called the *Gezireh*, or Island. This vast flat island is the granary of the Sudan.

If you want to bring a pet wart-hog or a giraffe home with you from the Anglo-Egyptian Sudan, you will first have to get a permit from the British authorities.

They watch over the wild game to save it from exploitation for commercial purposes. The hunting of elephants and ostriches for ivory and feathers is strictly controlled; trade in skins and trophies is prohibited. The exportation of captive wild animals for display in zoos and parks is kept within reasonable limits.

Egypt depends mainly on the Sudan for its meat supply, and thousands of acres of land have been put under pump irrigation to provide food crops for Egypt, whose people, as one investigator said, cannot subsist on bank notes and cotton.

Under the broken nose of the Sphinx, tourists converse with a local *fellah*, dwarfed by the 65-foot-high monument.

The Sudan, say the Egyptians, is an integral part of Egypt; but it was conquered, misgoverned, and lost by successive *khedives*, and for years and years it was exploited by Egypt for ivory, gold, and slaves. Both socially and ethnologically, it differs from Egypt.

The Sudanese do not like the Egyptians; their only common tie is that both live on the waters of the Nile. Just now, too, the project of building the new Nile dams in the Sudan is arousing much excitement in Egypt, where the fellaheen fear that they may be robbed of some of their ancient irrigation rights. And water, at best, is not always too plentiful in Egypt.

By virtue of an agreement made back in 1899, Great Britain shares the protectorate over the Sudan with Egypt; but Englishmen actually govern the country.

It is a region, apparently, of vast agricultural possibilities. If present projects are carried out, the Sudan may one day grow as much cotton as Egypt itself.

In Cairo and London, men think mainly of politics and agriculture when Egypt's affairs are mentioned. To most Americans, however, the name Egypt still means the home of the Sphinx and the whirling dervish, the land of the mummy and the scarab, a desert realm of camels and white-robed sheiks, where long ago the troubles of the Children of Israel first began.

And yet—you who know Egypt, you who have come under the spell of the Nile—you can forgive that Frenchman who wept when he saw the Pyramids! □

Military officers stroll through a market in Peshawar in what was then British India and is now northwestern Pakistan. Baskets above their heads hold fighting quail, the game cocks of this frontier town at the eastern end of the Khyber Pass.

PART TWO

THE HINGES OF HISTORY

1923-1960

With a few lines on a map, the modern Middle East takes shape: new nations, territorial mandates, and a Jewish homeland in Palestine. The magazine fills in the blank spots on the map.

MAYNARD OWEN WILLIAMS—1933

Baluchi traders pass the Little Buddha in Bamian, Afghanistan, 60 feet shorter than the nearby Great Buddha. Both were destroyed by the Taliban in 2001.

Cave dwellers in Matmata, Tunisia, escape the intense heat of the desert by moving their household underground. In Herat, Afghanistan, beams of light pierce the gloom in a crowded warehouse.

Blazing jets flare off surplus gas at Agha Jari oil field in Iran, one of the nation's most productive. Abundant oil supplies, industrialized by mid-century, were the key to the modern nation's riches.

THOMAS J. ABERCROMBIE—1961

Enterprising young Lebanese run a car-polishing business on one of the bustling, palm-lined avenues in Beirut that were legendary for cafés, nightclubs, and boutiques before war erupted in 1975.

■ As the ink was drying on the 1920 Versailles Treaty dividing the fallen Ottoman Empire into spheres of European influence, Junius B. Wood set out to explore the regions that the Hashemite Sherif of Mecca and his sons (who'd allied with Britain in World War I) were calling "greater Syria"—a pan-Arab dream nation stretching from present-day Lebanon to Iraq and western Arabia. In this excerpt, he interviews Abdullah, the sherif's second son, who was then the emir of Transjordan. Crowned the King of Jordan in 1946, Abdullah was assassinated in 1951 at al-Aqsa mosque in Jerusalem by a Muslim fanatic enraged by the king's negotiations with Israel. At his side that day was his 16-year-old grandson, who was later crowned King Hussein.

Junius B. Wood, "A Journey to Three Arab Kingdoms: Transjordania, Iraq, and the Hedjz Present Many Problems to European Powers," May 1923, pp. 535-568

Observing men playing chess in Amman, Wood writes: "Chess is the same the world over—when the game starts, conversation ceases."

Inventing Jordan

BY JUNIUS B. WOOD

Transjordania is a new country—a mere fleck of desert and trouble on the world map. It is so new that few persons more than 500 miles from its borders know where or what the kingdom is. The Versailles pastry makers, like many cooks, had some dough left over after the world molds were filled, and this was one of the odd cookies.

Theoretically, it is an independent Arab kingdom. Actually, it belongs in Britain's pantry. The Arabs can call it theirs, but they must not nibble it or permit any other nation to do so. It has been rechristened both Transjordania and Kerak, the former to give Western ears an inkling of its location, and the latter to soothe Mohammedan tastes.

When the leaders of the powers which rule the world sit in council it seems quite easy to create new kingdoms. Take a river, a mountain range, a few pencil lines and different shades of ink on the map, and the task is accomplished—so far as the statesmen are concerned. New maps are printed and school children are studying them before the people in the country itself realize what has happened.

Transjordania was among the easiest. It served a purpose. Lying just east of the Jordan River, only a few miles from Jerusalem, it is a buffer between the British mandate in Palestine and the Arabs of the desert, and at the same time an irritant to the French mandate in Syria. It was molded with the confidence of enduring for ages.

Amman is the capital of the new kingdom. That name alone might suggest that more than a new shade of ink on the maps and the discussions of distant statesmen are necessary to give a kingdom permanency. It has been a capital for ages.

The Ammonites, descendants of Lot, called it Rabbath Ammon when they ruled there. The creek which divides the village keeps its old name, Nahr Amman. Og's giant iron bed was a trophy in Rabbath Ammon.

Centuries later this city was the capital of one of the Greek republics of Decapolis; Ptolemy Philadelphus built an acropolis and renamed the place Philadelphia. The Romans and Crusaders came and it was one of their capitals. Others followed, until now it has new rulers.

Amman resembles Bisbee, Arizona, with its two main streets of Tombstone Canyon and Brewery Gulch—a creek in the valley with houses, shops, and footpaths struggling back up the hillsides.

Each evening during my short stay there, some neighbor would climb one of these steep paths to my host's home, sip a cup of coffee, and suggest a game of chess. Chess is the same the world over—when the game starts, conversation ceases. I could slip out for a stroll without being missed.

The main street winds around the base of the big hill which once was crowned by the massive Greek citadel, now a pile of ruined walls, fallen columns, and broken façades. In the center of the town, near the mosque, itself a ruin of the past, is the proscenium and arch of the later Roman theater.

Farther along, the road curves across the stone bridge, passes in front of the broken stone benches of the old Roman amphitheater, and disappears into the solitude of the desert.

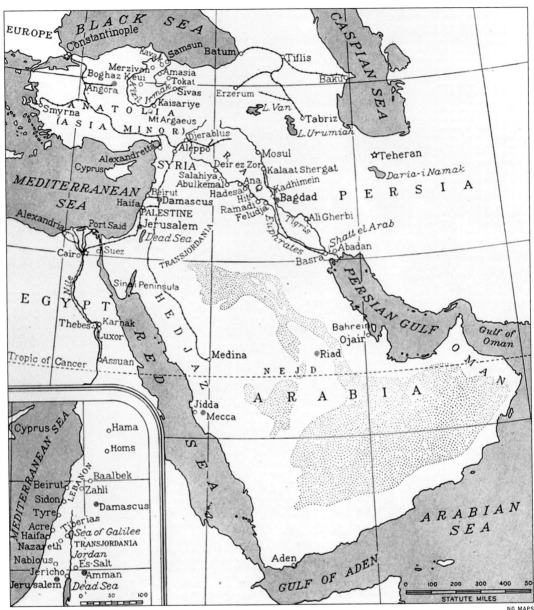

NG MAPS

The coping of the little bridge has been polished by the thousands who have loitered there since toiling backs first lifted the heavy stones into place. Under the moonlight the amphitheater stands out white and gaunt, concealing the scars of time. Croaking frogs and barks of distant dogs are the only sounds. A belated Bedouin gallops across the bridge, fading into a lengthening shadow in the distance.

Goats now are herded in the galleries through which the gay crowds passed to watch the sports of Roman days. In front of the Arab coffee shops marble columns from the Greek acropolis lie in the road for benches, on which dusty Bedouins sit to smoke and gossip.

The empires of the past which chose Amman as a capital built well, but they and their rulers have gone and been forgotten. The mighty powers which ruled it are a memory, but its life goes on just the same. Now it is chosen again, the kingdom has been baptized with a new name, and the maps reprinted as if it all were new.

Through all the cycles of time, the Arab has changed least of all. Those of the town play their chess in the evening as they have in quiet homes for hundreds of years. The Arabs claim they invented chess.

The Bedouin rides in from the desert, smokes his *nargileh*, drinks the cups of bitter coffee, and gallops out again into the void. As the seasons change he folds his tents and moves with his herds of goats. And camels. So long as the statesmen of Europe want to pay him for their pleasure in calling this or that portion of the desert a kingdom, it matters little to him. He knows nothing of maps and cares less. Should they attempt to make *him* pay, it would be different. Kingdom-making would not be so easy.

Emir Abdullah Ibn Hussein is the nominal ruler of Transjordania. His

court is the same as that of his forefathers—a cluster of tents in the desert, which he moves with the seasons.

By automobile it is only five hours from Jerusalem to Amman, but it is a change from the West to the East, and there are not many travelers on the road. Visitors are not generally welcomed in Transjordania. It is the threshold of Arabia, and once across its borders the law and authority of Europe are of the flimsiest.

An automobile can coast almost the entire distance from Jerusalem, along the steep hillsides, down into the valley of the Jordan. There is a glimpse of the Dead Sea on the right, and the road turns straight across the plains toward Jericho.

As one rides through that simmering, breathless valley, 1,200 feet below the level of the sea, the heroism of Joshua when he commanded the sun to stand still is impressed with stifling force. The farther end of the iron bridge across the Jordan is barricaded and a guard of soldiers stops the car. Unless word has been telephoned from the tented capital outside of Amman that a visitor in European clothes is to be permitted to pass, the car goes no farther.

While my companion was exchanging the inevitable cigarettes with the Arab officer in command of the guard, I started to take a picture of the international boundary. Their language was not understood by me, but the soldiers made it quite clear that the making of photographs was not allowed. The captain intervened.

"As long as you are not French, you can take photographs of anything you want," he explained, bringing the guard to attention as the first piece of scenery.

From the river the road climbs out of the broiling valley to the higher fertile plain. In winter Abdullah moves his tents and royal court here, near the Jordan, though he seldom crosses into the British mandate. To hold his people, he must play the role of the desert Arab.

Caravans of camels, sniffing in alarm at the automobile, jogged along the road. One train stampeded wildly, the drivers hilariously hanging on to the running-board of the machine during a frantic pursuit around curves and over dry creek beds to overtake the terrified leader.

Every man carries a long black-barreled rifle sticking up back of his ears—camel-drivers, peasants working in the little fields, and even the boys watching the herds of goats on the hills. Transjordania is of the desert, where everybody is his own policeman.

Workmen are leisurely clearing away the rubbish from the Roman amphitheater. Abdullah does not hope to restore it as in the days when shouting multitudes watched the games on the banks of the little creek, but the dirt and rubbish which now cover its battered artistic beauty will be removed.

Similar excavations will be made in the even larger ruins of Meshetta, a few miles from Amman. Other workmen are widening the streets and building roads in the country.

Amman is a station on the Hedjaz Railroad, much used between Damascus and the south. However, the country has few funds for internal improvements, and the eternal conflict with the desert is hopeless. Its area is only 16,000 square miles, with a population of 400,000, exclusive of nomads.

In Haifa, a mixed town of Arabs and Jews in Palestine, Arab women draw water from a community well. Now a thriving port city in Israel, Haifa in 1923 was part of the British mandate for Palestine issued by the League of Nations.

Somewhere in the
desert between Aleppo
and Baghdad, an auto-
mobile used by the au-
thor and photographer
provokes great curiosity
among Bedouin. Wood
noted that the nomad
"knows nothing of
maps, and cares less."

The annual budget amounts to $1,040,000, against a revenue of $500,000.
Great Britain makes up the difference, one of the many donations toward
maintaining an Arab policy.

Transjordania is a haven for the exiles and fugitives from all the nearby
territory. Under cover of night, they slip away from Damascus and
other cities in the French mandate, cross the desert with the assistance of
friendly tribes, until the long camel journey brings them into Transjordania.

Amman and the larger city of Es-Salt are full of men who have cheated
the already-overcrowded French prisons. Few of them have abundant
funds; all must be provided for. They are part of the brotherhood; poets,
merchants, editors, army officers, students, lawyers, and men and women
from every walk of life make up the number.

Some secure passports and continue into Palestine and Egypt; others are

given government appointments and remain in the desert kingdom, all awaiting a time when they can return to their own country and harboring an undying bitterness against the neighbor on the north. Salaries of officials are the big expense of Transjordania.

This is a fertile country and Abdullah, himself a strange mixture of desert and city, may make it prosper.

"We do not want this kingdom to be called Transjordania, for we consider it, with Palestine, Mesopotamia, and the Hedjaz, merely a part of the greater Syria," he said one day, as we sat in his tent, a picturesque figure in desert regalia. "We Arabs have lost our palaces and cities and are living in tents, as our fathers did. The Arabs have always been free and we will continue free, awaiting the time when we can take back the country which is ours. This portion of Syria has never failed in its duty to the Arab cause, and when opportunity comes we will be ready to do our part." □

■ *In the aftermath of World War I and the fall of the Ottoman Empire, the world of Muslims and Christians in the region was already in upheaval. Then came a war between Greece and the new nation of Turkey over Turkish territories where ethnic Greeks had lived for generations. Turkey's victory set in motion the migration of two million people—Turkish Christians to Greece and Greek Muslims to Turkey—every one bearing a story of tragedy and loss.*

Melville Chater, "History's Greatest Trek: Tragedy Stalks Through the Near East as Greece and Turkey Exchange Two Million of Their People," Nov. 1925, pp. 533-590

Journey of Sorrows

TEXT AND PHOTOGRAPHS BY MELVILLE CHATER

As Greek Muslims were making the trek to Turkey, newly arrived Turkish Christians were being loaded onto rail carts at Patras, Greece, and moved to the interior.

Ever since the expulsion from Eden, man has been trekking, and folk wanderings are the roots of his history; but with 1922 began what may fairly be called history's greatest, most spectacular trek—the compulsory intermigration of two million Christians and Moslems across the Aegean Sea.

This trek, brought about by the startling recuperation of Turkey after her defeat in the World War and her subsequent triumph over the Greeks in Anatolia, eventually developed into a regulated Exchange of racial minorities, according to specific terms and under the supervision of the League of Nations. But the initial episodes of the Exchange drama were enacted to the accompaniment of the boom of cannon and the rattle of machine guns and with the settings painted by the flames of the Smyrna holocaust.

After the Turkish offensive of August 26 the Greek army collapsed on a 150-mile front. The ensuing six months' cataclysm of fleeing peoples came as if there had been telepathically broadcast in great waves that swept Anatolia, Smyrna, Thrace, and Constantinople, the instinct of panic. The Greeks in these widespread areas suddenly awakened to find themselves on the brink of a whirlpool.

Refugees from anywhere within 150 miles inland herded seaward into Smyrna. At first they came in orderly trainloads or in carts, with rug-wrapped bedding, some little household equipment, and perhaps even a few animals. But as the distant military momentum speeded up, the influx became a wild rabble of ten, then twenty, then thirty thousand a day. Their increasingly scanty possessions betokened a mad and yet madder stampede from the scene of sword and fire, until September 7 saw utterly destitute multitudes staggering in, the women wailing over the first blows of family tragedy, whereby mothers with no food for their babies had been forced to abandon their older children in wayside villages.

By now Smyrna's broad quay swarmed with perhaps 150,000 exiles who camped and slept there, daily stretching their rugs as makeshift shelters against the sun, whose furnacelike heat was the mere forerunner to a terrible epic of fire.

All day long of September 8 and far into the night sounded the tramp of Greece's defeated troops surging toward the transports that chafed under full steam; then these, followed by the harbor's entire shipping, fled seaward. And, like a rising curtain, the dawn revealed only the grim hulls of neutral warships, come to "observe," across that commerce-deserted harbor, the catastrophe of Greece's Asian adventure.

A few hours later there came riding into Smyrna and past its close-barred shop fronts a body of Turkish cavalry, black-uniformed and scimitar-bearing, their left hands raised aloft, as in reassurance, while they called "fear not!" to the white-faced populace huddled in side-alleys.

Before nightfall the whole division was in, with two infantry divisions following.

A few days after the triumphal entry of the Turks, the army of quay-squatters saw flames dancing in the old, wood-constructed Armenian quarter, a mile and a half away. The dance became a fiery hurdle race, as the

American sailors help to move elderly refugees on a hand truck in Smyrna. All told, two million people were uprooted as Muslims and Christians changed places.

wind-fanned flames leaped from balcony to balcony across the narrow streets; then the race became a hungry conflagration whose roaring mouth ate through and gulped down that mile-and-a-half breadth of city down to where the refugee multitude huddled between a waste of fire and a waste of sea.

And now fresh multitudes were disgorged upon them—fleeing Smyrniotes laden, refugee-like, with snatched-up babies and bedding. The city had become a Titanic blast furnace, whose wind-driven flames fanned the quay with so dreadful a heat that the multitudes dipped their blankets in the sea and swaddled themselves. Maddened horses, their harness afire, ran amuck through the press, leaving a wake of crushed bodies, which roasted where they lay.

Estimates of the Smyrna disaster placed the loss of life at 10,000 and the property destruction at $300,000,000.

On September 23 an Allied note had retransferred to the victorious Turks

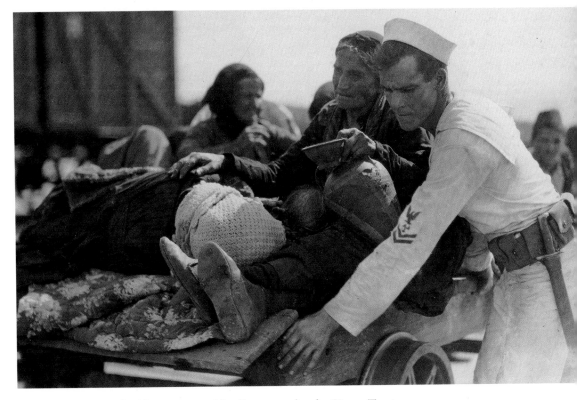

East Thrace, which had been annexed by Greece under the Sèvres Treaty. This triangular "backyard of Constantinople" stretched westward from 25 miles behind the city to the Maritza River and contained 600,000 Greek and Turkish farmers, in about equal racial proportions.

Bulletins giving a month's notice of the withdrawal of the Greek troops and the entrance of Turkish gendarmerie were to be posted in order to allay possible panic.

But panic was already abroad, as inextinguishable as Smyrna's. Within one week of the quayside evacuation, Thracian Greeks saw Greek troops striking camp and marching westward.

"You're coming back?" the farmers anxiously asked.

"No," was the response.

And within an hour villages were deserted. Household goods and sacks of seed grain were flung into wains, the oxen were hitched, then the little community trekked westward, out of the backyard of Constantinople.

Village by village the sight of the departing soldiers surprised women grinding at handmills, men on the threshing sledges, always with the same instant result—the dropping of tools, the crowding into hastily loaded farm wagons, the departure westward.

Many a local official ran out, protesting: "Turn back! Get your harvest! You've a month yet." Always the same, dull, fate-ridden response: "No. All is lost. We must move into Old Greece." Everywhere throughout the plain the word passed, the trek began, the endless caravan lines took form.

Ahead the sky grew dark. Rain fell in torrents, washing out roads and swamping fields, as this Christian hegira into Greece moved slowly, multitudinously on.

At Rodosto 28,000 trekkers descended the cliffs to camp on the wind-swept beach, waiting there for rescue ships until they were on starvation's verge—this while in the deserted interior their harvest mildewed.

Through Adrianople 60,000 poured during the first six days. So fast had action followed upon rumor that those trekking from nearest Constantinople saw throughout the entire line of march only moving caravans and deserted villages where, a few weeks later, starved cats and dogs were devouring each others' carcasses.

Men and women, trudging ahead to lighten the fast-miring wagons, bore shotguns; for thousands of the *comitadji*—those stormy petrels of the Balkans—were ambushing and raiding the emigrants. Many a wain entered Dedeagatch or Adrianople with the wife leading the oxen and her man's body stretched across the grain sacks.

And thus 300,000 crossed the swollen Maritza and strewed its western banks; and thus the third wave in the great trek, now mounting to 700,000 passed across the frontiers of Greece.

And meanwhile, behind Greece's officially closed doors? A small country of no great natural wealth, she had just emerged from ten years of continuous mobilization and intermittent wars, culminating in a recent defeat, only to be plunged into refugeeism on a colossal scale. Without reference to the total results of the Exchange, Greece had received within a year of the fall of Smyrna 1,250,000 exiles. This 25 percent leap in her population meant that to every four citizens throughout the land one homeless and usually destitute person had been added.

And now Lausanne came to the relief with a document, signed on January 30, 1923, entitled, "A Convention concerning the exchange of Greek and Turkish populations." It had come about by Greece's insistence that Turkey must accept the 450,000 Moslems resident in the Hellenic Kingdom in order to make room for the former's million or more refugees. It is safe to say that history does not contain a more extraordinary document.

Never before in the world's long pageant of folk-wanderings have 2,000,000 people—and certainly no less than 3,000,000 if the retroactive clause is possible of complete application—been exiled and re-adopted by a stroke of the pen.

Even if regarded as a voluntary trek instead of a compulsory exchange, the movement would be without parallel in the history of emigration. The

Klondike gold-rush peaked to only 22,000 in the year 1900, while that in California drew no more than 370,000 thither in 12 years.

Dealing with immigrant masses of about 1,500,000 each, the Irish movement took seven years, the Polish movement ten years, and the Jewish movement ten years, to land that number of their respective nationals in the United States. The highest human tide that ever reached our shores in one year (1907) was less than the Greek-Turkish shift by 750,000 people.

To everyone's surprise, this opening of the Exchange was effected with perfect harmony. The Moslem families, with their flocks and household goods, trekked to Mitylene's various ports, where small Turkish steamers were waiting. Taxes and passports were waived; minor offenders were released from prison; the women were even permitted to take with them their strings of gold coins.

Believers in a traditional Hellenophobia-Turkophobia would have stared

at the sight of the Mitylene Greeks spreading farewell meals for their departing neighbors, and later accompanying them to the quay, where Christians and Mohammedans, who for a lifetime had been plowing adjacently and even sharing occasional backgammon games at village cafés, embraced and parted with tears.

Then, seated on their heaped-up baggage, with their flocks around them—the women weeping, the children hugging their pets, the graybearded *babas* all dignity, as is their wont—the Mitylene Moslems set forth for unknown Turkey.

At Aivali, their "Ellis Island" of entry, interpreters speaking the familiar Greek and the unfamiliar Turkish installed them temporarily in waiting houses. Later they were distributed throughout the country according to

A tent city for Turkish refugees fills the plaza of the Theseum in Athens—a temporary annex for one of the best-preserved edifices in the ancient world.

trades and subject to a Turkish regulation limiting any village's increase, under the Exchange, to one-fifth of the population. While the family unit was preserved, the Mitylene communities were dissolved forever.

In November the Refugee Settlement Commission began its program in Greece. A month later the Mixed Commission's branches were preparing lists of exchangeable Moslems, filling out their declarations of property values, and supervising their transportation.

Throughout a year Saloniki's long quay beheld the mournful pageant of departing Moslems. Had the shade of Mr. Gladstone been present to witness his fiat of half a century ago being realized, he must have softened at that picture of dignity in misfortune, the Turks going "out of Europe, bag and baggage." Notwithstanding their new government's preparations to receive and care for them, many of the Moslems arriving in Asia Minor suffered even more than the exchanged Greeks.

Some of the former found themselves in a war-devastated region, others in villages whose best houses had been preempted and whose poorer ones had been dismembered for firewood by those who had remained behind after the flight of the Greeks.

Unreckoned tens of thousands died by malaria or exposure, while multitudes of disillusioned families declined the second-hand pick of farms offered them and became wanderers. To the question, "Where are you bound for?" addressed to ox-drawn caravans roaming through the

land, the answer would be, "We are looking for a tobacco field as good as ours at Drama," or, perhaps, "an olive grove like our old one on Mitylene." By May 1, 1924, 250,000 Moslems had been evacuated; then the westbound flow of 150,000 Greeks set in, these moving simultaneously with the remaining 200,000 Moslems until, eight months later, the Exchange was complete.

In this mechanized exiling of 600,000 souls the individual heartbreak was lost in the all-embracing swirl of things. Only here and there a glance, a gesture, a fragment of talk, revealed the undercurrents of this great Christian-Moslem drama.

Many a grayhaired shopkeeper beheld his lifelong customers dispersed, himself starting life afresh. And the old and honored public scribe—what use now his little writing box and literary flourishes, since his mother tongue would be as naught in yonder land of an alien speech? Many a village Evangeline and her parted lover would vainly seek each other in Greece's mountain-barred valleys or in widespread Anatolia.

Here a child sobbed for a lost pet, and there a grandmother wept at the thought of some tiny hill-topping cemetery henceforth abandoned to weeds and forgetfulness.

And few were the congregations who listened dry-eyed to their pastor's last sermon, or who without deep emotion fell in line outside the door of their dismantled church to follow in the wake of priest and sacred emblems down to the waiting ships. ☐

Ali Goes to the Clinic

TEXT AND PHOTOGRAPHS BY HERNDON AND MARY HUDSON

■ *For the devout Muslim, God is never far from his thoughts, his words, his day-dreams—even during a visit to a foreign doctor for a chronic, and slightly mysterious, stomach ailment. In this article, which appeared as is in the December 1946 issue, American doctor Herndon Hudson and his wife, Mary, render a portrait of life in newly independent Syria. The pair founded a hospital there in 1924.*

Herndon and Mary Hudson,
"Ali Goes to the Clinic,"
Dec. 1946, pp. 764-766

Ali El Hussein lives in the village of El Jadeed, Syria, a single row of straggling mud huts on the east bank of the Euphrates, 15 miles below Deir ez Zor. Having heard of the new American hospital in the city, he has decided to seek help there, for he has been sick for years.

Ali has no donkey or money to hire one, so he starts out afoot one morning before dawn with others from his village. Some of his fellow travelers are guiding and thumping diminutive donkeys which stagger under loads of wheat or corn; others carry inverted chickens, or a few eggs tied up in a ragful of straw.

Each woman carries a burden in her cloak, the two ends of which are drawn up over the shoulders and knotted across the forehead, forming a sack on her back. The burden usually consists of a baby, who often has to share its nest with a bushel of straw for sale.

Some women, in addition, have black pots balanced on their heads; these are destined for the booths of the whiteners. Everyone is barefoot, the men with loose cotton robes that reach the ankles, the women with dark-blue dresses that modestly cover their feet and trail in the dust.

There is little conversation as the party shuffles along in the heat. Toward mid-morning they finally reach the new bridge. It offers free passage over the Euphrates, in happy contrast to the old and expensive ferry, with its cursing boatmen so ready to cuff the awkward Bedouin.

Just across the bridge is the hospital to which Ali is bound, and he soon finds his way to the clinic door. There are many people already in the waiting room, but it seems quiet. He salutes the company with a bold

"*Marhaba*" (hello). But when he settles down against the wall he realizes that every one is listening to a voice reading.

The story is of one who had many sheep (ah, fortunate man!) and lost one (evil fortune, by Allah!). Of course he searched far for it until he found it in a *wadi* (gully), and, returning, he bade the rest of the village to rejoice with him (of course, for a sheep is worth a gold pound; more if a female and bearing young).

"And that," says the speaker, "is what God is like; His love seeks us out, though we stray far." Presently someone beckons, and, gathering his sheepskin cloak about him, Ali follows along to the examination room, whispering "*B'ism'illah*" (in the name of Allah) as he enters. "Marhaba," he says again, and the doctor replies, "*Marhabtein*" (double hello) as he indicates a stool for him to sit on.

But sitting on anything higher than the floor is a new experience, and Ali is also at a loss to know what to do with the staff he carries. Finally he drops it with a crash on the floor as he gingerly lowers himself onto the stool.

The doctor asks such irrelevant questions as how many children he has, and the state of his wife's health. Ali replies that he has no children.

"No children? Not even girls?"

"Oh, I have a daughter."

"How old?"

"She is still nursing, and with her mother. Your pardon for mentioning these unworthy females in your presence. May God—His name be blest and exalted—lengthen your years."

The question, "What is your trouble?" evokes the reply, "That is what I have come to you to discover." But when pressed for information Ali mutters, "God have mercy upon your father," bunches his fingers to claim attention, and, emboldened, tells his story.

"May God lengthen your forearm; do not be angered with me if I speak of

Face-to-face with ordinary Syrians, Herndon took the pulse of life in a Muslim society while his wife, Mary, noted their encounters with people like this unidentified man of the desert.

unworthy things! I have—far be it from you, O son of my brother—a pain here," and he solemnly lays his hand on his stomach. His story finally ended, Ali obediently removes his headcloth and rope coil, dumps them in a corner with his 25-pound *furwah* (sheepskin cloak with the wool inside), and steps forth in a cotton "nightgown" once white but now covered by many a telltale spot left by the denizens of his sheepskin.

His head—a stranger to soap and comb, with hair unkempt except where braided locks fall from his temples—is uncovered only because he realizes the extraordinary demands of the occasion.

Saying, "May he who looks upon your face see only good," and whispering a sibilant "Name of God," Ali mounts the examining table by first planting a leathery and dusty foot in the center of the white sheet. He next slips off a belt which carries a curved and sheathed knife and removes one or two leather-bound amulets hung around his neck. These may contain the

cabalistic writing of some religious sheik, or perhaps a hair from the Prophet's beard.

The examination over, the doctor explains to Ali that he needs to take some medicine and be "hit with a needle" every day for ten days. Ali replies immediately, "But my dwelling is far and my time is short," and asks if he cannot cut the time in half by taking two injections a day. It is explained that the injection is a daily dose and that he cannot expect a cure in less than ten days.

"Still," the doctor says, "there is no compulsion here, and the responsibility for treatment is on your own neck. Improvement is not the same as cure. We may strike the tail of the serpent, but unless we smash the head also we have failed."

"*Wallahi*" (by Allah), the Bedouin replies, sententiously, "the butter is in the head."

He is reminded that "Patience is the key to the door of relief," and he sighs, "Verily, patience is of God." Then comes the question of medicine—a tablespoonful three times a day after meals.

"What!" exclaims the doctor. "No spoon?"

"O long of years, we Arabs are wild beasts. We eat with our hands; we know not spoons."

So, with a glance at the size of his patient's hands, the doctor agrees that a palmful might do.

"And what shall I eat?" asks Ali, knowing full well that he has absolutely no choice in diet.

To please him the doctor begins, "Eggs, milk, vegetables, fruit." But these are not realities to Ali. He churns his milk for its salable butter; he sells his eggs, and raises neither vegetables nor fruit. So he breaks in:

"God guard your offspring! We Arabs, we eat corn like our asses. Know you not that the food of the Bedouin is corn, baked in the fire, and that even our sheiks eat only pounded wheat?" So the matter is closed.

And now for the supreme moment, the all-important question of cost. Ali knows he must bargain until the sweat runs down his forehead; nothing worthwhile has ever come his way without a price. To him free medicine means worthless medicine and scorn for the doctor who believes him such a dupe as to esteem it worth taking. The medicine must have a price, but— equally true—a reduced price.

At this point Ali rises from his stool and leans over in a confidential attitude. With one hand he makes a tentative gesture of supplication at the place where the doctor's beard should be, and in soft tones he says:

"Allah the all-powerful alone knows how poor I am; by your head and by my honor, I speak the truth. I came a long way this day because I heard it said that you in this place did works of healing as a gift to God. Should you heal me, I would praise you night and day; for I depend first upon God and next I put my trust in you! Maybe God will use you to work a work of healing in me. Perhaps God . . . By Allah (and be He exalted), I have not wherewithal to pay you one small flea!"

So finally, not too hastily, and with a proper regard for convention, doctor and patient agree upon terms, and one who exists just above starvation level secures at infinitesimal cost the offices of the best drugs that modern medicine can supply.

"God will give you healing," says the doctor, rising.

"The praise is to God," Ali replies, as he piously kisses the back of his hand and touches his forehead. "If God wills it," he adds by way of proviso, "and with your help, O protected of Allah."

"With the help of God," replies the doctor.

Ali must have the last word.

"God is generous," he whispers. □

In a field outside Aleppo, a family of grain growers lets the wind separate wheat from chaff. "A favorite place for drying grain is the surface of a main highway," observed the original caption. Trucks simply went around.

■ *Maynard Owen Williams is one of the Geographic's legendary figures, a former missionary in Lebanon and China who joined the staff in 1919. As a writer and photographer he ultimately contributed 97 stories—some 2,200 pages—to the magazine. This portrait of life in the new nation of Israel appeared in December 1950, 18 months after the founding of the state of Israel and the bitter war that ensued, which uprooted some 700,000 Palestinians, most of them Muslims. As a Christian, Williams is moved by the experience of visiting the Holy Land, yet he registers his admiration for the citizens of the new Jewish state and, noting the vast numbers of refugees in the lands later known as the West Bank, predicts the storms to come.*

Maynard Owen Williams,
"Home to the Holy Land,"
Dec. 1950, pp. 707-746

Barriers in Jerusalem, manned by Jordanian troops, stand as grim reminders of the 1948 war that brought forth the state of Israel. It left the city—and Palestine—divided between Arabs and Jews.

A Land Rich in Puzzles

TEXT AND PHOTOGRAPHS BY MAYNARD OWEN WILLIAMS

This is a simple traveler's tale of one who, coming home to the Holy Land, found friendship there at Easter time. Sitting below the hallowed walls of Jerusalem, I watched thousands of Christians, bearing banners and waving palms, going up to the Holy City.

A few rods away was a no-man's-land, outlined by barbed wire and bombed-out homes—grim reminders of the Palestine war. While Christians celebrated 20 centuries of Easters, an infant Israel danced in the streets to celebrate its second anniversary.

The places most significant and venerated in the life of Jesus Christ are now held by two new Middle East States, the Hashemite Kingdom of Jordan and Israel.

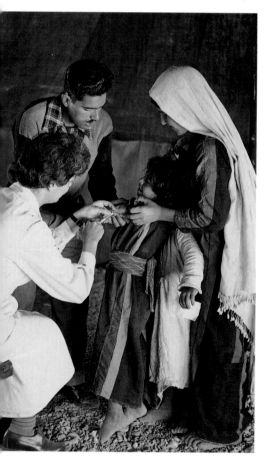

In a refugee camp near Jericho, a Palestinian mother gently grips two fearful children as they receive typhoid shots at a Red Cross tent.

Bethlehem, where the drama of the New Testament begins with the birth of Christ, and that part of Jerusalem where the last chapters end with His crucifixion are both in the hands of Arab Jordan. Nazareth, where Jesus spent His childhood and grew to manhood, is in Israel, as is Galilee, where He performed His many miracles.

Two Semitic nations, handcuffed by an uneasy armistice, guard sites revered by the followers of three great faiths.

What was Palestine is slowly but steadily recovering from the Arab-Jewish war. Bright spots dot the desert. But to attain a higher standard of living for more people, Arab and Jew must make fields grow more grain, cows produce more milk, hens more eggs, sheep more wool and meat, orchards more fruit, an agricultural land more industries, and industry more markets. A timeworn land must work harder under the same sun and rain.

How can this be done, with more than 700,000 Arabs displaced by the war and huddled in refugee camps, in tents, and in caves? How can it be done, with a half million Zionist immigrants, lured by the magic name of Israel, seeking a new and better life? This remains a huge dark puzzle for a land rich in puzzles. Probably not for decades will anyone know the solution.

Above the town of Jericho towers the Mount of Temptation, where the Devil led Jesus and "shewed unto Him all the kingdoms of the world" (Luke 4:5). Today Satan could show Him only human misery and suffering.

Below, the land is dotted with thousands of tents and thousands of ragged Arab refugees. These homeless men, women, and children, who fled Israel two years ago and cannot return to their homes until the issue is settled, huddle together in their despair and await their fate.

Their thirst is quenched from the same fountain which Elisha sweetened with salt (II Kings:19-22), but not their thirst for home.

The plight of these homeless souls is the saddest in all the Holy Land today. At 'Ain es Sultan camp, close to "where the walls came tumbling down" before Joshua's trumpets, I encountered the first of many Arab refugees I was to see. Most of them would starve if it weren't for UN and Red Cross relief.

"They talk of history," one of them said to me, "but what is history compared with a man's own home?" These restless, despairing Arabs are one of the world's touchiest problems today.

One day, with the permission of an Arab Legionnaire, I looked down into Israel from the Old City walls near Zion Gate. Officials in Washington had promised me every help, except that of bridging this 50-yard gap of no-man's-land between Jordan and Israel. If the information I got had been correct, I would have had to detour to Amman, Damascus, Beirut, and Cyprus before reaching this spot in Israel, below my very eyes.

Jewish friends in New York had urged me to attend the second anniversary of Israel, celebrated this year on April 23. There was no certainty that I could get back into Arab territory. But a national holiday, for which the wandering Jew had waited nearly 1,900 years, could not be ignored.

I finally obtained permission to make the crossing. I carried my equipment from Jordan to Israel and later came back the same way. Thus a 600-mile trip was shortened to a brief walk from one taxi to another.

I found myself standing in the New City, which has grown up in the last one hundred years outside Jerusalem's ancient walls. It is the de facto capital of Israel and is today as Jewish a city as any other in the country. There was a holiday air. A big military parade moved down Jaffa Road to celebrate Independence Day.

Legally, Israel is not at peace with any of the seven Arab countries it fought in 1948 and 1949. Yet there has been no active warfare for over a year and a half. The government of the young nation is functioning smoothly, even though rationing and price controls are in effect.

When the State of Israel was proclaimed, thousands more came from 52 countries in the four corners of the Earth. They came from countries with large Jewish populations, like South Africa and the United States. They also came from places like Greenland, Java, and Afghanistan. Each has his own story to tell.

My driver to Rehovot was a black-eyed Jewess wearing a shapely sweater, a checked skirt, and mannish boots. As we charged through traffic in the narrow streets of Tel Aviv and then hit the open road, she sang, first in a soft, crooning soprano, then in a full alto. From a pleading "Last Rose of Summer" she picked up momentum and roared out with the "Toreador" song.

A bit shy, this young woman in a refugee camp wears a traditional Palestinian dress. Others, says the author, make do with "sugar sacks and bean bags."

She was only 19 and a half years old. She escaped from Russia to Afghanistan, Bombay, Tehran, and then to Israel. She spent almost three years in the Israel Army, and in the Arab-Jewish war she doubled in jeep and machine gun.

"I'd drive to where the fighting was hot and then pop, pop, pop!" She had seven wounds in her right arm and a bullet in her right knee. She hopes to study music in New York. She speaks Arabic, Persian, Russian, French, English, and Hebrew. And when I took a seat in her cab, I wondered whether we would have to talk in sign language! Her name is Scheherazade.

World Jewry, largely centered in America, has poured in millions of dollars to develop the land in Israel. The Export-Import Bank in Washington loaned $35,000,000 for the purchase of agricultural equipment and $65,000,000 for public works and communications. The British Treasury also released the equivalent of $20,000,000 for the purchase of British goods.

Land of Muslims, Christians, and Jews, the Holy Land had new borders in 1950 to accomodate the Jewish state. In Jordanian controlled Jerusalem— holy to all three faiths— pilgrims and playful children wait for services to begin at St. James Cathedral.

Since imports exceed exports by eight to one, continued assistance from abroad is necessary if the huge number of Jewish immigrants are to be housed and put to work.

But as I drove north in spring time, in face and field Israel was a smiling land.

In great shiny sheds hens cackled. Brown-eyed cattle had full udders. Heavy-headed grain bowed to the reapers, and machines dropped their heavy bales of fodder with a hearty thud. As we climbed toward Nazareth I saw how Zionist funds had added value to the fruitful plain.

When the Jews declared their independence on May 14-15, 1948, they numbered perhaps 650,000 in all Palestine. Today there are well over a million in Israel, and new immigrants are arriving faster than the land is being tamed.

Still there is a manpower shortage, although new areas are constantly being developed.

More than 700,000 Arabs left the land and only 500,000 Jews have come in. Of these, 239,000 arrived in 1949. Half of them were from Europe, a third from Asia, a sixth from Africa, and 1,358 from the Americas. Immigration in 1949 was three times what Chaim Weizmann had hoped for in 1947.

Others have criticized little Israel for her unlimited immigration policy when the nation is still so young and not ready to receive newcomers. But some officials stoutly defend the "come one, come all" ruling.

"Israel was established," they say, "as a Jewish homeland. As long as a single Jew anywhere wants or needs to come here, the door must be open. If one person is refused admittance, we shall have failed in our purpose." President Weizmann says in his book: "The Jewish people would never produce either the money or the energy required in order to build up a wasteland and make it habitable, unless that land were Palestine."

The next day I set out for Galilee. Our first stop was at Onim, a children's village on the lush Plain of Sharon. There are scores of these settlements in Israel, most of them orphanages.

At Onim a teacher proudly pointed to a group of youngsters enrolled in the nursery school. "You are looking at Israel's most precious crop," he said.

Like a new grove of orange trees, these youngsters are given the most thoughtful and loving care. They are cherished and protected with patient attention. They get special diets and the best of food. Several months ago, butter was dropped from adult rations so there would be more for the children.

Israel stakes its bright future on its youth. It was the young people who fought the war. And in the children's villages and settlement schools youngsters are being trained for the future and for peace.

I was reminded of what an old rabbi once said: "The world is saved only by the breath of school children."

At Onim the children grow up in a cheery atmosphere, feeling that they are loved and that they "belong." They learn to live together and do most of their own work in the shops and gardens, with a minimum of adult supervision.

As we left, we picked up two French-speaking orphans who were leaving Onim to "go home," unaware that no parents would greet them there. As we left the flowery children's village, their guardian cuddled them close, to hide her tears. □

Parking is a new dilemma for visitors to downtown Amman at mid-century. Between 1945 and 1950 this ancient city, capital of modern Jordan, saw its population grow from 60,000 to 150,000 inhabitants. Many new arrivals were Palestinian Muslims displaced by Israel's War of Independence.

How the Kazakhs Fled China

TEXT AND PHOTOGRAPHS BY MILTON J. CLARK

■ *After the 1949 Communist Revolution in China, religious minorities—including the millions of Muslims living in western China—were subject to attacks by the Red Army as it fought for territorial control. In November 1954 the magazine published Milton J. Clark's encounter with a group of refugees under a subtitle that says it all: "Decimated by Chinese Reds and the Hazard of a Hostile Land, Nomads of the Steppes Trekked 3,000 Miles to Kashmir."*

Milton J. Clark, "How the Kazakhs Fled to Freedom," Nov. 1954, pp. 621-644

In storied Srinagar, cradled in the Vale of Kashmir, I spent a year among refugee Kazakhs, colorful tribesmen whose forebears have roamed the steppes of central Asia for 2,000 years. My wiry, high-spirited hosts were the remnants of hordes of saddle-bred nomads who had fled the Communist regime which Red China had imposed on their native Province of Sinkiang.

My wife and I became the good friends of a handful of tribal families, the homeless survivors of an overland journey that had been at once a triumph and a disaster: 4,000 families had set out from Sinkiang on their epic escape march; a pitiful 350 individuals reached Kashmir.

Who are these people? And what political storm set in motion the wave of crisis that dislodged them from their native land? Today the major domain of the Kazakhs, who blend Turkic stock with a mixture of Mongolian, is the Kazakh Soviet Socialist Republic. There several million of them occupy a vast territory stretching from China to the Caspian Sea.

Kazakh pastoral nomads also comprise, at present, about ten percent of the population of Sinkiang, China's westernmost Province. In 1949 semiarid Sinkiang, two and a half times the size of Texas with half as many people, came under the dominance of China's Communist regime.

Large groups of Kazakhs, their liberties in jeop-

Robed in the magnificent fur of a snow leopard, Qali Beg, a Kazakh chief, proudly rides into exile from his home in western China.

ardy, chose to emigrate, if necessary, from their dearly loved land rather than submit to Communist control.

Now, in the summer camp above Srinagar, Sultan Sherif was talking as a downpour pelted the felt tent.

"Almost in the beginning—it was early in the Year of the Tiger—our leaders Janim Khan and Osman Batir called us to a great council at Barkol in the eastern Tien Shan," he said, scooping up a gob of butter which he solicitously plopped into my newly filled bowl of hot tea. "The Communists were holding the reins of government in tight check. Our chiefs and leading men had to choose which way to turn."

During the fall and winter of 1949-50 the Kazakhs had dealt with the Communists, asking guarantees of religious freedom, preservation of tribal customs, and liberty to travel at will within Sinkiang. But the new regime let it be known that *it* would set the terms of Kazakh "cooperation."

Many of the Kazakhs made long journeys to reach the Barkol council. Then a winter storm killed much livestock; the sheep, which were lambing, could not be moved to shelter. It was the kind of time of which the Kazakhs say, "Ice is our bed and snow our blanket."

By March of 1950 the panorama at the rallying place must have been cause for pride and even reassurance. Kazakhs by the thousands populated the broad valley, still white with snow. Tents were strewn for miles across the landscape, the sons' placed around those of the fathers.

Within sight of Sultan Sherif's tent door were assembled at least 15,000 people, 60,000 fat-tailed sheep, 12,000 horses, 7,000 head of cattle, and more than 1,000 camels.

On March 28 in that Year of the Tiger a congress of 1,000 Kazakh leaders and family heads cast their vote to leave "the golden cradle of their birth" and make for the southern passes that led toward India.

A week later the council set up an autonomous Kazakh government, naming Janim Khan governor and Osman Batir commander in chief of the fighting men. Neither leader survived long enough to exercise his new authority.

At Barkol the threat of tribal destruction hung, like the Damoclean sword, over every tent, every horseman, every mother, every infant heir. Yet the Kazakhs clung stubbornly to the customs and ritual of daily life. The herders' work, the elders' prayers, the children's play—all went on as usual.

In mid-April the Communists swept down in a surprise attack on the Barkol encampment. Brief warning by outpost sentries scarcely gave women and children time to strike tents and head for the hills, driving flocks and herds before them.

Puppet troops in quilted drab poured into the valley in trucks, armored vehicles, and on horseback, heavily armed and plentifully supplied with ammunition.

For the spirited Kazakhs, used to unequal odds, even such formidable armament held no new terrors. Shouting battle cries and riding at full gallop, the warriors struck hard in righteous anger. "One shot, one dead enemy," states the Kazakh standard of marksmanship. But against an enemy equipped with modern arms, there could be no hope of victory. Kazakh fighting men died by the hundreds.

"*Janibeg!*" called out the chiefs at last, using one of the war cries that are old-time heroes' names. "Break off battle and flee!" Southward streamed the shocked, enraged, depleted company of tribesmen.

Sultan Sherif told me that 12,600 of the more than 15,000 of his people assembled at Barkol were killed, captured, or dispersed. Many fled to the hills, where some groups still may be precariously hiding out.

The survivors managed to rejoin the main body of organized refugees. Under the leadership of Osman Batir; Sultan Sherif, and Delil Khan, this group pushed southwest through Singsingsia and crossed out of Sinkiang into Kansu Province near Khara Nor.

Mile after mile the tribesmen plodded on, across steppes both green and sere, over stony mountain passes, through desolate valleys. Slowed to the speed of their flocks and herds, they could not outrun their pursuers. Small Communist bands attacked them at intervals. Only superb horsemanship and sharp shooting saved even the dwindled remnants of the tribes.

Meanwhile, to Timurlik had come another group of fleeing Kazakhs, perhaps 50 families, under Qali Beg, the chief who became my special friend. Pasturing among the mountains near Urumchi (Tihwa), Sinkiang's capital, these Kazakhs had heard of the disaster at Barkol. Leaders at once marshaled their families and got them under way southward through the Tien Shan. Their objective also was a rendezvous with Hussain Taiji's people.

Running the gantlet of enemy attack and natural obstacles, Qali Beg's skeleton "horde" endured even harsher trials than had the easterly tribes under Sultan Sherif and Delil Khan. My notes record reminiscences of Hamza, Qali Beg's deputy, about their anxious crossing of the exposed Lop Nor desert, eastern reach of the dreaded Takla Makan.

"Lacking maps, we followed a river to the salt at Lop Nor," Hamza said. "Hillocks we passed were strewn with bones of men and animals. Many among us thought the same fate awaited us, but I spoke what I believed: that death would be the destiny of our oppressors, not the Kazakhs. 'Let us follow our future,' I said, 'and trust in Allah.'

"Crossing the wintry desert," Hamza went on, "we huddled among our livestock as black sandstorms and snow squalls swept over us. We had to avoid known water holes, for the Communists would use them as lures, drawing us into ambush. Smaller water holes were frozen over. We broke the ice loose and carried it with us for melting as we needed it.

"Some became separated, lost their way, and couldn't even find ice. The need to keep moving made them sweat, even in the cold. First they drank the milk from their animals. Some slaughtered their cattle and sheep and quaffed the blood. Still many perished.

"At last, after seven days, we met Hussain Taiji's people. Our men and women danced and hugged one another and exchanged presents to celebrate their survival."

Four thousand families had set out from Sinkiang on their epic escape march; a pitiful 350 individuals reached Kashmir.

Early in the Year of the Hare (1951) the Communists swept down on Qali Beg near Timurlik. Routed by modern arms, he and his people fled for their lives into Tibet.

It was February when a mounted messenger brought to the Kazakhs at Taijinar Nor the word that Osman Batir had been captured and that the Communists had routed Qali Beg. Quickly the chiefs broke camp and led their people over the rugged Kunlun passes, then turned westward across Tibet. With the help of Allah they might reach Kashmir.

Even beyond the stormy Kunlun grass for the flocks and herds was hard to find. The animals grew thin, and many perished. Fortunately game—"by the hundreds and thousands," the chiefs told me—was there for the shooting. The men killed antelope, deer, and ibex; what was not eaten was smoked or frozen. Dung of the wild animals provided fuel in a land devoid of firewood.

The "manna in the wilderness," however, was the small, dun-colored horse known to the tribesmen as *qulan*. The Kazakhs hunted it from horse-back, killing scores for the flavorsome, nourishing meat.

Mountain illness, the bleeding death called *is*, was a special scourge during this part of the heroic trek. It killed or incapacitated the physically depleted Kazakhs by the dozen, especially while they were crossing the mountain passes into Tibet.

First symptoms of the disease often were a bad headache, dizziness, and nausea. In many cases treatment was in vain; futile even were the shaman's

efforts to exorcise the evil spirits believed to be causing the sickness.

Drastic treatment was sometimes followed by recovery. One victim told me of beseeching a shaman to free him from the misery of this illness. The shaman took a sharp knife, placed it against a vein in the man's temple, and flicked it to slit the blood vessel.

He let the blood, very thick and black, fill three cups. Then he applied some herbs and a bandage. In two days the patient was well again.

After ten days' travel the Kazakhs' outriders caught sight of a straggling band of men and animals quartering into their trail from the north. It was Qali Beg and the remnants of his group! Joyful was the reunion, calling for singing, wrestling, and dancing.

For safety, the united groups presently split again. Delil Khan and his people joined forces with Qali Beg, but Hussain Taiji and Sultan Sherif remained together, heading the other section.

Qali Beg told me his people suffered seven armed attacks during the ensuing crossing of Tibet, a portion of the trek that cost his families alone 42 killed in action, 22 dead of mountain sickness, and nine missing. Between the Tien Shan and the Kashmir border they lost in addition 3,000 sheep, 200 cattle, 73 horses, and 145 camels.

One day in the summer encampment above Srinagar, while we sat cross-legged in conversation, some of the young women were kneeling at the fringe of the group raptly engrossed in the men's talk. Suddenly Milya, Qali Beg's newest wife, turned to him saying, "*Erim* (my husband), do you remember the day the enemy came to the encampment when the men were away?" Qali Beg's eyes lighted up and, at his urging, Milya told the tale, flushed with pleasure as all eyes sought her out.

"My husband and his men were off fighting the enemy," she began, as her companions replenished the empty tea bowls. "Suddenly we saw troops galloping toward our camp. The women snatched up their young children and ran for their horses.

"I was last in the stirrups, and my horse balked, badly frightened. A Communist bullet grazed the animal's leg, and he bolted forward.

"I saw a child crying in front of a tent," Milya went on, helping break the round loaves of unleavened bread and spreading the chunks before us. "Slowing my horse, I leaned from the saddle and picked up the child, with the enemy close behind. Four bullets pierced my clothes, and I was much afraid. Luckily my horse was swift, and I lost my pursuers in the mountains. Soon I met Suleiman, a young man from our tribe who was herding sheep. I told him what had happened, and together we raced back to the camp by a short cut. We knew the enemy would return to loot the tents. We found two machine guns and lay in wait.

"As we expected, they rode up unsuspecting. We could see their startled looks when Suleiman commenced firing. I loaded one machine gun while Suleiman fired the other.

"We held off the foe for five hours, until my husband and his men returned and drove away the enemy. My husband told me I was very brave and that I had saved the camp. *Oi!* I shall never forget that day."

Even by forced marches the cruel 700-mile trek across Tibet consumed three months. To reduce the chance of attack, the ragged columns bypassed settlements that might harbor spies.

As for the Tibetans, they let the Kazakhs cross their land unopposed. The emigrants, in fact, hired willing shepherds as guides. Tibet at that time was in the throes of "adjusting" to the new Chinese Communist regime that was seizing their country, too.

There were streams to cross, and many Kazakhs cannot swim. Men and women rode the rivers tandem on the horses, infants in their mothers' arms. Young shepherds plunged into icy water and were swept across, clinging to the necks of two sheep.

At last, in the distance, rose the jagged, ice-draped Karakoram Range. To the weary pilgrims, by then nearly drained of hope, the mountains must have seemed a mirage.

Near Rudok, the last Tibetan village short of Kashmir, the Kazakhs pitched camp and invited the headman of the town to a meager "banquet." They gave their Tibetan guest a rifle; he reciprocated with salt, flour, and brick tea, showed the way to the border, and wished them well. Crossing into Kashmir near Pangong Tso, the weary refugees surrendered to the frontier guards and gratefully let their feet fall on the soil of sanctuary. ☐

In the mountains near Srinagar, Kashmir, Kazakh refugees relax with a *toi*, or celebration. According to the author, these wrestlers are continuing a struggle begun earlier on horseback.

■ *Few nations in the Muslim world have been as thoroughly terrorized as Algeria, where over the past decade more than 100,000 people—most of them innocent villagers—have died in a savage civil war between radical Islamist groups and an ironfisted government. When staff writer Howard La Fay visited for this June 1960 article , Algeria was in the throes of another guerrilla war—this one against the French, who had ruled there since the time of Napoleon. Algeria won its freedom in 1962.*

Howard La Fay, "Algeria: France's Stepchild, Problem and Promise," photos by Robert F. Sisson, June 1960, pp. 768-795

French Foreign Legion troops sprint to a weapons carrier in a practice strike against guerrillas near Sidi bel Abbes.

A Colony Erupts

BY HOWARD LA FAY   PHOTOGRAPHS BY ROBERT F. SISSON

The battle, when it came, was short, sharp, and typical. All afternoon the French commandos—30 sweating men in camouflaged fatigues—had pressed into the stark, lonely mountains of northwest Algeria. Their mission: to intercept a rebel band about to raid the fat farmlands of the Chéliff Plain.

A wound suffered in Indochina had left the captain with a small scar below his right eye and a permanent tic. He glanced at the darkening sky.

"Once the sun sets," he told me, "they'll slip past us like shadows. If we don't find them soon, we'll have several dead farmers by morning."

The skirmish line topped a rise and someone shouted: "There they are!" Simultaneously, the green-clad rebel band spotted the French. Machine guns clattered; rifle bullets cracked past my ears; grenades exploded gruffly, their fragments whining overhead. Then, as dusk deepened into night across the hills, the firing died.

"They've fled, *mon capitaine*," a corporal reported. "Back up into the mountains. We might have hit one or two, but in this light it's hard to tell."

The captain shrugged. "No luck. Well, take a squad and set up an ambush between here and the highway in case they try again. Keep me informed by radio."

As we trudged back the long, weary way we had come, the captain said, "It's always like this. You catch them, and they melt into the ravines. It's like trying to grab a fistful of quicksilver." He peered up into the black fastness of the mountains. "But don't think it's so easy for them. Cold, hungry, short of weapons, hunted like animals. Sometimes I think they're as sick of it as we are."

After almost six years of rebellion, all Algeria is sick of war. Daily acts of terrorism cloud the lives of the 10,600,000 people—90 percent Moslem, the remainder European settlers—who inhabit this country more than four times the size of France. The smoking bomb rolling into the café, the ambushed bus, and the morning obituary are the facts of Algerian life. So is the ominous predawn knock of police on a suspect's door.

The start of what Algerians call *les événements*—the events—on November 1, 1954, ushered in a grim struggle for independence by the Moslem Front de Libération Nationale, or F.L.N. The settlers just as grimly guard the old status quo. Caught between these implacable foes, the French Army fights thanklessly to pacify the bleeding country. Facing an estimated 50,000 F.L.N. guerrillas are 450,000 French troops; surprisingly, 150,000 of them are Moslem volunteers.

Other paradoxes abound. The anticolonial F.L.N. has slain nine times as many Moslems as Europeans, while the settlers who rally to the cause of French Algeria have twice taken up arms against France—toppling the Fourth Republic in May 1958, and shaking the Fifth Republic in January 1960. Finally, fewer than half these settlers are of French descent; most of the rest have Spanish, Italian, or Maltese origins.

In the capital city of Algiers you are never far from the strictures of war. Roadblocks bar every access to the city, soldiers with submachine guns patrol the thoroughfares, a nightly curfew clears the streets. To guard against time bombs, shoppers are searched at the entrances to stores,

In this automated pumping facility in the port of Algiers, push-button controls transfer Algerian wine from shore to ship. Winking lights track the wine's movement through the pipes.

movie-goers are forbidden to leave before a film ends, and the post office accepts no package not wrapped in the presence of a clerk. A doorman even searches the dinner-jacketed patrons of the city's plush casino before allowing them to try their luck at roulette.

Nonetheless, Algiers is a boom town. Soldiers, oilmen, refugees from the mountains choke the streets. New apartments spring up, but waiting lists continue to grow. Hotels are so overtaxed that every night some 600 visitors fail to find rooms. Harried city officials lodge them in passenger liners moored in the harbor.

The harbor itself, protected by three miles of jetties, is actually the dominant commercial pulse of the city, and its activities provide a revealing glimpse of the Algerian economy. Great ships glide in daily to disgorge coal, wood, steel, and cement, then cast off to replenish Europe's larder with fruits, vegetables, and wine.

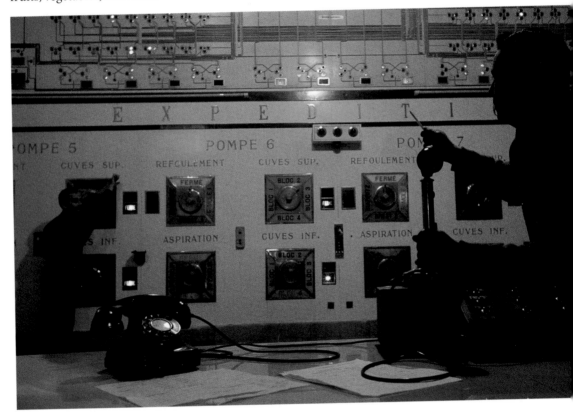

From the vineyards and gardens of lush Mitidja to the Atlas Mountains is no great distance, but in human terms it spans a thousand years. Until the start of "the events," isolated families of Berbers and Arabs followed their flocks across the bleak massif or sowed a sparse crop on some rocky slope. Now, however, the French have mounted a massive campaign to lift Algeria's nine million Moslems from the poverty that has ground them for centuries. The result, they hope, will be to win the allegiance of those who support the rebellion.

As a first step, the army gathers all families in a given area into a "regroupment village." There soldiers, civilian volunteers, or officers of the government's Specialized Administrative Sections begin the war upon misery.

Since many if not most regroupment villages are in rebel-infested territory, the danger is great. Death lurks no farther than the next clump of trees.

Still, the program has caught the French imagination. Every year hundreds of youths from both Algeria and metropolitan France enlist for the risky business of nursing and teaching the Moslem population. One such is Mademoiselle Françoise Carbon, a young graduate of the Sorbonne's Faculty of Letters, who spent several months as a volunteer nurse in the regroupment village of Aïn Tida.

With Mlle. Carbon I set off one day to see the program in action. From Algiers we went by train to Affreville. A government official, wise in the ways of survival, suggested that we take the *inoxydable*, the express with stainless-steel coaches. "Though one must pay a supplement," he explained, "the inox gives much more protection than wooden coaches if it strikes a mine."

Via inox, therefore, we proceeded to Affreville, thence to the dusty agricultural town of Carnot, where we joined the weekly truck convoy bound to Aïn Tida, high in the hostile Dahra mountains. The convoy—bristling with machine guns—had formed in front of Carnot's school for girls. Inside the big glass windows I could see European girls, their hair in pigtails, and Moslem girls, their hair hennaed a vivid red, sitting at double desks.

To my surprise, Charles Boyer commanded both the convoy and Aïn Tida. But this Charles Boyer, I soon learned, had never seen Hollywood; he was a sinewy captain of the 42d Artillery Regiment. As the trucks growled up into the brown hills, he told me: "I've been in the army for 14 years now. And always there's been a war. First Germany, then Indochina, now here. France is the one place a French officer rarely visits any more."

As our convoy wound higher into the hills, a silver fighter plane kited in from the south to fly cover. Zooming low, the pilot hedgehopped the road ahead, searching for any sign of a rebel ambush. Periodically, he flashed an "all clear" on the radio.

When we finally swept into Aïn Tida, a tidal wave of children engulfed Mlle. Carbon. While she renewed acquaintance with her onetime patients, Captain Boyer showed me through his village of 150 mud huts—called *gourbis* in Arabic—housing 790 people.

He knocked on a door. After a moment it opened, and a smiling Berber woman invited us into her windowless habitation. The air was close, furniture was pitifully scarce, but the house was as clean as hands and brooms could keep it.

"These gourbis are temporary," the captain said. "We hope eventually to provide every family with a new two-room house. Meanwhile, we've built a school and an infirmary, and we've set up one of the villagers in the grocery business."

Captain Boyer's pride and joy proved to be a pipeline that his men had built between the village and its spring, some two and a half miles distant. "The women of Aïn Tida," he told me, "no longer have to trudge five miles a day for water and carry it home on their shoulders. Now water is no more than one hundred yards from any house.

"Of course, the rebels harass us. Once they cut the pipeline, but we managed to repair it in an hour. Another time they fouled the spring itself. All they accomplished in both cases was to alienate the villagers.

"Soon," he added enthusiastically, "I'm going to use the surplus water to irrigate these

Veiled shoppers haggle over chickens at a hole-in-the-wall shop in the Casbah, Algiers' teeming—and much romanticized—Arab quarter.

slopes. Someday Aïn Tida will be the most prosperous village in the Dahra!"

"For a professional soldier," I observed, "yours is an odd assignment."

"True," he grinned. "But this is an odd war."

An hour's drive south from Oran brought me to a small, walled city steeped in romance: Sidi bel Abbés, home of the French Foreign Legion. Bel Abbés, as legionnaires call it, owes its existence to the Legion: legionnaires built the city as a garrison in 1847, and the training of Legion recruits remains its chief industry.

Behind an imposing sand-colored wall in the center of Bel Abbés, young men—and some not so young—receive an arduous initiation. Founded in 1831, the Legion has left its dead on battlefields from Norway to Madagascar. The flag of the Legion's 3d Foreign Regiment is the most decorated in the French Army.

Burnoose-clad customers at El Oued's Friday market inspect mountains of oranges and greens. In an oasis where timber is scarce, adobe construction predominates.

Twenty thousand men from more than 40 nations now swell Legion ranks. Thousands serve under assumed names. "The Legion," an officer told me, "is a thermometer of the economic and political ills of Europe. After the Spanish Civil War, we had an influx of Spaniards; the post-World War II period brought us Germans and Italians; recently we've been doing very well with Hungarians."

The Legion motto, *Legio Patria Nostra*, means "The Legion is our Homeland," and for the dispossessed it is just that. The Legion feeds its men, clothes them, pays them, even gives them an annual Christmas present. In return, legionnaires swear allegiance not primarily to France but to the Legion.

In Algeria the Legion does the bulk of its fighting in the east near Constantine, where the European population is submerged in a sea of hostile Moslems.

I found Constantine a city besieged. Concertinas of barbed wire stood ready to seal off each street leading into the central Place de Nemours. Elaborate screens protected every large café from grenades. The police, bedeviled by a terrorism that has killed or wounded thousands since 1954, had completely barricaded certain sections of the Moslem quarter. To go from one house to its neighbor, I frequently had to detour completely around a district.

What, in the end, are the images that one carries away from Algeria?

. . . A bitter Moslem in a village square pointing to the blind and the lame pleading for alms. "For centuries of this," he says, "there is a justice that awaits us. The Europeans exploit us. They grow richer while we grow poorer. But now we will have justice."

. . . A small, pretty girl in a pinafore amid the throngs on Algiers' Rue d'Isly. A rebel bomb has just killed her. The girl is eight years old. The day is Christmas Eve .

. . . A young couple on the Oran-Algiers train—the inox, of course. The girl stares out the window. Leaning over, her escort asks, "Why so sad, _chérie?_" Without turning her head she replies very softly, "Because this is a sad country." □

Worry beads click
in the hectic currency-
and-securities trading
room of Gulf Interna-
tional Bank in Manama,
Bahrain, a city of
148,000 with some 130
financial institutions.

PART THREE

ISLAM RISING

1961-1990

Colonies no more but still not free: Facing tyranny
at home and an increasingly material world, Muslims
embrace traditional values and rally around their faith.
Keeping pace with the times, our coverages grow
longer, deeper, darker.

Veiled women shopping in Kohat represent the Muslim heritage of Pakistan, which sees itself as a leader of Islam. In the cities women enjoy greater freedom and opportunity, becoming teachers, journalists, doctors, and diplomats.

Kentucky Fried Chic

Far from his old Kentucky home, a cardboard Colonel Sanders brings his "finger-lickin'" fare to Abu Dhabi. With fattened paychecks from the oil boom of the 1970s, many Persian Gulf Arabs had plenty to spend on products from Japan and the West.

As time goes by, Saddam Hussein's grip on Iraq has outlasted many predictions. President since 1979, he still leads Iraq's ruling Baath Party.

A king-size portrait of Oman's Sultan Qaboos bin Said bin Taimur towers over workmen hoisting it onto the side of a hotel in the capital city of Muscat.

Expressing monumental grief and pride, this 150-foot-high tiled Baghdad dome, split in half, commemorates Iraqi soldiers killed in Iraq's war with Iran during the 1980s.

STEVE McCURRY—1985

The Sword and the Sermon

TEXT AND PHOTOGRAPHS BY THOMAS J. ABERCROMBIE

■ Beginning with his first Middle East assignment (Lebanon) in 1957, Minnesota native Tom Abercrombie made himself at home in the Muslim world, where his Geographic career took him about once a year until he retired in 1994. Prowling backstreets and villages from Yemen to Casablanca, Cairo to Istanbul, Abercrombie learned to speak Arabic, steeped himself in Islamic history, and embraced the faith of Muhammad. In 1970 he set off on a yearlong journey to render the faith in words and pictures and gave readers of the July 1972 issue an extraordinary experience— a personally guided tour of the world of Islam, led by "Abu Kareem Bey."

Thomas J. Abercrombie,
"The Sword and the Sermon,"
July 1972, pp. 3-45

Wrapped in humble pilgrim's cloth, I stepped through the Gate of Peace and into the immense courtyard of Islam's holiest shrine, the Great Mosque of Mecca.

Lofty stood its seven minarets; its marble and granite galleries gleamed in the white-hot desert sun. Around me the pious from all the Muslim world paid homage to God in the birthplace of their faith. A circle of schoolboys cradling Korans chanted their catechism; joyous pilgrims splashed themselves with water from the sacred Well of Zamzam; the very old, with eyes on the next life, washed winding cloths and laid them in the courtyard to dry. A trace of incense wafted on the reverent murmur of a thousand prayers.

In the center of the courtyard the stark cube-shaped Kaaba, draped in black silk, loomed fifty feet above the worshipers. At God's command, it is told, Abraham built the first shrine on this spot. From the edge of the courtyard I bowed through two prayers, then followed my *mutawwif*, or pilgrim guide, into the churning multitude.

Seven times we circled the shrine, repeating the ritual devotions in Arabic: "Lord God, from such a distant land I have come unto Thee . . . grant me shelter under Thy throne." Caught up in the whirling scene, lifted by the poetry of the prayers, we orbited God's house in accord with the atoms, in harmony with the planets.

Thus, with a pilgrimage to its fountainhead, I set out to trace the once mighty, and still awesomely vast, empire of Islam.

For many years a traveler in Arab lands, I

Eyes fierce as a desert hawk's, a Saudi Arabian embodies the faith that gripped Muhammad's first converts—and sustains Islam today.

have now fulfilled a dream of traversing that empire—more far-flung at its zenith than ancient Rome's—from Spain to Soviet Central Asia, from Sicily to the southern Sahara. And wherever Arab armies fought, and Arab scholars taught, I found a remarkable modern legacy of their power and learning. For the blood of desert-born conquerors still flows in the veins not only of sheiks and sultans, but of matadors and nuns and Bolsheviks as well.

After completing the seven circuits of the sanctuary—part of the *umra* ritual required of all visitors to Mecca—I jostled through the crowd to kiss the Black Stone, perfumed and set in silver into the eastern corner of the Kaaba.

A story is told of this ancient relic, revered even in pagan times before Islam, when Meccans worshiped such diverse deities as Uzza, goddess of the morning star, and Awf, the great bird.

When the elders of Mecca renovated the shrine—sometime in the late sixth century of our era—they fell into argument: Who would have the honor of resetting the sacred stone into the masonry?

It was agreed that the next man to enter the sacred precincts would judge the dispute. First to appear was a young Meccan merchant whose wisdom and honesty had already won him the nickname of "Al-Amin—the trustworthy." He was a lean man, strong of bone and muscle. His thick beard framed an oval face set with dark, serious eyes. His laugh was rarely more than a smile.

He called for a cloak to be spread on the ground and had the Black Stone placed upon it. With a noble from each of Mecca's leading tribes pulling a corner of the robe, the sacred stone was raised. Then, with his own two hands, the young man set the stone into its niche, where it remains to this day. The man's name was Muhammad.

Born in Mecca into the prominent Quraysh tribe about A.D. 570, Muhammad was orphaned at six and reared by a grandfather and then by an uncle. In his youth he worked as a shepherd, and later rode with the camel caravans that carried frankincense and silk through Mecca north to Syria. Although unlettered, he gradually gained respect as a businessman. At 25, he married Khadija, a wealthy widow many years his senior.

Of his next few years little is known except that he devoted much time to contemplation. Often he climbed to a small cave among the rocks of Mount Hira, just north of Mecca, to spend days in fasting and meditation. There, in the year 610, a revelation overwhelmed him: a blinding vision that frightened him to his knees.

"Recite: In the name of thy Lord who createth," the vision commanded, "Createth man from a clot... Who ... teacheth man that which he knew not."

Springboard to empire, Medina now crowds around the Mosque of the Prophet, where minarets rise above the green dome that marks Muhammad's tomb. Fleeing persecution in Mecca, Muhammad founded the first Islamic community in Medina at this date-palm oasis in A.D. 622. Like Mecca, Medina is closed to nonbelievers.

Troubled, Muhammad returned home to Khadija. God had spoken to him, had appointed him His messenger . . . or was he losing his senses? His wife consoled him, believing in his call, and soon became his first convert. The revelations continued, and would later form the Koran, the Muslim holy book. His circle of believers grew, but his preachings angered the Meccans. By condemning their deities, he offended not only the consciences of the Meccan leaders, but also their pocketbooks. More and more he was openly scorned, even threatened, on the streets.

Finally the Prophet and several trusted friends slipped away from Mecca under the veil of a moonless night. Mounting camels, they embarked for the oasis of Yathrib, more than 200 miles north across the desert. It was the year 622.

Islam's calendar dates from this hegira, or emigration, of Muhammad. Who could have guessed the event would signal a momentous era? Within a hundred years the banners of Islam would span three continents, from the rim of China to the Pyrenees.

Long before history began, the Arabian Desert was home to the cultural ancestor of these conquerors—the Bedouin, whose flocks of sheep and camels earned him a meager living from the unforgiving wastes. Often he rode out on *ghazwas*—raids—to settle feuds or to rustle camels from rival tribes. In this crust of a land a man's name was often his only wealth, and he guarded it carefully. Says an early Arabic poem: With the sword I will wash my shame away, Let God's doom bring on me what it may!

Yet a Bedouin's love of freedom was bridled by loyalty to clan and tribe; both were tempered by an unblinking submission to his destiny. This stern code left an indelible mark on Muhammad's new religion.

It took Muhammad and his companions about ten days to reach the safety of Yathrib after their flight from Mecca. They had traveled fast and rested little, avoiding the main tracks and caravan wells. Alerted to his coming, the small band of Muslim converts living at the oasis had waited days at the southernmost fringe of palms.

"He has come! He has come!" they shouted, tears staining their cheeks. Many offered him their homes, but Muhammad said Allah would guide his

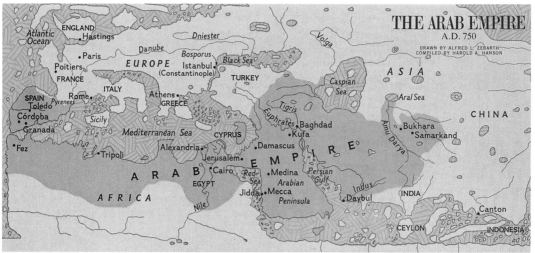

NG MAPS

camel to a chosen spot; the beast stopped and knelt near a small barn used for storing dates.

Here, with his own hands, Muhammad helped his followers build the world's first mosque. The oasis would become known to the world as Madinat al-Nabi—City of the Prophet, or simply Medina.

Around the extraordinary personality of Muhammad, the small Muslim community began to crystallize into a political force. The Prophet's revelations continued. Set down later in the Koran, they detailed how a Muslim should conduct his prayers, his business, his marriage, his wars—the whole spectrum of his life. They became the kernel of Islamic law that today governs much of the world.

Allah had commanded Muhammad to make war against nonbelievers. The first target was the annual caravan marching south from Damascus, a thousand camels laden with goods of his enemies, the Meccan merchants. Forewarned of the Moslems' plans, the Meccans rushed reinforcements to rescue the caravan. At the wells of Badr, near the Red Sea coast, they surprised Muhammad's army of 300.

"All who die today will enter paradise!" the Prophet shouted over the slashing of swords and the whistle of arrows. Outnumbered three to one, the Moslems fought savagely and routed the Meccans. "It was not ye who slew them," Allah revealed to Muhammad. "It was God."

A year later, at Mount Uhud near Medina, the Meccans retaliated, nearly killing Muhammad himself. He was wounded in the face by a stone, then a sword glanced off his helmet and he fell, bleeding. Companions carried him to safety.

Slowly, by treaty and by skirmish, Muhammad converted the Bedouin tribes of the surrounding desert, mustering their swords and swift camels to his cause. Not until the year 630, two decades after his vision, did Muhammad the conqueror reenter his native city, now leading an army of 10,000. Mecca surrendered without a fight.

The Prophet walked to the Kaaba, touched the Black Stone, and made the prescribed seven circuits. He ordered the idols smashed, then declared a general amnesty. Meccans filed past to swear allegiance to the Prophet of God. Within two years much of Arabia was united under the banner of Islam.

But the Prophet's personal mission was nearing its end. Back in Medina he fell ill of fever. Weakening with each passing day, he had to delegate Abu Bakr—later to become his successor, the first caliph—to lead the public prayers. On June 8, 632, in the arms of his favorite wife, Aisba, Muhammad whispered his last devotions, then peacefully surrendered to Allah's will.

The centuries have enlarged the sanctuary Muhammad built in Medina of palm logs and sun-dried brick. The galleries of today's Prophet's Mosque are lined with marble and graced with stately minarets and a high green dome that marks Muhammad's tomb. Facing the brass grill-work of the sepulcher, I paid my respects to Islam's founder. Praying to Muhammad is strictly forbidden, but visitors pray that Allah grant the Prophet eternal peace.

Outward from the mosque fans the modern city of Medina. Television sets blare from coffeehouses; fashionable shops and air-conditioned hotels line wide avenues. But five times each day, on the call from the minaret, the hectic rumble of traffic falls silent. Shops close and streets empty as towns-people converge on the Prophet's Mosque.

"There is no better place to savor the full measure of Muslim faith than here in Medina," said my friend Daoud Abdullah, a student at Medina's Islamic University. "The footsteps of the Prophet of God still echo in these narrow streets."

I had to agree as we strolled in early evening through the labyrinth beyond the bazaar. Overhanging balconies almost met above our heads. Veiled women passed, lugging home baskets of onions and turnips, and school-boys carried books wrapped in their prayer rugs. A donkey squeezed a bulging load of alfalfa past a young lamplighter carrying glowing lanterns. Such scenes had changed little since the Prophet's time. "As-salaam alaykum!" we greeted the lamplighter. "Peace be upon you." "Wa alaykum as-salaam wa rahmat Allah wa barakatu!" he replied. "On you peace; and the mercy of Allah and His blessings."

This was the language Muhammad spoke, the incomparable Arabic preserved forever by the Holy Koran. It still serves as the lingua franca of the people I met in Medina's international community—pilgrims from Morocco and Indonesia, black Sudanese street vendors, the refugee carpenter from Soviet Turkistan, a Syrian scholar passing a quiet afternoon

Arab scholar Al-Idrisi sent agents throughout the known world in the 12th century to gather information for the original of this chart, here shaded to show the Arab sphere in A.D. 750, 118 years after Muham-mad's death. Using their reports, Al-Idrisi located distant places such as the Chinese city of Canton and Hastings, England.

in the library behind the Prophet's Mosque.

"A Turkish sultan built this library 125 years ago," said the director, Sheik Mahmud Akinli. "The Ottoman Turks ruled Medina and Mecca for 400 years, until World War I."

Leaving my sandals at the door, I walked across thick carpets to browse through the priceless collection of manuscripts in tall, mahogany bookcases. Sheik Mahmud showed me a tattered volume of gazelle-skin parchment. "This Koran was copied only a few years after the Prophet's death," he said, reverently turning the worn pages. "It is one of the earliest copies known."

The first Arab thrusts from Medina were little more than Bedouin raids. But Moslems were forbidden to attack brother Moslems. Instead they united against the infidels to the north: Byzantium and Persia—both weakened by years of mutual warfare.

In Palestine and Syria the desert warriors of Islam's most famous general, Khalid ibn al-Walid, clashed with armies of Byzantine Emperor Heraclius. Against the better disciplined and more numerous Byzantine soldiers, the Arabs pitted their greater mobility and unbridled zeal. In 636, at the battle of Yarmuk near the present border between Jordan and Syria, the Arab army, outnumbered two to one, faced 50,000 Byzantine troops in one of the decisive battles of history.

The Byzantine infantrymen took oaths to "stand or die" and chained themselves together, ten on a shackle, 30 ranks deep. On the other side, the women accompanying the Muslim soldiers stood ready behind the lines with tent poles and stones to punish any cowards who turned from battle. They goaded their men:

We are the daughters of the night . . . If you advance we will embrace you; If you retreat we will forsake you.

Amid shouts of "*Allah akbar!*—God is most great!"—the emperor's troops fell like ripe wheat under the flashing Arab blades. His army annihilated, Heraclius retreated to his capital on the Bosporus; the Byzantine Empire had lost the Holy Land and Syria.

The city of Damascus, then Christian, had surrendered after an earlier six-month siege. And Khalid had issued terms that served as a model for future Arab conquests:

"In the name of Allah, the Compassionate, the Merciful. This is given by Khalid ibn al-Walid to the people of Damascus . . . safety for themselves, their property, their churches, and the walls of their city . . . as long as they pay the *jizya.*"

Those who converted to Islam were exempted from the jizya, a yearly head tax—one dinar and a measure of wheat.

Today people of both faiths live side by side in Damascus, though now the Muslims form the majority. I mixed with both as I pressed through busy Al-Hamidiya, the covered bazaar in the center of the Old City. Crowded shops overflowed with famous Damascus wares—copper, inlaid tables, silver filigree, and fine silk brocades. Outside, I adjusted to the grim reality of present-day Damascus. Chill winter rains grayed the capital. It was Ramadan, the Muslim month of fasting, when gaiety is always constrained.

Not far from the big mosque I ducked into the warmth of the coffeehouse Nafura. Here, each evening, blades flash and heroes bleed when Abu Ali mounts his podium. Abu Ali is a *rawi*, or storyteller—among the last of

"Rich carpets of beauty" await the faithful in paradise, promises the Koran. Like a foretaste of that reward, just-washed Persian rugs dry near Tehran, Iran. The vibrant colors and complex designs add luxury to farmers' homes and nomads' tents. With the smaller rugs, Muslims claim a private place for prayer.

his breed. For centuries rawis have mesmerized Arabs with heroic tales of Antar, the sixth-century Lancelot of the Bedouin. Such epics of bravery and romance, carried back by Crusaders, sparked the age of chivalry in medieval Europe.

I squeezed into a seat between two old men in long robes and headcloths. The waiter brought Turkish coffee and a tall water pipe, sterilizing the mouthpiece for me in a dish of scalding water. We hushed as Abu Ali donned his horn-rimmed glasses, pushed back his red fez, and began booming

out the latest chapter: *To prove his love for the fair damsel Abla, Antar would fight the lion . . . .*

"Oooah!" We held our breath.

But to prevent Antar from escaping, his feet were bound by the villain, Munzar . . . .

"May Allah sever his head!"

The lion sprang, looming large as a camel, but Antar met him in midair with his sword and cleaved him in two.

"Ya Allah! Ya Allah!" the crowd chorused: "Oh God! Oh God!"

His courage won him freedom, and Antar set out once more to win his true love, this time facing single-handed an army of 40,000 . . . but that story tomorrow night.

Heroic in battle, the Arabs could be noble in victory. Their magnanimity at Damascus was not lost on Sophronius, the Byzantine patriarch of beleaguered Jerusalem. He sued for peace.

Caliph Omar, the second successor to the Prophet, came personally to accept the surrender and to promise Jerusalem security for its people and its churches. Jerusalem was a holy city for the Moslems, too; they included Jesus Christ among their many prophets. Muhammad himself first prayed toward Jerusalem, but after the Jews in Medina turned against him, he changed the direction of prayer to Mecca.

IT IS HE [ALLAH] WHO HAS SENT . . .
AN APOSTLE FROM AMONG THEMSELVES . . .

The patriarch took Caliph Omar to the Holy Sepulcher. They arrived at the time of prayer, and a soldier started to spread Omar's prayer mat on the floor of the church. But the wise caliph declined, stepping outside for his devotions. He knew that if the Prince of the Faithful prayed here, later Moslems might be moved to convert the sacred site into a mosque. Today a small mosque does mark the spot where Omar prayed. Daily the minaret moves its shadow across the holiest shrine in Christendom.

During the rule of Caliph Omar, the Arab conquest gained its greatest momentum. In ten years most of the Middle East fell to his armies, fanning out simultaneously into Persia and North Africa. In Iraq, Saad ibn Abi Waqqas withered the forces of Yazdegird III like a searing desert wind and took the fertile island between the Tigris and Euphrates. The King of Kings fled northward to Merv, in what is today the Soviet Union, and Persia ceased to be.

The wealth and luxury of Persia dazzled its rustic conquerors. Many of the Arabs innocently exchanged "yellow" money for "white;" silver they had always used, but gold was new. One of Saad's soldiers was said to have captured a nobleman's daughter, then sold her back for 1,000 dirhams. When told he could easily have demanded many times the ransom, he replied he had never heard of a number more than ten hundred.

If the Arabs had worlds to learn from the 1,500-year-old civilization of Persia, so, too, had they much to teach. Under stable Arab power and inspired by Islam, Persian art and science continued to thrive, and over the centuries the cultures fused. By the tenth century a new Persian language, alloyed with a wealth of Arabic words and penned in the Arabic script, had emerged with a literature of its own. The Persian provinces bred some of Islam's greatest poets and scholars, men such as Hafiz, Saadi, and Omar Khayyam.

"Khayyam is famous in the West for his *Rubaiyat*, or quatrains, but he was foremost a mathematician and astronomer," said Dr. Seyyed Hossain Nasr at his office on the modern campus of Tehran University. Dr. Nasr wrote his doctorate at Harvard on the history of Islamic science.

"It is no coincidence that Persia's traditional scholars were what you in the West call 'Renaissance men,'" Dr. Nasr continued. "As you know, the torch of Islamic learning, especially in Spain and Sicily, lit the lamps of Europe's medieval scholars."

The opening of the 17th century in Persia saw a golden age of Islamic art and architecture—especially in Isfahan. The serene blue domes and minarets of the city, immaculately preserved by the Iranian Government, still rival the sky, a tribute to the prolific builder, Shah Abbas the Great.

It is still a delight to stroll down the avenue of Chahar Bagh, literally the "four gardens." Here, and in the nearby covered bazaars, hundreds of shopkeepers display Persia's finest—ceramic tiles, carpets, miniature paintings, jewelry, block-printed textiles, and brassware. In one dusty antique shop I browsed through stacks of illuminated manuscripts, then bargained for a 12th-century brass astrolabe, a Greek astronomical device perfected by the Arabs.

While the early Arab conquerors came to terms with the Christians and Jews—even with the followers of the Persian prophet Zoroaster—the first crack soon appeared in their own faith. It rends Islam to this day.

The rift began in 656 after the murder of the third caliph, Othman. Ali, son-in-law of the Prophet, succeeded him. Duly elected in Medina, Ali soon moved his capital to Kufa, in Iraq, in order to rally his eastern forces against Muawiya, the powerful governor of Syria, who was challenging the succession. Moslems turned their swords against Moslems in a conflict that shattered the empire. In 661 Ali died under an assassin's blade, and Muawiya emerged as caliph.

As descendants of the Prophet, Ali's heirs still command the allegiance of the Shias, some ten percent of the Muslim world. Muawiya's dynasty ruled from Damascus for nearly a century, and the Sunnis, his adherents, today are the overwhelming majority of Moslems.

According to one tale, it was an act of piracy that prompted the Arabs' first move into India. Pilgrims traveling to Mecca from Ceylon were dragged off their ship while in the harbor of Daybul, in the delta of the Indus. They were imprisoned there by the local raja.

Outraged, the Arab viceroy in Iraq sent an army under Mohammed ibn Qasim. This remarkable general led his men on a 1,500-mile march across the deserts of Baluchistan and Sind. The Arab force stormed Daybul and killed the raja, then marched up the Indus Valley. General Ibn Qasim was 17.

Though the Arabs had thus sown Islam in India, it was left to later dynasties to reap the harvest. Sweeping out of Afghanistan three centuries later, the Ghaznavids—named for their ancient Afghan city, Ghazna—built a lasting Muslim presence on the subcontinent.

In Lahore, religious and cultural capital of Pakistan, Muslim shrines have replaced the ancient temples, but many of the Hindu rites survive. Late one hot, humid afternoon I mingled with the thousands of supplicants who gather every Thursday near Bhati Gate to visit the domed tomb of Hazrat Data Ganj Baksh Sahib, a revered mystic.

Near the entrance musicians played drums; harmoniums and finger cymbals accompanied the *quwwals*, or chanters, who intoned melodic prayers to the saint. A young dervish had been thrashing since noon to the monotonous rhythm and was lost in a trance.

"I usually stop at the tomb each morning on my way to work" said Ali

The blood of desert-born conquerors still flows in the veins not only of sheiks and sultans, but of matadors and nuns and Bolsheviks as well.

To the far-riding Bedouin of Arabia, shown here in their daily life of sun and sand, hospitality even to an enemy is a sacred duty. The Bedouin were among the first to rally to Muhammad's cause, eagerly obeying Allah's commands to convert nonbelievers.

Azmat, a Lahore accountant. Ali had introduced himself in fluent English and kindly offered to escort me through the chaos. "It is known that one's prayers are stronger today, the eve of our Friday Sabbath."

We followed the scent of roses and jasmine to the line of stalls selling offerings for the tomb—bright garlands of marigolds and batches of sugar candies. At the bier we recited together a *Fatiha*, the opening chapter of the Koran, and left our flowers.

These "pagan" rites that color Islam in Pakistan would appall the Muslims

of, say, Saudi Arabia, where gathering at tombs—except that of the Prophet himself—is strictly forbidden. Even King Abdul Aziz al-Saud, the founder of the country that bears his name, lies in an unmarked grave.

Near the Kashmiri Bazaar I hailed a tricycle taxi that Pakistanis call a ricksha, a motor scooter with an enclosed back seat for two. A roller coaster has yet to be built that can equal the bald terror of a ricksha ride through rush-hour traffic in Lahore.

Throwing handlebars hard over and squeezing the throttle, my driver plunged into the melee of horse-drawn wagons, bicycles, barking dogs, and trucks. Oxcarts jostled double-deck buses. I heaved a sigh of relief when the traffic—and my driver—slowed to a crawl. Ahead, a small naked boy hurled dung at his water buffaloes, blithely driving them through an intersection.

As Islam was raising its first banners along the Indus, a thousand miles across the Hindu Kush to the north the caliph's governor of Persia, Qutayba ibn Muslim, crossed the Oxus River and the deserts of Turkistan. His fierce cavalrymen quickly captured the oases of Bukhara, Samarkand, and Tashkent before marching on, some accounts say, into China itself.

Samarkand had long prospered as a trading center on the silk route from China. In Samarkand the Arabs captured Chinese artisans and from them learned the art of papermaking. From Samarkand and Baghdad papermaking traveled, via Arab Spain and Sicily, into Christian Europe.

Weighted by its Asian provinces, the center of gravity of the Arab Empire gradually shifted eastward. By 762 the Abbasids, a dynasty descended from Abbas, an uncle of the Prophet, had massacred the ruling family in Damascus and founded a new capital on the Tigris in Iraq: Baghdad.

Only 50 years later the Baghdad of Caliph Harun al-Rashid—immortalized in *The Thousand and One Nights*—reflected the prosperity of Arab civilization at its peak. Muslim historians describe a reception for envoys from Byzantium in which 700 chamberlains, 7,000 eunuchs, 160,000 cavalrymen and footmen, and a parade of 100 lions took part. The palace was hung with gilded curtains and 22,000 rugs, while in an artificial tree fashioned of gold and silver, mechanical birds chirped metallic songs.

Such wealth and splendor drew skilled poets and musicians to the city of the Abbasids. The humble life followed by the first caliphs was forgotten. In the lines of Abu Nuwas, a poet companion of Caliph Harun:

How can you but enjoy yourself When the world is in blossom, And wine is at hand?

Philosopher-physician Abu Ali al-Husayn ibn Sina (known in the West as Avicenna) wrote his *qanun*, an encyclopedia of Greek and Arabic medical lore that, translated into Latin, would remain Europe's standard medical text for four centuries. At Baghdad, Hunayn ibn Ishaq translated Plato and Aristotle. Galen's priceless *Anatomy*, much of it now lost in the original Greek, survived only through Ishaq's Arabic rendition.

Hindu scholars brought to Baghdad the numerals we still refer to as "Arabic." Baghdad's scientists bequeathed to our language such Arab words as "cipher," "azimuth," "zenith," "alkali," "amalgam," and "alcohol." Arab astronomers updated Ptolemy, plotted the orbits of planets, and accurately measured the size of the Earth.

Caliph Harun sent envoys to his contemporary, Charlemagne, at whose court—as one historian put it—"they were dabbling in the art of writing their names."

Religious fervor remains a dominant force in Arab life today. Yet it is pale compared to the zeal that drove Arab conquerors across North Africa to the gates of Christian Europe.

From the Nile the Arabs pushed their frontiers west. In 682 a bold general named Uqba ibn Nafi led his cavalry on a whirlwind sweep across North Africa through Tunisia, Algeria, and Morocco. On a sandy beach near

Agadir the flamboyant Uqba, nearly 3,000 miles from the Arab capital in Damascus, finally galloped into the surf of the Atlantic.

"Lord God, bear witness," he shouted over the breakers, "were I not stopped by this sea I would conquer more lands for Thy sake!"

Uqba's successors established an Arab presence in North Africa that endures to this day. One by one the last Byzantine coastal strongholds—Tripoli, Carthage, Tangier—crumbled; Arab fleets soon made the Mediterranean a Muslim sea.

It was caravans, not cavalry, that carried the message of Muhammad south across the vast Sahara. Long lines of camels, driven by Tuareg nomads, took cloth, brassware, sugar, salt, and fine leatherwork to Kumbi and Gao and Timbuktu, returning with ivory, gold, and slaves. So, over the centuries, the seeds of Islam sprouted; today, Muslims outnumber Christians in Africa two to one.

The Atlantic stopped Uqba ibn Nafi's drive across Africa, but Europe lay only nine miles across a strait. In 711 Tariq ibn Ziyad landed an army of 12,000 near the rock that still bears his name, Jabal Tariq (Mountain of Tariq): Gibraltar.

In a savage battle near Cádiz, the Muslims overwhelmed the Visigoths and their king, Roderick. The Christians relinquished their tenuous hold on the peninsula, city by city, until within six years Spain was Arab.

In 732—exactly a century after the Prophet's death—the great Arab wave crested; a raiding party reached Poitiers, deep in France, there to be repulsed by Charles Martel.

Having passed the torch that helped to light Europe's Dark Ages, the Arabs slipped into a long and fitful sleep, from which only now they are rubbing their eyes. Since World War II, freed at last from centuries of alien rule, blessed with new oil revenues, and borrowing back from Western technology, the long-divided Arab peoples again grope for unity.

Nahda, the Arabs call it—renaissance. So far it is merely a feeling, a beginning, a spirit one senses throughout the Arab world. I discussed it one evening with a Meccan friend.

"The days of the empires are over," he told me. "But surely we Arabs will, Allah permitting, flourish once more under our common religion, culture, and language."

And he recounted the story about the skeptic who taunted Muhammad about Islam's promise of resurrection: "What possible power could raise a man to life again from mere dust and bones?"

"That power which, from clay, created him in the first place," the Prophet had answered calmly. □

■ *When* Geographic *staff writer John Putman set out to report on the Arab world in 1974, the United States was reeling from its first brawl with OPEC, and business, not religion, was on the minds of the leaders he encountered. His story reminds us of why the Muslim world and the West are so inextricably linked, and how a handful of Arab nations grew fabulously rich while others, the majority, were left coughing in the dust and fumes.*

John J. Putman, "The Arab World, Inc.," photos by Winfield Parks, Oct. 1975, pp. 494-533

The Arab World, Inc.

BY JOHN J. PUTMAN   PHOTOGRAPHS BY WINFIELD PARKS

Teletype dispa
a hotel lobby i
Qatar, link a re
that tiny Persi
state with the
political and fi
happenings ab

He was tall, with great presence, and I sensed in him a hint of the mystic. He moved well, yet age and illness were revealed in pale, almost translucent skin, the weariness in his face, the slump in his shoulders when he sat.

I had watched him for several days: in the Riyadh Government Palace, where he listened to simple tribesmen petition for relief in land disputes; in the reception rooms of the Royal Palace, where he greeted foreign dignitaries; and in the small office where he worked alone, the only sound the scratch of his pen as he read and signed document after document.

King Faisal ibn Abdul-Aziz Al Saud was at that moment one of the world's most influential men; the ruler of one of its wealthiest nations, Saudi Arabia; and custodian of the world's largest known oil reserves.

As such, he had to make the decisions that allowed the members of the Organization of Petroleum Exporting Countries (OPEC) to raise the price of oil more than fourfold in 12 months and begin a massive transfer of wealth from the industrialized nations to those that produce the oil. Last year OPEC's oil revenues—and its petroleum bills to consumer nations—reached 90 billion dollars.

Thus to many he symbolized a world turned upside down, in which once-destitute desert sheikdoms threatened the prosperity and power of the industrial nations.

One day he motioned me to a chair beside him. We talked of his youth. At 16 he had led one of his father's armies in the campaigns to create a united Saudi Arabia. "Indeed I felt a great responsibility"—but he had no interest in recalling the excitement of combat.

"The essential thing in any role a man can play is good intentions, sincerity, a good purpose. Then, as now, I had always before my eye the interests of my people."

As for the increased oil revenues: "We have great hope in God Almighty for a bright future. We seek prosperity, a good and comfortable life. It is only just that we share in those things that our oil makes possible."

Within six weeks he was dead, shot down by an assassin. On the day that his body was borne to an unmarked Islamic grave, crowds in the streets—those who had known they could bring the pettiest of their problems to him—cried: "Where goes our knight? Where goes our protector?"

In Faisal's court I had begun my journey on the Arabian Peninsula, a three-month journey in search of answers to these questions: What are the Arabs doing with their money? Who are the decision makers? And what may we expect of them in the future?

The search would take me the length of the "Arabian Gulf"—it is never called the Persian Gulf in these proud Arab lands—to tiny sheikdoms with musical names like Abu Dhabi and Dubai. I would find answers—and more questions—in travels throughout Saudi

In tune with tradition, the Bank of Oman in Abu Dhabi attracts women customers by offering a separate facility to ensure privacy. Under *sharia*, or Muslim law, women are entitled to family inheritance and can accumulate significant wealth.

Middle East oil reserves
IN BILLIONS OF BARRELS

TURKEY
U.S.S.R.
SYRIA
MOROCCO
TUNISIA
ISRAEL
IRAQ
IRAN
AFGHANISTAN
ALGERIA
LIBYA
EGYPT
SAUDI ARABIA
KUWAIT
QATAR
U.A.E.
PAKISTAN
INDIA
Jidda
Mecca
SUDAN
OMAN
Salalah
YEMEN
(ADEN)

8
4
27
35
173
81
6
34
6
66

OTHER MIDEAST COUNTRIES

TOTAL WORLD RESERVES

MIDDLE EAST
444 BILLION
BARRELS

REMAINDER OF WORLD
272 BILLION BARRELS

Most of the world's known oil reserves lie beneath the sands and waters of the Middle East. To demand greater returns for their resource, Saudi Arabia, Kuwait, and Iraq, along with the non-Arab oil nations of Iran and Venezuela, founded the Organization of Petroleum Exporting Countries in 1960. Despite the vast flow of wealth into Middle Eastern nations since then, Muslim traditions remain strong—even in an auto showroom, where a *muezzin*'s call is promptly answered with prayers.

Arabia and inevitably, the trail of Arab billions led me to the banking centers of London and New York.

In Faisal's court I had learned that in order to assess the Arabian states' deployment of wealth, it is necessary first to learn something of the men who govern those lands and of the past that shaped them.

Sheik Shakhbut is an old man now, and dwells comfortably at the oasis town of Al Ain, 90 miles from the coastal city he once ruled, Abu Dhabi. That he is an old man—his three predecessors were assassinated—is due to the kindly nature of his brother Zayid, who took over the rulership from him, and to the wisdom of their mother, Sheika Salama. Years before she had made her sons vow not to kill one another.

Shakhbut lost his sheikdom because he could not come to terms with the oil money that began to flow in during the early 1960s. "A tightfisted old devil, but shrewd," one friend remembered. Another recalled "a fear of sudden change, a feeling for the old ways." The years of penury—the sheikdom's total annual income in the 1930s was only about $75,000—had stamped him indelibly.

He kept his growing revenues in a room at his fort; some of the paper currency was later found damaged by insects. A British bank manager finally persuaded him to deposit some of it in the bank: 5,000 pounds for one week. In seven days the manager dutifully brought the money back in a suitcase. Shakhbut counted it: "What's this extra money for?" "Interest," the manager replied, and explained the benefits of bank deposits.

Shakhbut was impressed and let the manager take the money back, this time for a month, and later for longer periods.

But Shakhbut wouldn't spend. The oil money was piling up, the sheikdom was desperately in need of schools, water systems, electricity, every basic need. The pressure became intolerable.

And so one day in 1966 Zayid and his supporters confronted Shakhbut in his palace: He must depart quietly; his financial future would be assured. Shakhbut flew off to exile, living mainly in Iran until he was allowed to return to Al Ain.

If Shakhbut couldn't spend, it is sometimes said that his brother cannot help but spend. On helicopter or Land-Rover tours into the desert, where he goes to persuade Bedouin to move into the sheikdom's new housing projects, he sometimes spies a need and instantly orders it met—a well here, a road there. A widow is given three houses; the rents will provide for her old age. Developing nations seek aid: Zayid earmarks millions for loans and grants to them.

For years he dreamed of having a "proper army." On the third anniversary of the United Arab Emirates (U.A.E.), the federation of seven sheikdoms formed in 1971 to provide unity and strength after the British ended their treaties of protection, Zayid watched proudly as squadrons of jet fighters, helicopters, and transports flew over the city. No matter that the pilots were Pakistanis—Abu Dhabi in time would develop her own. One hundred million dollars' worth of air-defense missiles were on order.

But it is the city itself that best bespeaks Zayid's aggressive spending. Fifteen years ago Abu Dhabi was just a cluster of fishermen's houses and Shakhbut's old fort. Now with its corniche, or waterside drive, and high rises it seems bent on rivaling Beirut's seafront glitter.

But what I saw is only the beginning, I was told. Town planner Abderrahman Makhlouf, an Egyptian, led me through a series of rooms crammed with models of future projects: "Our new Sports City, 250 million dirhams (63 million dollars); our new Summit Conference City, with 50 villas for heads of state, 20 million dirhams; our new 'Wall Street' area, already under construction; a new satellite city with free houses for U.A.E. citizens.

There'll be shopping malls, lots of green. If we ever want a university, it should be sited there."

There were other plans: a new jet airport, a new beach road, a second bridge to link the island city with the mainland, a new police-and-defense-force housing complex. At Al Ain new projects include a 1,000-house development, a second hospital, a cement plant, an Intercontinental Hotel to pair with the elegant Hilton already there, and further improvements to the zoo—"which is a special interest of His Highness."

Stepping from Dr. Makhlouf's cool, quiet model rooms into the bright sunlight of Zayid II Street, I blinked. Not at the sunlight, but at the boldness of Zayid II's plans.

I wondered: How is an "instant city" created? How are monthly oil-company checks translated into buildings, wealthy families, commerce? One observer said: "Construction. When you find oil, you need facilities to get it

Inheriting the windfall, a Bedouin family of Abu Dhabi pitches a goat-hair tent while awaiting the completion of their government-built home next door.

out—roads, pipelines, a port, housing for workers. The money starts moving.

"When Abu Dhabi began to take off, the leading families—those close to Zayid—set themselves up as merchants to import construction and consumer goods. I remember one chap who for a number of years operated a *dhow* for a diplomatic mission and one day decided to go into business. He was close to Zayid and so could not go wrong. Today he is among the wealthiest merchants."

Like a great suction pump, Abu Dhabi's wealth has drawn in workers from poorer lands: Pakistanis to lay the concrete blocks of new buildings, Indians to man offices and hotels, Baluchis to dig ditches, Omanis and Yemenis to drive cars and trucks. You will find Lebanese merchants and contractors, Palestinian and Egyptian teachers, Americans and British staffing the oil companies and rigs. Foreigners now comprise two-thirds of Abu Dhabi's 140,000 people.

Their wages vary: A "coolie," or unskilled laborer, may claim 30 dirhams a day, about $7.50; an oil consultant with special skills, $250 or more a day. There's no shortage of banks to serve them: Abu Dhabi city has 31.

Abu Dhabi's economic whirl was powered last year by oil revenues of 3.5 billion dollars, according to John Butter, a Scot, Director General of the Abu Dhabi Finance Department. "Of that, one billion was spent in Abu Dhabi and the U.A.E., one billion went out in loans and grants, and the balance was either invested or added to our short-term reserves."

The investments are crucial, for Abu Dhabi has little hope of providing for the nightmare every Persian Gulf state fears—the day the oil runs out— except for income from wise investments in other countries.

Last year 40 percent of Abu Dhabi's investment funds were placed in equities and properties through the government's Investment Board. It includes experts from New York's Morgan Guaranty Trust Company, Robert Fleming & Company of London, and the Banque de l'Indochine of Paris.

Another 40 percent was placed in bonds, and in a small amount of gold, through the Union Bank of Switzerland and Britain's Crown Agents. Most of the remaining 20 percent went in loans to foreign governments, and to institutions backed by them, in France, Austria, Finland, Spain, and South Korea.

Despite the splashy publicity attending its purchase of 44 percent of London's prestigious Commercial Union Assurance Building and smaller purchases in Europe and the United States, Abu Dhabi failed to reach its target in real estate investments. Buying property while avoiding risk takes time. Considerable sums are kept liquid so that, even with the fall in equity and bond prices, the government ended 1974 "roughly square," with long-term investments valued at about 1.4 billion dollars.

If the smaller states of the Arabian Peninsula proclaim their new wealth with glittering new buildings and the dust of construction, they remain—in the words of one oilman— "small potatoes" when compared with Saudi Arabia. Last year that kingdom received 23 billion dollars in oil revenues.

The bonanza seems unlikely to end soon. The country has proven reserves of 173 billion barrels, and possible reserves of 250 billion—enough oil to last for 40, perhaps as many as 90, years. And the oil that Saudi Arabia sold for $10.40 a barrel came out of the pipe for about 17 cents in production costs.

Riyadh, the capital, boasts a new hotel complex and the 200-million-dollar King Faisal Hospital (234 single, TV-equipped rooms, banks of computers, and villas and squash courts for its foreign staff). The Queen's Building, owned by Faisal's widow, towers over Jidda, and tall construction cranes herald a huge twin airport, one side for regular travelers, the other for pilgrims to nearby Mecca. In the east the ultramodern University of

Symbol of vigilance, a mounted tiger guards the desk of Sheik Muhammed, Minister of Defense for the U.A.E.

Petroleum and Minerals marks the skyscape of Dhahran. Still, in Saudi Arabia, the glamour buildings are relatively scarce; the signs of wealth are mute.

Saudi Arabian money has gone into roads, power lines, education, social services, the strengthening of the defense, and internal security forces. As Faisal himself lived modestly and quietly, he shaped his country that way. Custodian of Islam's holy shrine, Mecca, he declared that the first premise of any development plan must be "to maintain religious and moral values."

What then did Saudi Arabia do with last year's 23 billion? Some six billion was spent internally and for imports. About three billion went out to Arab or developing nations.

This left a surplus of 14 billion, much of which went into official reserves. These reserves, 3.9 billion at the start of last year, rose to 14.2 billion—surpassed only by those of West Germany and the United States.

The agency handling this surplus is the Saudi Arabian Monetary Agency,

housed in an old two-story building near the Jidda airport. SAMA's small staff keeps busy on the phone searching out the best rates on their favorite instruments: bank notes and U. S. and British treasury bills.

To the world financial community, this treasure is a worrisome thing—both threat and opportunity. The sudden shifting of those funds could injure a bank or a nation. Both businesses and governments around the world look at that 14.2 billion as a possible source of capital, investment, and purchasing. It could build plants, create jobs, shore up flagging economies.

Yet the money sits there, manipulated by a handful of Arabs and a battery of high-powered foreign advisers.

But, I learned in Riyadh, Saudi Arabia was ready to move. A second five-year plan would change the face of the country, provide vast opportunities for foreign companies, and diminish those short-term deposits and reserves that bothered so many people.

I called on Hisham Nazer, 42, President of the Central Planning Organization, to ask about the 70-billion-dollar plan. "Seventy billion? That was last week. Now it's 142 billion. That too may become outdated."

The plan had been shaped under Faisal. "He never rejected a plan; he asked only that we achieve more."

The plan, said Mr. Nazer, reflects two basic premises: "Oil supplies 70 percent of our gross domestic product, 99 percent of our exports, and 95 percent of government revenues. One day it will be gone; we must prepare an economic base for that day. Secondly, we aim to provide every Saudi citizen with a minimum standard of living; the good life above that is 'a prize to be striven for.'"

To meet the long-term manpower problem, the ambitious five-year plan calls for increasing the number of students in elementary and secondary schools from 943,000 to 1,400,000; vocational students from 4,000 to 31,000; university students from 14,500 to 49,000. Other increases include: hospital beds from 7,600 to 19,100; doctors from 1,900 to 4,200; first-class roads from 2,560 miles to 8,100; port berths from 26 to 72. Even fun is carefully drawn into the plan, which projects a tourist city in the south, zoos, and Disneyland-like parks.

A whopping 17 billion will go to develop industry. ("The private sector has proven too slow," said Mr. Nazer.) Some

Doing business on the fly, a group of *kaffiyeh*-clad entrepreneurs buzz Dubai in a helicopter. Arab nations along the Gulf turn a significant share of oil dollars into military hardware.

three billion of that will go to oil-related industries, such as a vast system to collect the four billion cubic feet of natural gas flared off daily in the kingdom. ("The oil companies thought it was not economic to harness that resource; we do.")

Last year Saudi Arabia acquired 60 percent control of the production facilities of the Arabian American Oil Company, which developed and operates most of its oil fields. The government aims at eventual 100 percent ownership. Aramco's American participants—Exxon, Mobil, Texaco, and Standard Oil of California—now seek new roles in partnership with the Saudi Arabians to build and operate new petrochemical industries.

The scent of profits has encouraged literally hundreds of other U. S. companies to bid for supply contracts, construction jobs, or joint ventures: Marcona to build a steel plant; Bechtel Inc. to design Riyadh's new airport; Gulf, Dow Chemical, and Shell to put up new petrochemical complexes.

Americans should be well positioned. The U. S. Army Corps of Engineers administers contracts for nearly eight billion dollars' worth of military construction, while U. S. Government teams work on a joint economic commission with the Saudi Arabians to provide technical assistance.

But other nationals jam Riyadh's hotels—Germans, French, Japanese, British. One American grumbled: "The Japanese send 40-man delegations; they stay awhile, then leave. You wonder what they do—are they just fishing?" So countless feasibility studies are commissioned, countless letters of intent initialed; but many fewer contracts are signed.

On one of my last journeys in Saudi Arabia, I visited the fishing village of Jubail, the planned hub of the nation's biggest industrial complex. It seemed a near-ghost town. The streets were empty, many houses deserted; the dhows lay like tilted sea gulls on the mud flats of low tide. For some years Jubail's inhabitants have drifted off for jobs in the refineries and larger surrounding towns. There were a few signs of change—construction machines rumbling in the distance, wooden stakes marking off sites in the desert. But it was difficult to envision the quarter of a million housing units planned for workers, the dozens of plants.

Can the Saudis do it? Will they do it? "Historically," one banker said, "they have been better at talking than at performance." So the world waits as businessmen come and go, their briefcases crammed with intent.

W hat do the Arabs want? Ian Seymour, a respected editor of the Middle East Economic Survey, had told me in his Beirut office that he thought it was "simply a seat higher up

Marked for tragedy, Saudi Arabia's King Faisal held a weekly *majlis*, an open-to-all audience in the manner of a desert sheik. At such an occasion in 1975, he was shot and killed by a nephew.

the table. The next ten years will be their period of maximum bargaining. If they don't use that time well, they won't get anywhere."

As for the transfer of wealth, "It's really all that hardware arriving every day at every Gulf port—the steel rods, the air conditioners, the cars. One can trace the roots of Western resentment to this: We have to produce more and more to buy the same amount of oil."

In personal affairs, as in history, change is a constant. The ignorant sometimes learn; the poor become rich; the powerless, influential. It is a test of life, as old Shakhbut's fate indicates, to come to terms with change; neither to hide from it, nor to waste too much time in protest.

As for the future, few undertake to make predictions when they concern the Arabian Peninsula or the international oil business. But the motives of the Arabs are easy to discern. As one Arab minister said: "Nobody cared about us before the oil came, nobody will care about us when it is gone." □

■ *Making the annual hajj, or pilgrimage, to Mecca is one of the five Pillars of Islam required of all Muslims if they're able. And for most of the two million pilgrims who stream into Saudi Arabia each season, this trip to the birthplace of the Prophet is the long-cherished dream of a lifetime. It was no different for Muhammad Abdul-Rauf, an Islamic scholar who'd memorized the Koran as a boy of eight in Egypt.*

Muhammad Abdul-Rauf,
"Pilgrimage to Mecca," photos
by Mehmet Biber,
Nov. 1978, pp. 581-607

Radiant with faith, pilgrims by the thousands throng the Grand Mosque in Mecca, waiting their turn to enter and approach the Kaaba, holiest shrine in Islam.

Pilgrimage
to Mecca

BY MUHAMMAD ABDUL-RAUF

PHOTOGRAPHS BY MEHMET BIBER

Here we come, O Allah, here we come!

Here we come. No partner have You.

Here we come! Praise indeed, and blessings, are Yours—the Kingdom too!

No partner have You!

This *talbiyah*, recited by more than a million Muslim pilgrims one recent December, marked the formal beginning of our pilgrimage. Etched in memory is the scene at the airport in Beirut, where we waited all night for our flight to Jidda in Saudi Arabia. My son Faisal and I, each clad in two pieces of seamless white cotton terry cloth, bareheaded and wearing sandals, and my daughter Aisha, with only her face and hands exposed, were among hundreds similarly clad.

How spoiled we were! The thought of the African herdsman who had walked much of the way, and the Indonesian peasant who had invested his life savings in making this pilgrimage by sea, shamed us into thanking God for the ease with which we were performing our *hajj*.

At dawn we boarded: "First-class passengers, then tourist class . . . ." How awkward that there should be such a distinction on this journey. Trappings of class here were more a cause of embarrassment. I remembered savoring the feeling of equality on my first pilgrimage 25 years earlier, when I rode from Kuwait in the back of a truck.

Now in a state of *ihram* (restriction)—forbidden to clip our nails, cut our hair, hunt, argue, or engage in sexual activity—we were eager to join our brethren converging on Mecca from all over the world. There we would perform a major duty in our religion: the pilgrimage to the Kaaba, originally built, Muslims believe, for the worship of God by Abraham and his son Ishmael, ancestors of our Prophet Muhammad.

The annual pilgrimage, instituted by Abraham, was continued by succeeding Arab generations, for it brought wealth and prestige to Mecca. Pagan practices, however, were gradually introduced until the religion of Islam, with its dedication and submission to God, came in the seventh century A.D., restored the hajj to its purity, and made it a deeply spiritual journey.

In two hours we were in Jidda, and by late morning we began the 45-mile drive to Mecca. Busloads of pilgrims were around us, and what a variety of features—Oriental, Negroid, Caucasian, and all the blends brought by generations of intermarriage.

On the way we stopped at the Mosque of Hudaybiyah, site of a treaty marking the political turning point of Islam in its battle for survival in the seventh century. Here Muhammad concluded a truce with the Quraysh, the polytheistic inhabitants of Mecca among whom he was reared and to whom he first delivered his message: God is One.

The Quraysh had responded with unrelenting persecution, forcing Muhammad to emigrate from Mecca—the Hegira, A.D. 622, which begins the Muslim era. The treaty halted the battles waged against the Prophet and his new town, Medina, more than 200 miles north, allowing him and his community to practice their faith in peace.

Continuing on our way, we passed a white pillar that marked our entry into the sacred territory, a circle around Mecca in which no wild animal may be hunted. Chanting the talbiyah, our excitement mounting, we came to the city's outskirts. In one of these buildings the *kiswa*, the embroidered black cloth covering the Kaaba, is made anew each year.

Finally we were in Mecca, Islam's holiest city, crowding a barren valley walled by harsh hills. Accompanied by Adeeb Tilmissan, a courteous young Saudi student assigned to us by our host, the Muslim World League, we drove through teeming shop-lined streets to the Sacred Mosque to perform the *tawaf*, the prescribed seven counterclockwise circumambulations of the Kaaba. Entering through the Gate of Peace, we were met by a hum of chanting. In the middle of the mosque's large open court our eyes fell on the Kaaba, majestically towering over a sea of humanity.

It is impossible for any pilgrim to forget that first sight of the black-draped shrine. Five times daily in our prayers, from whatever part of the world we are in, we face toward the Kaaba, longing for the moment we can cast our eyes on it and touch it.

Each pilgrim reacts to seeing the Kaaba in his own way. In my first experience I became suddenly dazed. My wife clung to my arm, trembling and sobbing. This time my daughter shuddered as if an electric current had shot through her, and my son was speechless. He later told me he was struck by deep feelings of sweet tranquillity.

Caught up in the ecstasy of devotion around us, we recited together:

O Lord! Grant this house greater honor, veneration, and awe; and grant those who venerate it and make pilgrimage to it peace and forgiveness. O Lord! Thou art the peace. Peace is from Thee. So greet us on the Day of Judgment with the greeting of peace.

W hy this veneration of a stark cubelike building of gray stone? It is not a striking piece of art, nor is it adorned with precious stones. And no Muslim endows it with power to benefit or to hurt. The Kaaba is the House of God, dedicated to His worship by Abraham. Near it the Prophet Muhammad was born about A.D. 570. Forty years later the archangel Gabriel descended with the revelation of the truth—that there is but one God—calling Muhammad to cleanse the Kaaba of idols. And here, eight years after his emigration from Mecca, the Prophet triumphantly yet humbly returned to see those idols toppled at his beckoning and the purified Kaaba rededicated to the worship of the one God.

We plowed through the crowded court toward the Black Stone. This sacred rock, 12 inches in diameter, is set in silver in the east corner of the Kaaba. The only remaining relic from the original building of Abraham, it is the starting and end point of the tawaf. Pilgrims are eager to touch or kiss it, as if it represents the right hand of God, with whom they are renewing their covenant. Reading the golden Koranic lettering embroidered on the Kaaba's black cover reminds us of its original builders, Abraham and

From noon until sundown on the ninth day of the final *hajj* month, Muslims converge on the Mount of Mercy (left) where, standing under the scorching sun, they pray and recite verses of the Koran, asking that their sins be forgiven. Below them, the Plain of Arafat (following pages) blooms with believers as the crowd halts and bows towards Mecca for the midday prayer.

Ishmael, and their prayers to God to raise from that area a messenger of peace, learning, and wisdom.

At last we came close, but the crowd was too thick for us to touch the stone, except Aisha, aided by the police officer in charge. Swept along by the human tide, we kept chanting prayers, struggling to touch the stone or the Kaaba whenever possible.

Coming opposite the Black Stone on each circuit, we raised our right hands to it and recited: "In the name of God; God is most great!" The Kaaba loomed over us as if it were an ear of God absorbing the earnest prayers of His human creatures. Like subjects appealing for their sovereign's favors at the foot of his throne, we circled our Lord's House, shedding tears, seeking blessings and mercy, and yearning for His company in paradise.

On completing the tawaf rituals, we went to drink from the Well of Zamzam, with its rich mineral water with which Ishmael and Muhammad had quenched their thirst.

Ishmael and his mother, Hagar, the tradition goes, were left alone in a desolate valley by Abraham with only some dates and water, which were soon exhausted. Seeing her infant writhing with thirst, Hagar desperately searched everywhere for water. She had asked the departing Abraham, "Has your Lord instructed you to leave us here alone?" When Abraham answered affirmatively, she said, "Then God will not abandon us."

God did not abandon them. Zamzam was revealed to them, and beside it Abraham and Ishmael in time built the House of God, and the town of Mecca grew up around it.

After the greeting tawaf, performed on arrival in Mecca at any time of the year, pilgrims proceed to the ceremony of the *sa'y*, making seven trips between the hills of Safa and Marwah, now inside the mosque. This ritual reenacts Hagar's search for water before she was led by an angel to Zamzam. During the seven journeys of the sa'y, a pilgrim recites prayers, his heart closely in communion with God.

Whether they arrive early or late during the 70-day pilgrimage season (which begins annually with the start of the tenth month of the Muslim lunar calendar), pilgrims spend the eve of the ninth day of the 12th month in the village of Mina, four miles east of Mecca. Following the practice of the Prophet, they rest there before the day of the "standing." During this high point of all hajj rituals, pilgrims stand on the Plain of Arafat and pray from noon until sundown.

By the time of our arrival Mina had become a crowded tent city. After dawn prayers, we joined the rush of one-way traffic flowing to the Plain of Arafat, eight miles farther east, greeted by the bright colors of sunrise.

Pilgrims crammed cars, buses, and trucks and rode on the backs of camels and donkeys. Often those on foot seemed to make the fastest passage. By noon all would make it to the hot desert plain, all clad in the same simple attire, rulers and subjects, rich and poor, men and women, black and white.

It was a scene to last in memory: a million and a half people assembled for the day on this barren, rocky plain, leaving all wealth and fame behind, praying for salvation and for our brethren's deliverance. Thus we reinforced the sense of equality before the Lord and reminded ourselves of the day to come when all will be raised and gathered for accountability, leading to eternal bliss or affliction.

Some pilgrims climbed to the spot where the Prophet, from the back of his camel, delivered his farewell sermon. In it he reiterated some of the basic teachings of Islam and bore witness to his companions that he had given his message and fulfilled his burden of prophethood. Three months later, in Medina, A.D. 632, he died.

Shortly after sunset the reverse rush toward Mecca began. On the way back to Mina pilgrims halt for the night at Muzdalifah. There they offer prayers, as the Prophet did. And there they collect pebbles to throw at the three "Satan's stoning points" in Mina during the following days. These pillars symbolize the forces of evil, and casting stones at them symbolizes our lifelong struggle against evil.

On the tenth day of the month pilgrims celebrate the 'Id al-Adha (Festival of Sacrifice)—which marks the end of the pilgrimage season—by sacrificing an animal, thus commemorating Ishmael's deliverance.

During the annual hajj season, the Kaaba's gold and silver door opens for the sacred ceremony of washing the interior. According to Islamic tradition, in A.D. 630 Muhammad cleansed the Kaaba of its idols, reaffirming Islam as a faith of the one God, or Allah.

We drove from Muzdalifah to Mecca soon after midnight, halting briefly at Mina for the first part of the stone-throwing ceremony. Then we returned to the Sacred Mosque to perform the post-Arafat tawaf in the same way we had made the greeting tawaf, followed by the sa'y ceremony. Then each of us had a lock of hair clipped, symbolizing the end of ihram.

Afterward we could have returned to our room, had a shower, and resumed our regular clothes, but we decided to stay in the Sacred Mosque until dawn, then join the 'Id prayer congregation.

We stationed ourselves on the balcony overlooking the Kaaba as throngs began to fill the vast court of the Sacred Mosque. I sat by the railing, reciting the Koran as the rapidly increasing crowd of pilgrims flowed under the bluish glow of light. I could not discern faces or heads, only a sea of human waves revolving around the gracefully draped House of God.

Hypnotized by the scene, my mind floated over the immense influence of the humble man behind this spiritual fervor, whose teaching has molded the daily lives of these multitudes, giving them spiritual and moral guidance, certainty, and comfort and drawing them here from all corners of the globe.

I pictured the Prophet kneeling in prayer inside the Kaaba, cleared of the idols that had desecrated it. I felt as if my eyes penetrated those very walls before me, surveying the empty expanse within, gold-and-silver lamps hanging from a ceiling resting on three wooden columns. Would that I had the privilege of praying under that roof, prostrating myself on that marble floor. Only on rare occasions is the Kaaba opened, notably for its ceremonial washing, which is attended annually by the king of Saudi Arabia himself.

Oasis of comfort in the midst of an implacable desert, the Mecca Inter-Continental Hotel caters to the more affluent pilgrims, some of whom enjoy a sumptuous buffet following one of the hajj rites.

What is it that impels the Muslim to make this journey involving great sacrifice, hardship, and cost, yet doing so ardently and lovingly? What meaning do the rituals have?

We each carry within our hearts a divine element. Torn from the womb of existence and ushered, crying, into this world, we spend all our energies in the pursuit of a state of happiness. This restless, incessant drive is no more than that divine element within us seeking its origin.

The joy of Islam lies in its recognition and fulfillment of man's various needs. Unburdened by and innocent of the sin of any other, we are encouraged to pursue our material, emotional, and intellectual urges and are rewarded by God for fulfilling them. Yet we must not forget our origin, God our Creator, unto whom will be our return. Toward this end we perform ritual obligations called the Five Pillars of Islam: belief, prayer, almsgiving, fasting, pilgrimage.

These embrace the recitation of *shahadah,* confirming our belief in God and His angels; in resurrection for final judgment; in God's messengers, beginning with Adam and concluding with Muhammad; and in His sacred books, including the Torah, the Psalms, the Gospel, and the Koran, the word of God revealed to Muhammad through the archangel Gabriel.

They also include prayers five times daily in which we face the Kaaba wherever we may be and, without intermediary, pray directly to God, kneeling and prostrating in humility; the giving of alms, 2.5 percent of our income and savings, as an expression of sympathy to the poor and a sharing in God's blessings; fasting during Ramadan, the ninth month of the lunar calendar; and making this pilgrimage in which the Kaaba, focal point of Islam and symbol of our unity, becomes immediate and touchable.

In these common beliefs and observances, simple and clear, a Muslim feels united with his brethren in faith, now more than three-quarters of a billion worldwide.

He is also conscious of a common religious heritage with Judaism and Christianity, the other great monotheistic faiths that rose amid the deserts of the Middle East. For to a Muslim, Islam is God's revelation made to Adam and Noah; the religion revealed to Abraham and Moses; the religion of David and the Prophets of Israel, and of Jesus and the Twelve Apostles. For the final time, in its purity, the true religion was revealed to the Prophet Muhammad.

A Muslim yearns to escape, at least once in a lifetime, from the conflicts and vagaries of daily life to the birthplace of his Prophet and the House of his Lord. There he seeks, with his brethren, spiritual nourishment and deliverance.

Pilgrims swarm through Mina on their return to Mecca from Mount Arafat and then head home, exhausted and exhilarated. On the road, passengers riding in the open air sprout umbrellas to shield against a scorching sun.

The pilgrimage symbolizes the return to our origin. We taste the joy of this return, and that drive within our hearts is somewhat contented and fulfilled.

Divine wisdom selected the arid region of Mecca, stripped of all botanic luxuriance, purely as a focus of faith. God commanded Abraham to take his infant son Ishmael and leave him with his mother in this desert valley. On a later visit, the Koran tells us, Abraham was commanded to sacrifice him, and here Ishmael was saved at the last moment, a sacrificial ram being substituted. Here Abraham and Ishmael raised the first Kaaba. The rituals of pilgrimage recall these events, and the austerity of this site underlies its sacredness.

Soon there was no more space in the mosque. *"Allah u akbar!*—God is most great!"—came the call to prayer. The flow around the Kaaba ebbed to a stop. The human particles formed concentric circles around it, and the hum of chanting melted into silence. All I could hear was the distinct voice of the imam leading the dawn prayer, the rustle of clothes as we performed our prostrations, and the echo in my heart:

"O God! Let this not be the last time we pray before the Kaaba!" □

■ *Foreigners making war in Afghanistan. Israel at war with the Palestinians. Radicals wielding Islam as a weapon against Arab moderates and the West. These themes, familiar as today's headlines, run through this story by Tom Abercrombie that appeared more than 20 years ago in* National Geographic. *Especially chilling is his final comment: "In Islam's anguished heartland, some fear, lie the bitter seeds of global war."*

Thomas J. Abercrombie,
"Islam's Heartland, Up in Arms,"
Sept. 1980, pp. 335-345

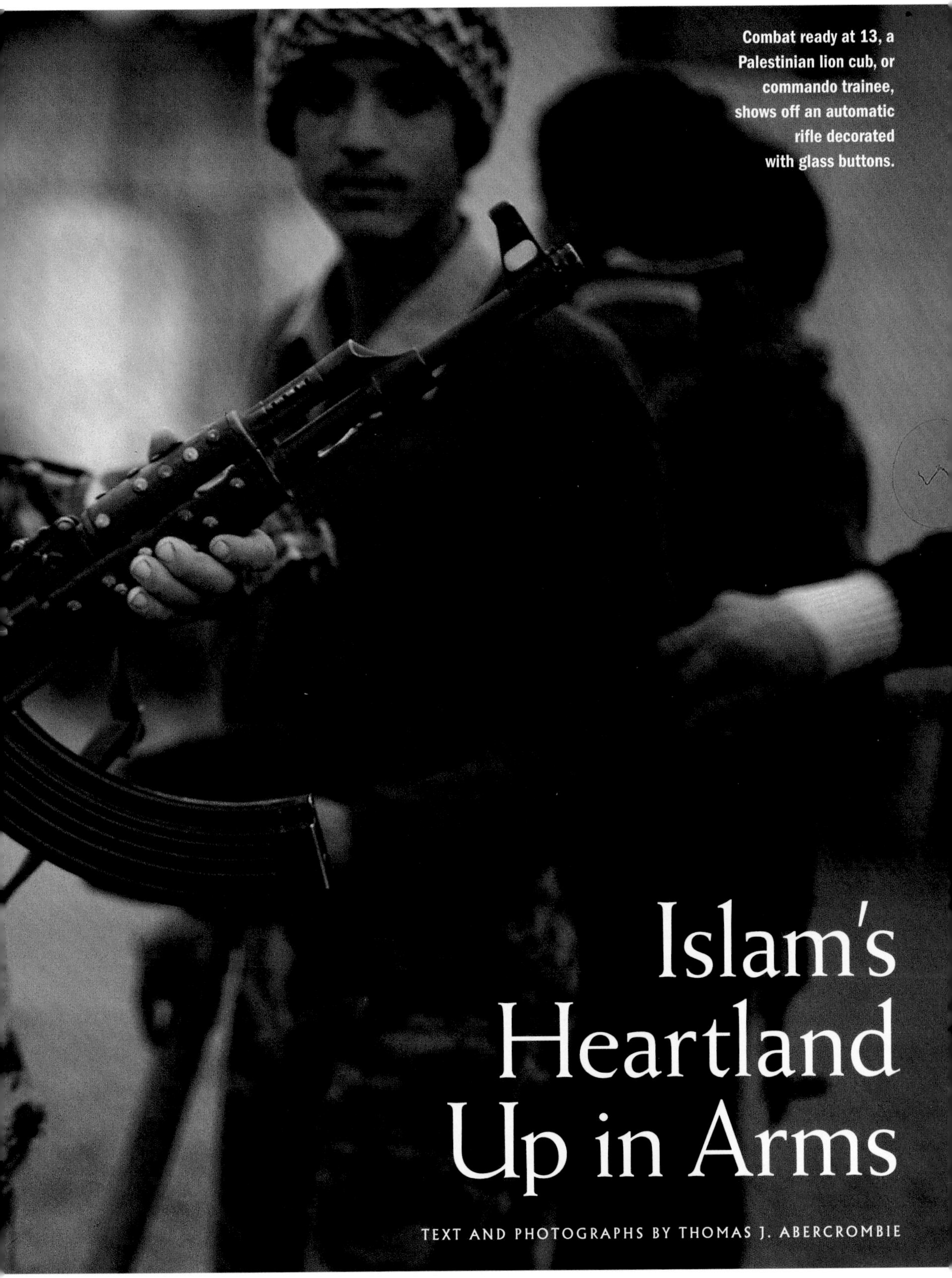

Combat ready at 13, a
Palestinian lion cub, or
commando trainee,
shows off an automatic
rifle decorated
with glass buttons.

Islam's
Heartland
Up in Arms

TEXT AND PHOTOGRAPHS BY THOMAS J. ABERCROMBIE

KABUL, AUGUST 1967. Music blares, bright lights and fireworks flare as Afghanistan celebrates 48 years of peaceful independence. Yet the winds of cold war already blow from the north: Soviet-made tanks and rocket launchers rumble along Akbar Khan Street, and MIGs scream overhead to highlight the military parade.

To an army brigadier I express my surprise. How could his nation, traditionally neutral, trust its colossal northern neighbor to train and equip its armed forces? His reply is beautifully Afghan:

"When you ride a good horse, do you care in which country it was born?"

QANDAHAR, MARCH 1980. Aloft somewhere over Afghanistan's Dasht-e Margow, the Desert of Death, we throttled back and buckled up for the descent into Qandahar, the southern Afghan city where I would spend the night.

Authorities at Tehran's airport had refused to let the plane wait there any longer, and our destination, Kabul, on the edge of the Hindu Kush, was still closed by blizzards. We looked like a flying rerun of the Orient Express: the Turk with a diplomatic passport, the striking lady from Lisbon, two Pushtun tribesmen in robes and turbans, a strung-out German hippie, the bald Lebanese always taking notes, and an American reporter revisiting a dozen familiar cities caught up in the wrenching turmoil of 1980.

I had earlier inquired of our pilot, sipping coffee at the galley, after an old friend who also flew for the Afghan airline. "He's dead," he said sadly. "They shot him in front of his house."

"They," of course, meant the Soviet-supported regimes that have ruled the country since 1978. Among the thousands who died in the ensuing tumult was U.S. Ambassador Adolph Dubs. Last December Afghanistan's revolutionary president Hafizullah Amin, suspected of making overtures to the West, was assassinated, and the Red Army, 80,000 strong, poured across the border.

Armies and borders are the oldest of all stories in the Middle East, that crossroads where three continents meet. The region, when I first visited it, was relatively peaceful, with big-power attention focused on Southeast Asia and later Africa. Now the nations between Morocco and Pakistan provided a new chessboard on a grand scale. And again the lives of the people across a vast area were being influenced by decisions made elsewhere.

We touched down on a long runway built with U.S. aid but now guarded by Soviet tanks and anti-aircraft missiles. We taxied to the terminal past rows of dart-like MIG-19s and MIG-23s slung with rockets—64 jets in all, poised only 650 miles from Persian Gulf shipping lanes.

Bused from the airstrip into Qandahar, I found only a handful of green-grocers halfheartedly selling tangerines and apples from pushcarts. A few local taxis, three-wheeled Vespa scooters embellished with mottoes from the Koran, huddled near the hotel. Otherwise, merchants protesting the Soviet occupation had shuttered the city tight.

"It is a tragedy. Afghanistan will never be the same," one of my fellow passengers, a Kabul man in a business suit, volunteered in a guarded voice as we warmed our hands over the fire in the lobby. "Praise God, I got my family out. As soon as I settle my affairs, I will leave too."

When our flight finally reached Kabul next day, turbaned street crews were digging out from under two feet of snow with crude wooden shovels. Wraiths of steam billowed from trucks and armored cars

marshaling along the road to Charikar.

I looked up a high official in the Foreign Ministry, a longtime friend who had spent 20 months in prison following the 1978 coup. "These are difficult times, even painful, and they will not end soon," he said. "But this is not the first crisis wished on our nation by outside forces. We must persevere. Afghanistan will survive."

My driver, a rough-hewn Hazara from the rugged Hindu Kush, best summed up the fears of his deeply religious countrymen. "Look what happened to our brothers north of the border. Their mothers were Muslims, their fathers were Muslims—but the young men have all been brought up *kafirs* (nonbelievers). Is that the fate of Afghanistan?"

Here I found another major change between the Middle East I had known and the one that now confronted me. As the Western powers lost first their colonies, then their influence in the area, Muslim leaders moved gradually to fill power vacuums, sparking an international resurgence of Islam. Only under the Russians and the Israelis has Islam waned. Now one of these religious leaders—Ayatollah Ruhollah Khomeini—has overturned a government, and others exert potent political influence in places like Saudi Arabia, Egypt, and Libya.

Jerusalem: reunited or occupied? Dominating the skyline, Israeli-built apartments rise beyond Arab suburbs and the golden Dome of the Rock shrine, where Muslims believe Muhammad ascended to heaven.

TASHKENT, SOVIET CENTRAL ASIA, 1971. I am impressed by the many ambitious Soviet development projects: electric buses, the large university, parks, a building boom. Still, many of life's basics are missing. Shoppers wait in long lines, only to find store shelves nearly bare; travel requires a government permit; bookstores are stocked mainly with bound volumes of Lenin's speeches. And the faces in the street—those same Tajik, Turkoman, and Uzbek faces one met in the Kabul bazaar—never smile.

Despite the U.S.S.R.'s official atheist policies, I found many there seeking comfort in their Islamic culture and religion. In Samarkand, 14th-century capital of the conqueror Tamerlane, I joined crowds at the splendid azure-tiled shrines of Shah-i-Zinda. Trees were festooned with strips of white cloth, prayer offerings left by the faithful visiting a tomb believed to hold a cousin of the Prophet. Such local pilgrimages are popular. Last year, of the Soviet Union's 40 million Muslims, only 25 were allowed to visit distant Mecca.

At one mausoleum a long-robed Uzbek villager and his son watched me with curiosity while I copied an elegant Arabic inscription into my notebook.

"Tarif al-lughah al-arabiyah?" the old man ventured in the Arabic of the Koran. "Do you know the Arabic language?"

"Yes, a little," I answered in kind, then added the universal "as-Salaam alaykum."

"And upon you, peace," he replied. From him I gleaned glimpses of a hard life on the steppes: three bad harvests and a collective farm committee that put too much land in cotton, too little in grain; religion discouraged by the government but still observed at home; six sons, two in the army.

The soaring birthrate of Soviet Central Asia's Muslims—their numbers grow some three percent a year, or five times faster than the Russians themselves—may well be viewed with misgivings in the Kremlin. Indeed, some observers conclude that one of the main reasons for the massive march into Afghanistan was to stifle, by unmistakable example, any thought of unrest among the growing Muslim population in Central Asia.

BEIRUT, LEBANON, 1972. I savor a stroll through the Paris of the Middle East. The neighborhood along Avenue des Francais seems a second home to me. I return the wave of Chartouni, the shirtmaker; browse among the Roman coins at Petit Musée antiques; pick up a Herald Tribune at Antoine's book shop. Over arrack at the sleek Hotel St. Georges, I watch water-skiers cut slaloms on the glinting blue Mediterranean.

But now the St. Georges was a blackened shell. It stared emptily at a cannon-pocked Holiday Inn a quarter of a mile inland.

"Opposing factions fought for months for these two hotels," said my escort from the National Movement, a leftist coalition. "Cannon and rockets. You see the results."

The herds of tourists were gone from Beirut, and many students, bankers, businessmen, artists, and writers. They began to flee in 1975, when civil war ravaged the city.

The delicate Christian-Muslim balance, with political powers apportioned by the constitution, had long guaranteed tiny Lebanon a genuine, if fragile, republic, but the balance was upset by the half million refugees driven from Palestine. Denied repatriation, confined to crowded camps,

Rugged as the mountains that conceal him, an Afghan guerilla looks down on a government fort in a valley of Nangarhar Province. When this story was published, the *mujahidin* had been fighting communist regimes in Kabul for about two years.

they grew more militant and allied themselves with Lebanese leftists challenging the Christian-dominated power structure. Beginning in the late 1960s, the Israeli Army, battling Palestinian commandos, made spasmodic, sometimes extended, incursions into southern Lebanon, exposing the impotence of the small Lebanese Army and sending more waves of refugees north to Beirut.

Throughout the country dozens of political factions—Christians, Druzes, Socialists, Muslims, Palestinians, Falangists, Nasserites—armed themselves. In Beirut sniper attacks escalated into full-scale war—a war that, so far, has claimed 60,000 lives and left the city in shambles.

Halfway along the no-man's-land of Rue Allenby, a squad of battle-ready Syrian soldiers from the Arab peacekeeping force screeched up behind us in a bullet-riddled Mazda station wagon.

"Get out of here, you fools! This area is dangerous," one shouted, then began arguing with my escort. A block away children were playing. Two blocks east I heard the crack of rifle fire and a round of artillery.

Life in the city goes on, especially in fashionable Ras Beirut, still largely unscathed. On every wall, posters of Gamal Abdel Nasser, Yasir Arafat, Ayatollah Khomeini, and Palestinian martyrs compete for space with spray-can graffiti in Arabic: "The Land Belongs to the Steadfast"; "Revolution Is the Road to Liberation"; "No U.S. Bases in the Middle East." Yet American and Egyptian films pack theaters along Rue Hamra. Supermarkets are well stocked. Nearby, one still finds Paris couture at Milady, works in English at Uncle Sam's Bookstore, fast food at Kentucky Fried Chicken, and fast ladies at the Dolce Vita or the No Name Bar.

What chilled me was how many in Beirut had adapted to the anarchy. At a friend's apartment on Rue Madame Curie I heard horror stories: a cousin cut down stepping out of her car; the small grocery on the first floor bombed, smashing most of the building's windows. To get home that night, my host had to detour around a shoot-out.

A machine gun crackled outside. I jumped. "Take it easy," my friend smiled. "It's probably just a wedding celebration."

STEVE McCURRY

BEIRUT, JANUARY 1975. Armed soldiers lead me through labyrinthine back streets, up a dark stairway to a midnight rendezvous. Only a bare bulb lights the temporary command post; Yasir Arafat, chairman of the Palestine Liberation Organization, seldom dares spend two days in the same place.

"Our argument is not with the Jews," he tells me. "We are both Semites. They have lived with us for centuries. Our enemies are the Zionist colonizers and their backers who insist Palestine belongs to them exclusively. We Arabs claim deep roots there, too."

Two decades ago Palestinians were to be found in United Nations Relief Agency camps at places like Gaza and Jericho, in a forlorn and pitiable state. While Palestinian spokesmen pressed their case in world capitals, the loudest voice the world heard was that of terrorists, with whom the word Palestinian came to be associated. Jordan fought a war to curb them. The disintegration of Lebanon was due in part to the thousands of refugees within its borders.

Prospects for peace brightened, however, when President Anwar Sadat of Egypt, most powerful of the Arab countries, made his historic trip to Israel in November 1977. A year later Sadat and Israeli Prime Minister Menachem Begin signed the Camp David accords, a framework for the return of the occupied Sinai Peninsula to Egypt. The former enemies established diplomatic relations and opened mail, telephone, and airline communications.

The Camp David accords also addressed the all-important Palestinian question but left it vague. Sadat insists that any lasting peace depends on an eventual Palestinian homeland in the Israeli-occupied West Bank and Gaza. Israel agrees to limited autonomy for those regions, but, fearful of a new and hostile Palestinian state suddenly planted on its borders, insists that Israeli troops must maintain security there.

Crowded Rashidiyah refugee camp, set among orange groves south of the ancient Phoenician port of Tyre in Lebanon, lies on the frontlines. Frequent pounding by Israeli military jets and warships seeking PLO targets has war-hardened its population, some 13,700 Palestinians.

At the schoolyard I watched a solemn flag raising. Uniformed *ashbal*, or lion cubs, stood rigid as color guards briskly ran up the green, white, and black Palestinian flag. Ranging in age from 8 to 12, they might have been Cub Scouts—except for the loaded rifles they held at present arms. Behind them stood two rows of girls, *zaharat*, or little flowers. Same age, same weapons.

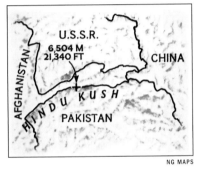

NG MAPS

In Badakhshan Province, Afghanistan, yak herdsmen climb a trail to summer pastures in the Hindu Kush. Towering above them, the frozen peak of an unnamed 21,000-foot mountain (map, above) overlooks three other nations: the (former) Soviet Union, Pakistan, and China.

A fter crossing the Allenby Bridge from Amman, I drove across the fertile Jordan Valley through Arab Jericho and past some of the controversial new Jewish settlements: Mitzpe Jericho, Tomer, Maale Adumim, Shilat. Then as I climbed through the steep stony hills to Jerusalem, I saw that it too had changed. A ring of highrise apartments and offices was growing inexorably around the occupied Arab side of the walled town. Within the wall, too, scores of Arab houses had been leveled during extensive reconstruction.

"Already 64 settlements have been built on the West Bank," said a Christian Palestinian agriculturist working for an American church group in Jerusalem. "And another 10 are planned," he said. Unfolding a copy of the master plan prepared in 1978 by the World Zionist Organization, he read: "Realizing our right to Eretz-Israel . . . with or without peace, we will have to learn to live *with* the minorities . . . ."

The Israeli Government has reaffirmed the policy. In Prime Minister Menachem Begin's words: "Settlement is an inherent and inalienable right. It is an integral part of our national security."

"Security" is a word deeply etched into the Israeli psyche. The country has lived for 30 years as an armed camp, always on guard against PLO raids and terrorist bombings. Whenever such incidents occur, the response is quick: even greater retaliation.

In Jerusalem I met with David Eppel, an English-language broadcaster for the Voice of Israel. "We must continue to build this country. Israel is our lawful home, our destiny. We have the determination, and an immense pool of talent, to see it through."

I drove out of the Old City in the dark of morning and arrived a few hours later at the nearly finished Israeli frontier post, whence a shuttle bus bounced me through no-man's-land to the Egyptian terminal. As a result of the Egyptian-Israeli treaty, it was possible for the first time since 1948 to travel overland from Jerusalem to Cairo. An Egyptian customs man opened my bags on a card table set up in the sand. I took a battered taxi into nearby El Arish, to a sleepy bank that took 45 minutes to convert dollars into Egyptian pounds. Then I hired a Mercedes for the 200-mile run across the northern Sinai Desert, the Suez Canal, and the Nile Delta. By sundown Cairo was mine.

Despite official government optimism, I found many in Cairo worried that President Sadat's bold diplomatic gestures might fail. The city was noticeably tense as Israel officially opened its new embassy on Mohi el-Din Abu el-Ez Street in Cairo's Dukki quarter. Black-uniformed Egyptian troops guarded the chancery and nearby intersections as the Star of David flew for the first time in an Arab capital. Across town, police with fixed bayonets were posted every ten feet around the American Embassy. Others were posted at the TV station and the larger hotels. Protests were scattered, mostly peaceful. None disturbed the cadence of the city.

Welcoming ever larger delegations of tourists and businessmen from Europe and the U.S., Cairo was busier than ever—and more crowded. Despite a building boom, many Egyptians migrating from the countryside, perhaps 10,000 a month, still find housing only by squatting among tombs at the City of the Dead, the huge old cemetery on the southeast side of the capital.

Even with the new elevated highway and wider bridge across the Nile, half-hour traffic standstills are common. Commuters arrive at Ramses Station riding even the roofs of trains, then cram buses until axles break. Cairo smog, a corrosive blend of diesel fumes and hot dust from surrounding deserts, rivals tear gas.

Despite the rampant blessings of progress, Cairo can still charm. In the medieval Khan el-Khalili bazaar near Cairo's thousand-year-old Al-Azhar University, I sought out Ahmad Saadullah's sidewalk café. I found that 30 piasters (45 cents) still brings hot tea, a tall water pipe primed with tobacco and glowing charcoal, and the latest gossip. The turbaned gentleman on the carpeted bench opposite was unusually talkative; we dispensed with weather and the high cost of living and got right to politics:

"Of course I am behind President Sadat, but he is taking a great risk. The Israelis have not fully responded. If Sadat fails, no other Arab leader will dare try for peace again for a generation."

Across town at the weekly *Akhbar El-Yom* newspaper, one of the largest and most widely read in the Middle East, chief editor Abdel-Hamid Abdel-Ghani drove home that same point.

"What worries me most is that President Sadat's agreement with Israel has isolated Egypt from our brother nations," he told me. "When Saudi Arabia broke with us, it was a heavy loss. The Saudis are our close neighbors. Now they have canceled pledges for hundreds of millions in development aid to Egypt. Some 200,000 Egyptians—teachers, doctors, engineers—live and work in the kingdom.

"And Saudi Arabia, guardian of the holy cities of Mecca and Medina, remains for Muslim Egypt a spiritual homeland."

MECCA, FEBRUARY 1965. Across the rooftops from the highest minarets peal the calls to early morning prayer: "Come to salvation. Prayer is better than sleep . . . ."

I am swept up in the largest religious gathering on Earth, the annual pilgrimage to Mecca. Pious crowds surge through narrow streets and covered markets to the great Sacred Mosque, heart and focus of the holy city. We come from a score of nations and cultures, but each of us now wears the humble ihram, *the simple pilgrim costume of white cotton. Inside the shrine, blacksmith, banker, Bedouin—prime minister or pauper—all bow in unison, all equal in the eyes of the Almighty.*

Those narrow streets seemed unusually quiet this time. Around Islam's holiest shrine hundreds of masons and carpenters labored, repairing the heavy doors, filling gaping shell holes in the minarets, replacing scarred marble panels.

A few weeks earlier an armed band, led by a radically fundamentalist Muslim from Saudi Arabia's hinterland, had seized the Sacred Mosque, protesting the moral corruption and modernization efforts of Saudi leaders. Outrage swept the Muslim world. In Libya and Pakistan, fired by false rumors that the United States was involved in this sacrilege, mobs attacked U.S. embassies.

In Mecca the forces that had profoundly changed the Middle East I knew became clearer in the face of the most profound force of all—the largest transfer of wealth in human history. Industrialized nations poured untold billions in oil payments into the coffers of governments that ruled populations whose values sprang from relative poverty, simplicity, and faith.

To protect those societies from moral crumbling under the assault of wealth, fundamentalist religious leaders had risen—with potent political impact.

Jiddah, the kingdom's commercial capital, a small desert seaport when I first landed there 19 years ago, had swelled to a metropolis of perhaps a million people. Overwhelmed by oil prosperity, it has become, according to a recent survey by the Union Bank of Switzerland, the most expensive city in the world.

With students of King Abdulaziz University in Jiddah, I attended a lecture by Dr. Ghazi Algosaibi, the Saudi Minister of Industry and Electricity.

"We must not depend on foreigners to run the machinery of our country," Dr. Algosaibi warned. "They neither understand nor care about our culture.

"We are blessed with revenue," he continued, "but unless we develop skills, money will not solve our problems."

All across the Middle East I saw this clash between Western-style modernization and traditional values. Now new external pressures build as the oil-seeking superpowers maneuver for position around the wells.

Encircled by events beyond their control, the Muslim nations fear that the Soviet Union will maintain its hold on Afghanistan, and that United States countermoves will make pawns of the region's nations. Internal strife gnaws away at Iran, Iraq, Lebanon, and other nations with strident minority groups. Continued Israeli settlement on the West Bank, over official United States objections, threatens Sadat's peace initiatives, as do continuing PLO raids.

In Islam's anguished heartland, some fear, lie the bitter seeds of global war. □

All across the Middle East I saw this clash between Western-style modernization and traditional values.

■ *One of* National Geographic's *most graceful and prolific authors, Bill Ellis covered Pakistan a number of times during his 28-year career as a staff writer and editor. In 1981, two years after the Soviet invasion of neighboring Afghanistan, Ellis found Pakistan overrun with Afghan refugees and weighing the same dilemma it faces today: whether to make alliances with the West and risk antagonizing a poor—and increasingly volatile—Muslim population.*

William S. Ellis, "Pakistan Under Pressure," photos by James L. Stanfield, May 1981, pp. 668-701.

Pakistan Under Pressure

BY WILLIAM S. ELLIS   PHOTOGRAPHS BY JAMES L. STANFIELD

She had lived behind the veil for most of her 25 years, and now, in death, she lay covered by a red-and-gold blanket. Probably it was her grandest possession, that blanket, and when the services were over—when the words had been spoken and the body committed to final rest—it would be returned to her family and perhaps one day be passed along to the son born to her in the final minutes of her life.

She died in exile, in Pakistan. As one of the estimated 1.5 million persons who have fled across the border since Soviet troops entered Afghanistan late

The pall-covered body of an Afghan refugee woman is borne from the Aza Khel refugee camp to burial on a knoll more than a mile away.

in December 1979, she had taken up residence in a makeshift camp in the rugged North-West Frontier Province of Pakistan. With her tribesman husband, a Pathan, she had trekked more than a hundred miles to the camp, and that cost her the strength needed for childbirth.

She had made the crossing in winter, when heavy snows in the high country thinned the ranks of refugees as they attempted to escape bombings and strafings of their villages by moving east until the mountains were behind them. But even on the other side they were dogged by bitter cold.

So it was on this morning. The four men carrying the body pushed against a chilling wind as they walked out of the camp, across the road, and along a dirt path to a hillside burial site more than a mile away. There were but few gentle words of remembrance in the graveside eulogy. Rather, the speaker exhorted those in attendance to vow to drive the Russians from Afghanistan. He cried for revenge. The hawk-faced Pathan tribesmen replied as one: Revenge would be theirs.

As the second anniversary of the invasion approaches, cries of outrage have softened, and the presence of 85,000 Soviet troops in Afghanistan has taken root. For those opposed to the spread of Soviet influence, one blessing may be counted in all of this: Neighboring Pakistan has survived.

Seldom in its short and troubled history as a nation has so much worldwide attention been visited on Pakistan as it was during the early phases of the turmoil in Afghanistan. The Western world embraced Islamabad—Pakistan's gleaming modern capital—and whispered of delicious things forthcoming: aid and arms and nourishments enough to make the country a rock of strength. Or, failing that, to get the armed forces in a position where they could handle border skirmishes and put down any Soviet-inspired tribal uprisings within the country.

Then, as now, Pakistan was under martial law imposed by the military regime of President General Mohammad Zia ul-Haq. The press was censored, and the jails held hundreds of political prisoners. Waves of unrest and anger over the execution of former Prime Minister Zulfikar Ali Bhutto surged through the cities.

Pakistan was created in 1947 as a separate Muslim state carved away during the partition of India. The bond of Islam, however, was not strong enough; 24 years later the eastern portion of the country, separated by more than a thousand miles of Indian territory, broke away to become Bangladesh.

The gap between the two cultures—predominantly Punjabi in the west, Bengali in the east—was too vast to be bridged by a shared faith.

What remains is a country with a landmass equal to that of Texas and Ohio combined. In the south the provinces of Baluchistan and Sind share 500 miles of

Bundled against the predawn chill, Pathan tribesmen of Pakistan guard the legendary Khyber Pass; its dual roads, impassable in winter, separate camels and cars.

Arabian Sea coastline. The North-West Frontier Province and the portion of Kashmir now under Pakistani control carry the country to the breathless heights of the Hindu Kush and the Karakoram mountains. A fourth province, the Punjab, abuts India north of Sind. And through much of the land runs a deep warrior tradition.

There was great bloodshed during the partitioning of India, and again when Bangladesh wrenched itself away. Indeed, has not Pakistan in all 34 years of its nationhood come to be synonymous with tragedy? War, hunger, poverty, and the shattered dream of uniting 120 million Muslims; all that, and yet there is a magic about this place.

It is a magic of landscape, for one thing, of mountains, including K2, that punch through the clouds to heights of more than 25,000 feet, and deserts where the highest thing above ground is the hump of a camel.

There are lakes stained pink with flocks of stately flamingos, and valleys

called Swat and Hunza where the play of breezes in flowering apricot trees is a grace note to the gurgle of sweet and glistening river waters.

There is a magic, too, of people and history. With a present population of 87 million, Pakistan not only fills but overflows the Asian mold of massed humanity. In the streets of the major cities of Karachi, Lahore, and Rawalpindi the throngs are like human slipknots as they manage barely to escape anatomical entanglements. And somehow, in those same streets, with horns butting and blaring, water buffalo dispute the right-of-way with '68 Chevys.

It is not unsavory chaos, however, for it all seems as a reflection of the times when this land was crowded with the legions of emperors, and with merchants who traded in the riches of the Orient. One walks here in the footsteps of Alexander the Great, and in the paths of caravans that carried silk and gold, ivory and jewels, to and from China.

Change has come slowly to Pakistan, and because of that, there is a lingering sense of the drama of the past—especially in Peshawar, sprawled upon a plain east of the Khyber Pass.

Here is a city where the streets are paved with shards of history. Many believe that Herodotus referred to it in the fifth century B.C., calling it Kaspaturos, but it may well have been there even before that, as provocative and colorful a place as could be found in all of Asia. Great armies came to grief in and around Peshawar at the hands of tribesmen that Herodotus called "the most warlike of all." They were probably ancestors of the Pathans.

Pathans of the Afridi tribe are the custodians of the Khyber Pass, and Peshawar its gateway city. So it has been all through the centuries, at times when Kushan, Turk, Mongol, Mogul, and others spilled through the passes with conquest in mind. The Afridis have never been truly conquered, not even by the British in the days of empire.

In the Khyber Pass on a day in January of last year, I walked with a group of Pathans along the main road toward the town of Landi Kotal. They talked of a shooting several weeks earlier, and when I asked if anyone had died, one man replied, "Forty." It was a matter of revenge, he told me, and therefore permissible under the Pathan code of justice. It is part of a life-style they call *pashtunwali*, or the way of the Pathans, and it is structured on dignity and pride.

Meanwhile, activity at the border crossing in the Khyber continues as usual. People in droves are moving back and forth between the two countries, while off in the distance trains of camels and donkeys freighted with refrigerators and television sets plod along the smugglers' route.

Money changers are seated in a line on the Pakistani side, fingering stacks of paper currency gone grimy and tissue thin with age. They sit facing the sun, and when the third one from the end smiles, the light dances on a tooth of gold. Generally he smiles at the conclusion of one of his transactions, as indeed he should.

There is a discernible pattern to the traffic across the border. They come from Afghanistan with empty sacks and satchels, and they return with bodies bent low under the weight of their purchases (rice costs twice as much in Afghanistan as it does in Pakistan). A boy of no more than five made three crossings in less than an hour, each time filling a five-liter tin with cooking oil. He would deliver the oil to an Afghan merchant who would dump it into a large tank and then send him back across the frontier for more, and back again until the tank was filled.

On his last trip the boy was stopped by a border guard who cuffed him smartly across the cheek. He was a Pathan, but being only five or so, the spirit of pashtunwali had not yet taken hold of him. So he cried.

The border is often referred to as the Durand Line, after Sir Mortimer Durand, the foreign secretary of the Indian government who in 1893 signed the agreement with Emir Abdur Rahman for a line of demarcation between British India and Afghanistan.

The boundary meant little to the Pathans then, and it means little to them now. They come and go as they please, for their loyalty is not so much to nation as it is to tribe. Many say they will have their own nation one day, and they will call it Pashtunistan.

The Baluch, too, find fealty to tribe more important than nationhood. "We are Muslims, but we are not fanatic about it," said Jamil Bugti, a tall, heavyset man with a beard the color of topsoil. He is 31 years old and the second-born son of Akbar Khan Bugti, chief of the 100,000-member Bugti tribe centered in Baluchistan Province. "I was born a Muslim, I will die a Muslim. That's OK. But Islam plays no role as far as Baluch politics is concerned.

"We ask ourselves what has Pakistan done for us, and the answer is they've killed 8,000 Baluch men, women, and children." Bugti, of course, speaks for only a portion of the tribal population in the province. In northern Baluchistan, for example, most of the tribesmen are Pathans, and they tend to put themselves apart from Baluch unrest.

Still, Bugti's sentiments are widespread.

For four years, from 1973 to 1977, there was a war in Pakistan that gained little notice in the world. On one side was the Pakistani Army of highly trained soldiers, on the other Baluch irregulars. They fought in the bleak hills of the sprawling province in the southwest corner of the country. Before the guns were silenced—not by a truce but a cease-fire only—close to 10,000 had died.

The bitterness remains.

Of Pakistan's four provinces, the Punjab holds the great bulk of population. The queen city, Lahore, is there, as is the national capital of Islamabad.

It is in the Punjab that the ghost of British rule does its heaviest haunting—from the tall, erect Punjabi soldier with Sandhurst bearing to the government functionary speaking in Oxford-accented English. In the cities the three-piece suit is as much a fashion as the baggy trousers and the turban.

The construction of Islamabad began in 1961, and by the end of that decade it had taken over the role of national capital from Karachi and from the interim seat at Rawalpindi, only ten miles away. They are called twin cities, Rawalpindi and Islamabad, but they hold scant resemblance to one another.

Rawalpindi is an old cantonment city. The new capital is a study in orderliness, of white office buildings set in striking vistas against the Margala Hills.

Lahore, the nation's cultural center, was Pakistan's prized inheritance at

Public flogging is permitted; at times a microphone is placed before the criminal so that his moaning and cries of pain can be heard by the assembled crowd.

the time of partition. Had the boundary with India not been drawn just 15 miles from the city, it likely would have been designated the Pakistani capital.

The grandest era in Lahore's 2,000 years of history, when Mogul emperors held court in palaces of marble, lasted from the late 16th century into the 18th. The Moguls swept down out of central Asia to conquer India, and their legacy still survives. They left a finery of architecture. They left pavilions and halls of mirrors, waterfalls and gardens sweetened by the fragrance of a thousand exotic blooms. They left to Lahore an enduring aura of regal character.

As in most countries with a history of riot and revolution, student activity is closely monitored in Pakistan—and more so in Lahore, home of the nation's oldest university, than in most cities. And what are the students saying, now that Pakistan is on the front line of the upheaval in Afghanistan?

This:

"It's good that the West wants to help us now, but they should have done that long ago. Anyway, it isn't so much the Russians that I worry about. Our problem, it seems to me, is on the other border. I don't think for a minute that India is going to let China, the United States, or any other country make Pakistan a fearsome military power." And this: "Just yesterday I saw an officer in the Pakistani Air Force wearing one of the coats sent here for the Afghan refugees. It was shameful. But then you have to stop and consider how far we've come as a civilized nation. The answer is pretty clear when you realize that the government has resumed the practice of flogging prisoners in public. How do you Americans feel when you give money to a regime that promised free elections but gave us the stave instead?"

One of Ali Bhutto's last acts as prime minister was to institute severe Islamic laws in the country. General Zia has since moved to further tighten government control over the manners and morals of the people.

Consider: Any liquor found in a traveler's luggage is confiscated until he leaves the country.

Public flogging is permitted; at times a microphone is placed before the criminal so that his moaning and cries of pain can be heard by the assembled crowd.

Gory penalties for serious crimes are now lawful, although not a single doctor in the country seems willing to inflict the most gruesome: amputation. (Muslim Shia and Sunni sects also disagree on a thief's sentence: Shias maintain the fingers should be cut off only to the first knuckle, thereby allowing the punished to continue to help himself from the communal food bowl. Sunnis say the hand should come off at the wrist.) In July of last year the government announced it would collect a 2.5 percent tax on savings accounts over a certain amount.

This tax, known as the *zakat*, would then be distributed among the poor, as the Koran prescribes. Many in Pakistan (mostly those who will be required to pay the tax) claim it should be voluntary.

Judges of the Supreme Court, high courts, and the federal Shariat court are now to be addressed as "Sir" and "Janab Wala," instead of "My Lord," and they will wear traditional black *sherwanis* and Jinnah caps while attending court and official functions.

Pakistan has become an artery in the vast, sinister network of international narcotics traffic. "Until four years ago, the Golden Triangle of

A warrior mentality stalks the highlands, where "just about everybody carries a gun," says the author. A storefront armory in Bara sells bullets, shotgun shells, and "fountain pen" guns that can fire a single slug.

Southeast Asia was the leading producer of opium for export," said Reza Husnain, former director of operations of the Pakistan Narcotics Control Board.

"But that distinction now belongs to the Iran-Afghanistan-Pakistan area, and the disturbances in the first two mean that Pakistan's potential may be exploited further." Until recently, Husnain explained, most of the opium was grown in Afghanistan and marketed through Pakistan. "Now it is the other way," he said. "Not too long ago we intercepted 250 kilograms of morphine being transported on a road from Quetta to Iran.

"Hauls of such size were unheard of before the troubles in Afghanistan and Iran. In addition, our laws having to do with drugs are lenient compared to those of, say, Iran," Husnain said. "If we are to keep this thing from getting out of hand, we have to come down hard now, as we are starting to do." According to Husnain, his country's annual production of opium normally ranges from 200 to 300 metric tons.

"All around there are countries in turmoil, and so Pakistan is left to fill the gap as far as providing narcotics is concerned," Husnain said. "It is a very serious situation, and it has even started to result in the spread of addiction here. In northern Pakistan now you can find whole villages on hashish or opium."

The use of opium seems to be heavier in the villages than in the cities of Pakistan. In the largest city of them all, Karachi, the sweltering, swollen hub of the nation's industry and commerce, the apathetic stupor of an addict would go little noticed amid the bustle of millions of people in movement.

Seven million now live in Karachi, with another 500,000 added each year. By the end of the century this Arabian Sea port city may well overtake Calcutta as the most populous place on the subcontinent.

"We simply cannot keep pace with what is happening here," said Umar Yusuf Deda, deputy mayor of Karachi. "Our major problems are transportation, water supply, and housing. A third of the city's population lives in substandard housing." A century ago Karachi was a settlement of fishermen. But, sitting on what is perhaps the finest natural harbor on the southern coastline, it grew as only a port city could at a time when ships were the workhorses not only of the international trade but also of travel.

"I sailed to Karachi from Bombay 30 years ago," said an old man who was peddling oranges from a pushcart. "It took 36 hours and the fare was two dollars. My grandfather made the same trip in 1920 for 50 cents." We talked for several hours, and when he sold the last of the oranges to a woman who kept her money knotted in the corner of a handkerchief, he invited me to his home for tea.

"As you can see," he said when we approached his house, "it is only a hut. I have lived here since I came to Karachi in 1950." It was a boxy structure of one story with a concrete floor, and frayed gray blankets hanging over the openings between the two rooms. On one wall was a picture of Clyde Beatty holding a raised chair in the face of a snarling lion. A kerosene heater offered up a smelly breath of warmth.

"My five children are still home, so there are seven of us living here," he said. "Three of the five are sons, and they will take care of me when I can no longer work, *inshallah*. Still, I suppose I will live in this hut until I die. Do you know the man in the picture, the one who looks in the mouth of the lion?" □

"Peanuts!" said President General Mohammad Zia ul-Haq when he spurned a U.S. offer of 400 million dollars in aid after the Russians invaded Afghanistan. Above, a portrait of Muhammad Ali Jinnah, founder of modern Pakistan.

■ *In the autumn of 1981, staff writer Harvey Arden and photographer Kevin Fleming were on assignment in the Sinai Peninsula, working on a story for the magazine. Egypt's President Anwar Sadat paid a ceremonial visit to the region, where a decade earlier he'd battled Israel in the Yom Kippur War. Yet it was the peace accords with Israel, signed at Camp David in 1978, that was to be his lasting legacy. That day in Sinai, as Arden and Fleming watched, a group of radicals including Ayman al-Zawahiri (now linked to Osama bin Laden) shot Sadat to death.*

Harvey Arden, "Eternal Sinai,"
photos by David Doubilet
and Kevin Fleming,
April 1982, pp. 444-461

Egypt Loses Sadat

BY HARVEY ARDEN

Traded away for peace, the Israeli settlement of Yammit changed hands when Egypt reclaimed the Sinai as part of the 1978 Camp David agreements. Egypt's President paid for that peace with his life.

DAVID DOUBILET

T he unthinkable had happened: Peace had come to the eternal battleground of the Sinai Peninsula, and never had things seemed so confused or uncertain. It was late September 1981—a time like no other in this place like no other.

I had arrived in the midst of a dizzying transition. After 15 years of occupation and controversial settlement, the Israelis were in the process of preparing for their final pullout. The Egyptians, meanwhile, were still tentatively moving in.

Within seven months—by April 25, 1982, if the terms of the Camp David peace accords were to be kept—Israel was scheduled to have withdrawn its military forces and settlers from the third of Sinai it still occupied, returning the entire West Virginia-size peninsula to Egyptian sovereignty for the first time since Israel had seized it during the six-day Arab-Israeli war of 1967.

But in still-occupied eastern Sinai, ultranationalist Israeli zealots, defying the embarrassed government of Prime Minister Menachem Begin, were moving into homes abandoned by outgoing original settlers, vowing to disrupt the withdrawal from Sinai at all costs, even to the point of outright physical violence.

Prowling through clouds of dust, an Israeli tank commander trains his crew. Egypt and Israel fought one of history's largest tank battles in Sinai in 1973. Sadat was acclaimed for his role in launching the campaign.

During their 15 years here, the Israelis gridded the desert with roads, found new oil off Sinai's western coast, discovered vast, still untapped subterranean deposits of fossil water, constructed some of the world's most sophisticated military bases, resettled many of the 50,000 or so Bedouin, founded a score of Jewish settlements with long-range plans for tens of thousands more inhabitants, and—in the process—won the near unanimous condemnation of friends and enemies around the world.

In Cairo and other Egyptian cities, Muslim extremists were loudly shrilling their fanatic opposition to Egypt's unilateral peace with Israel, which they considered a betrayal of the Arab cause.

Photographer Kevin Fleming and I had hoped to see Egyptian President Anwar Sadat at the annual military parade near Cairo—a display of pomp celebrating Egypt's 1973 breakthrough into Sinai.

Sadat's fate had been intertwined with Sinai ever since his early years as an army officer at El Qantara, El Arish, and Rafah. Into this desert, in 1973, he had launched the war that won him the title, Hero of the Crossing. Here he came to worship at the foot of Mount Sinai on the second anniversary of his bold visit to Jerusalem. Here, too, he built a lovely retreat where he could retire for rest and meditation. And here, he once said, he hoped to be buried.

I could hardly have conceived that the laminated plastic identity card issued to me the morning of October 6 in Cairo would be a press pass to an assassination.

At the parade grounds, after placing a wreath and praying at Egypt's Tomb of the Unknown Soldier—built after the 1973 war—Sadat took his seat at the center of the reviewing stand. He seemed relaxed, chatted, puffed at his pipe, sipped tea. From his neck dangled a medallion commemorating the 1973 war. There was an exceptional beauty about his dark, complex face, noble as a pharaoh's. Removing his military hat to wipe his brow, he revealed on his forehead the *zabiba*—the visible dark spot common to devout Muslims who press their heads to the floor during prayer five times a day.

When the shooting started, Kevin and I had drifted about 25 yards to Sadat's right. Crowds blocked our view of the assassins as they leaped off a parade vehicle. Our first thought was that fireworks were going off. But no.

Tumbled chairs. Tumbled dreams. The images return to mind again and again. Bodies sprawled like rag dolls. The moans of the wounded. The astonishing brightness of their blood. It has a dreamlike intensity about it even now.

Over the heads of the crowd near Sadat I saw objects flying—hand grenades. I never heard them go off because a squadron of jet fighters was screaming overhead, releasing rainbow trails of colored smoke. The thought crossed my mind: Might they be dropping bombs?

We had no way of knowing whether this was an attack only on Sadat or a general insurrection. Crowds lunged out of the reviewing stand, tumbling over hundreds of wooden chairs. Bullets skipped off the tarmac. People lay wounded to both my right and left. Amid the fleeing spectators, a young man in army fatigues, his eyes wild, ran right past me, fleet as a gazelle. In moments half a dozen soldiers hauled him back, savagely beating his limp form. A suspect had been caught.

But where was Kevin?

I made my way back to the grandstand, where blue-bereted troops had formed a security cordon.

Kevin had slipped behind the cordon. While gunfire still crackled, he was coolly photographing the aftermath of violence: bloody bodies, captured assassins, stunned spectators. He had come to photograph a parade; he left with history in his camera. ▫

Sadat was attacked as he sat on a ceremonial platform reviewing troops. Just 25 yards away, photographer Fleming had barely captured this image of a wounded ambassador when a soldier pushed a gun into his face and screamed "No!" He didn't pull the trigger.

■ Muslims revere Jerusalem as the third holiest site in Islam, after Mecca and Medina, in part because they see their faith as a culmination of Judaism and Christianity. The Prophet Muhammad also spoke of a mysterious night journey he made to a hilltop in Jerusalem, and from there to heaven. After the armies of Islam conquered Jerusalem in A.D. 638, the site of Muhammad's ascent was sanctified with a mosque, called the Dome of the Rock, over the ruins of the Jewish temple that had been destroyed by the Romans in the first century. Control of the Dome and a second mosque, al-Aqsa, passed to Israel when it wrested Jerusalem's Old City, including the Temple Mount, from Jordan in June 1967.

Joseph Judge, "This Year in Jerusalem," photos by Jodi Cobb, Apr. 1983, pp. 479-515

This Year in Jerusalem

BY JOSEPH JUDGE   PHOTOGRAPHS BY JODI COBB

During a shopkeepers' strike in East Jerusalem, a woman vents her rage at the arrest of a Palestinian by hurling a rock at Israeli police.

T he sky over blessed and accursed Jerusalem sometimes seems on supernatural fire. Thunder explodes through gusts of snow. Darkness whelms the deep Valley of Kidron, from which will rise the many dead on the last of all days—and yet beyond, a light of stars, space, and time sets distant Abu Tur aglow, as though truly elsewhere.

When the Old City of golden stone puts on its magic act, one does feel that it is the hill nearest heaven, where a man can cup his hand to the wind and hear the voice of God. Faith: Here an angel stayed the hand of an obedient father about to slay his son. Faith: Here the Prophet of Allah arrived on a winged steed and climbed to heaven, into the presence of God. Faith: Here the Son of God was killed on the Cross and rose from the dead to save us all from sin. Faith: Here the Ark will be found, the Temple rebuilt, and the true Messiah come at length to lead mankind toward Paradise.

So they say.

And as long as men believe what they believe, and act, piously or with cold cruelty, upon that belief, the dream and the tragedy of this unique city will go on and on.

From its ancient gates, roads lead away as they have for millennia, down toward the Mediterranean seacoast westward, steeply down to the Dead Sea eastward, south along mountain ridges toward Bethlehem, where Jesus and David were born, and to Hebron, where lies Abraham, and north toward the home of the old empires, Assyrian, Persian, Roman, Byzantine, that periodically smashed Jerusalem and enslaved and slaughtered its devout people.

But the *true* road to Jerusalem is passion; the gates are faith; the streets are memory; the inner sanctuary is the yearning soul. It is a place where myth may be reality and truths are mendacious, where men who remember persecution walk in narrow, safe paths of their own careful making; a city of walls within walls, of locked gates, bolted doors, of windowless first stories, of iron and stone, stone and iron.

And yet when the sky clears over the highest of all peaks, that to the northwest called in Arabic Nebi Samwil, the Prophet Samuel (who, it is said, is buried there), one remembers its other name—Mount of Joy, thus christened by Crusader King Richard the Lion-Hearted for the emotion he felt at his first sight of the distant city of Jesus.

The Christian kingdom the Crusaders erected in A.D. 1099, over the bones of the Jews and Muslims they exterminated after their victory, lasted only a century before Arab armies took the city back and Muslim potentates— from Cairo, Damascus, Istanbul—ruled on until 1917, when a British army, under Gen. Sir Edmund Allenby, entered the Old City. Allenby, in a memorable moment in Jerusalem history, chose to walk humbly through old Jaffa Gate as a sign of respect for the sanctity of the place.

The British Mandate came to a confused and bloody end after decades of Arab revolt and Arab and Jewish guerrilla war that erupted into open combat in 1948. The British flag was no sooner pulled down from the staff before Government House and the last lorry had barely rolled away from the barbed-wire compounds that set off large sections of the city when

Ancient lessons of sacred Jewish writings and traditions are passed on to yet another generation of boys at a *yeshiva*, a private religious school, in the old and ultra-Orthodox neighborhood of Mea Shearim.

Jewish and Arab forces opened fire. Jerusalem was the prize. Jerusalem, the holy, the sanctified, demanding again the blood sacrifice.

Lt. Abdullah Salam, leading an armored column of the Arab Legion down the height of Sheikh Jarrah, stopped his sand-colored command car and threw himself down to kiss the ground when he first saw the city sacred to Islam. (He was dead before he reached it.)

The Arab Legion held on to the Old City. A United Nations cease-fire left it divided, with a wide no-man's-land running under the walls, and thus it remained for 19 years. In those years, Israel built a modern city in West Jerusalem while Jordan held the east, a land of pastoral villages. Until June 7, 1967—the third day of the Six Day War.

On a wintry day last year a former colonel of the Israel Defense Forces sat with me in a warm bar and remembered.

"Who forgets such a thing?" he said. "We rushed St. Stephen's Gate. In the Israeli Army, always the officers first. We thought the Arab Legion would be there in force. In an hour, I was at the Wall. I wept."

On that day, for the first time in more than 1,800 years, a Jewish state and a Jewish army commanded all Jerusalem, and the prayers of Passovers beyond recounting had been answered in gunfire.

For the numberless Jewish dead of the centuries, for whom persecution flowed with their mothers' milk, and especially for the victims of the Nazi Holocaust, this moment at the Western, or Wailing, Wall—Judaism's most sacred site, all that remains of Herod's magnificent temple—was one of redemption, of a bursting pride and resurrection of self-respect. It was the closing of a long contract: The Lord had led them into this land always promised to them.

I asked my friend if it had turned out the way he thought it would.

"No," he said. "Our hopes were too high." Then he opened his left palm, bobbed his head a bit, shrugged, and said: "But . . . not so bad. We said we would build a Jewish state in the Land of Israel. And we built it."

For most of the world's people, the Old City is Jerusalem, that square kilometer within the magnificent walls of Suleiman, of such spiritual density that its magnetic field covers a planet, a neutron star of the human need to believe.

From atop the ancient wall near Damascus Gate, where tourists now walk, it seems one organic structure that grew, stone by stone, wall by wall, house by house, roof by roof, dome by dome, tower by tower. It is a labyrinth of 120 named and countless unnamed narrow paths and lanes, only a few of which—those that trace the Roman streets of the second century A.D.—run straight, and these are the ones lined with more than a thousand tiny shops and stalls. It is a dense human habitation of 29,000 people. Woven into it are the bits and pieces of its turbulent past: Crusader arches shadow the steep steps to Ramban Synagogue; a Roman square forms the basement of the Convent of the Sisters of Zion; the city wall of King Herod holds up an Ottoman Turkish wall at David's Tower; Byzantine paving stones catch rain in their rippled surface near the Mosque of Omar. Maps traditionally divide it into four quarters—Christian, Muslim, Jewish, and Armenian—but in reality it has three centers of gravity.

For almost 2,000 years, Jews have struggled to live close to the Western

Wall. In today's Jewish Quarter (largely rebuilt after being destroyed during the fighting of 1948 and Jordanian occupation) are left ten of the 70 old synagogues and dozens of religious academies.

For 2,000 years, Christians have wanted to live close to the Church of the Holy Sepulchre, site of Christ's death on the Cross, burial, and Resurrection. In the Christian Quarter today are dozens of churches and scores of monasteries and other religious institutions belonging to the more than 20 Christian sects here, among them Roman and Greek Catholic, Greek and Armenian Orthodox, Anglican, and Coptic.

For 500 years, Muslim devout have wanted to live near the Haram esh Sharif, the great platform on which the Temples of Solomon and Herod once stood and where now stand the glorious Dome of the Rock, Islam's oldest religious structure, and al-Aqsa Mosque, the third holiest in all Islam. Their mosques and *madrasahs*, or schools of religion, clustered along the old retaining walls of the Temple Mount, along with the Governor's House, the courts of law, and libraries.

It took a good 1,700 years to make the Old City; one small piece of it would be the glory of any congregation on Earth. And this not to mention the surrounds: Mount Zion on the southwest, where is located the reputed tomb of David, and, just above, the room of the Last Supper; or the Mount of Olives to the east, paved with the tombstones of devout Jews and the reputed tombs of Mary and Joseph, and the church built over the rock where Christ agonized in the garden. All in a stunning setting of hills below racing clouds, plunging valleys, rolling brown desert, and spectacular vistas. As the Talmud says, of the ten shares of beauty in the world, Jerusalem has nine.

I must admit I like the place in foul weather, in spitting snow and cold. The few tourists huddle in damp coffee shops, pressing their noses against frosted windows. A few Orthodox Jews march resolutely to the Wall, but in general the Old City is quiet, cold as a tomb. Arabs in shops crouch over charcoal braziers and wrap their hands around small coffee cups. Outside the walls, the traffic of West Jerusalem churns around one-way streets, blowing horns as though an expectant mother were in each car.

Then is the time to set your foot upon the Via Dolorosa, the Way of the Cross, going into the Old City by Damascus Gate, not St. Stephen's. For if you go in by way of St. Stephen's, you will have to consider the veracity of this way and its Stations of the Cross.

"Christ did not go that way," a scholar once confided in me. "He was tried by Pilate near where the Armenian church is today. He then carried His Cross—just the crossbeam, not the whole thing—down St. James and up Habad, the Cardo Maximus of the Romans, and out the Garden Gate, which stood where David Street hits the bazaars today. That's the true Via Dolorosa."

"Can you prove that?" I asked.

"No. I only have archaeology, history, and common sense on my side."

Whereas, if you go in Damascus Gate, you can cut straight through to Abu Shukrei's small but warm restaurant (four tables), where his sons carry on the reputation for Jerusalem's best *hummus*, and look in on the antiquities shops, which sell museum seconds. A Canaanite goddess. A pot from Hebron. A coin from Jericho.

I n a city of so many places, everyone sooner or later finds one special. For Protestants, who came on the scene so late they enjoy only minimal privileges at the Holy Sepulchre, it may be the Lutheran Church of the Redeemer in the ancient district of Muristan, from the belfry of which is one of the Old City's finest views, or Christ Church, a sober, appealing Anglican establishment of 1849 across from David's Citadel near Jaffa Gate—the first Protestant church in the Ottoman Empire.

Beyond is the Armenian Quarter, a small city within a city behind thick walls and a strong gateway that is locked and bolted each night at ten.

There is something especially poignant about the Armenians, because this Jerusalem compound is in fact the spiritual capital of a stateless nation of people living in their own diaspora. They were in Jerusalem in the fourth century, and their Cathedral of St. James is the Old City's most beautiful and authentic—a Crusader survival, a vast cave of a place hung with gleaming golden lamps, smoky with incense, spread with magnificent rugs, filled with the baritone chanting of the priests. James, the brother of Jesus and the first bishop of Jerusalem, rests under the main altar.

For a visiting Jew, a special place has to be Rivca Weingarten's house because she is still sitting in it.

"The army called me in 1967," she told me. "I was the first person back

When an Israeli soldier opened fire in the Dome of the Rock in 1982, killing two Muslims and wounding many more, Arab youths clashed with police in the compound of the mosque and in the streets. Despite the threat of a prison term, a young Arab raised the Palestinian flag—outlawed in 1983, legal today.

Dominating the heights like fortresses, Israeli housing developments settle Jewish populations in land largely confiscated from Arabs. Such seizures have been declared legal under Israeli law.

into the Jewish Quarter. I came immediately to this house, where so much history had happened."

This house is at No. 6 Or Ha-haim Street, in a neighborhood now completely rebuilt in lovely but heavy stone. In 1948, though, it was the residence of Rivca's father, Rabbi Mordechai Weingarten, the patriarchal figure for the 25,000 Jews then living in the quarter, and the man who surrendered it to the Arab Legion.

"What could he do? They were women and children and an army of boys," Rivca said. "Afterward, my father's heart was broken. He never again laughed or smiled. We could not play the radio, not even the piano, in his presence."

With the help of the Jerusalem Foundation, Rivca has converted the old house into a museum of Jewish life as it was lived in the quarter long before the destruction of 1948. It is a compelling and beautiful memory—a

Although their two acres of olive trees were confiscated by Israel for a housing complex, the Salameh family kept their home; they were one of four Palestinian families to remain after the complex was built. Their forebears came here in 1948, refugees from the fighting in West Jerusalem.

bedroom with many beds, including two sizes of cribs; a kitchen where one can all but smell the baking and the cooking that went on in small, tin, coal-burning stoves; the guest room with its gilded mirror and couch made from boards and crates; the inner courtyard where most of life was lived.

In a separate room, the worn but lovely objects by which men earned their bread—the reeds and quills of the scribe, the copper shoeshine stand, the wheel of the knife sharpener, the stake and lasts of the cobbler.

Simple and fundamental, this series of rooms touches any human heart, for it reflects the endurance of the small against the mighty forces of history.

"We called it the Old Yishuv Courtyard Museum," Rivca continued. "The term is used to designate the group of Jews that came to Jerusalem around 1700, mostly from Spain, long before the so-called First Aliyah, or wave of immigration, which came in 1882. Ours is the fifth generation of Jews to live in this house.

"There were always riots, it seems, when I was a girl here. Always trouble, and the house was bombed more than once.

"At the same time, between the troubles, there was a common life. Many

Jews had Arab landlords. I remember that at Passover our Arab friends brought us food, and we did the same for them during Ramadan."

There is another special place that touches the heart, but this one with rue. It is the Khalidiya Library on the Street of the Chain, that ancient thoroughfare that carries the Muslim pilgrim to the precincts of the sacred Haram.

The Khalidi family came to Jerusalem with Sultan Omar ibn al-Khattab, the second caliph of the Prophet Muhammad, in A.D. 638. It was Omar who built a small mosque where the Dome of the Rock would rise 50 years later.

Scholars, lawyers, and government officials, the Khalidis assembled over the years a magnificent library on Arab history. But now the door is shut and bolted. A few doors away Dr. Haidar Khalidi admitted me to his house, some yards from the main passage to the Western Wall from the Old City. We went upstairs to a room that overlooks an open courtyard, its roofline ringed by barbed wire put up by the Israeli authorities. This I took to be an unsubtle reminder that perhaps Dr. Khalidi should move to where he would be more welcome.

"I will not discuss the present situation," he said in a kindly but firm tone, "because you are an American, and because it is too complicated." We had strong coffee and spoke of Arabic history. But downstairs, in the Street of the Chain, waited a man perfectly willing to discuss the situation.

He said:

"When the word came to us in 1921 that the British, who had been only four years in this land, were going to give it away to the Jews, my eyes were opened. We ran into the streets with the madness of young people, thinking to end this injustice with a club.

"Why must we Palestinians continually pay for the sins of you Christians? If your conscience was stricken, why didn't you take the Jews out of the gas chambers? Why did you send them here with guns, tanks, and planes to take our land?

"The Zionists want me to go away, but I will die and be buried in the land of my fathers and grandfathers."

A few days later I called on a young Jewish couple recently moved into the new neighborhood of Ramot. It occupies the lower slope of the highest hill (875 meters) in the entire region—Richard the Lion-Hearted's one-time Mount of Joy. From the approach road across the deep Valley of Soreq, the four- and five-story apartment blocks in rank after rank loom like a fortress.

Tamy and Joseph Koren's apartment is well furnished, comfortable, warm with rugs and wall hangings. Though she can see French Hill, in "down-town" Jerusalem, from Ramot and can get there in ten minutes, Tamy still feels that she is somewhat isolated, perhaps because she was born in a comfortable and secure suburb of Jerusalem. Ramot, new, big, and still only half finished, has a feeling of being not really a part of anything.

"Our families helped us," Joseph said, when I asked him about the cost. He makes a good living as an environmental designer, but . . . "If you don't have families to help, it is very difficult to find a good place to live."

A flat in Ramot, or Gilo, or Maale Adumim on the way to Jericho now costs the equivalent of $50,000. The government will lend a qualified buyer as much as two-thirds; the rest has to be negotiated with the seller. With inflation now at 130 percent a year, prices keep rising.

Still, it is far more difficult to find an apartment to lease. Some so-called key-money flats are held by longtime tenants who cannot be dislodged while alive if they meet the rent payments.

The lucky ones live in the old sections of Talbeiya (formerly middle- and upper-class Arab houses, the best in town) and Rehavia, a pleasant, shady, Jewish section where establishment types years ago found large, comfortable places at low monthly rentals and are fixed in them for life. They can even pass on the lease as part of their inheritance.

Like other young Jerusalemites I met, the Korens were weighed down by the air of tension that inhabits the country, the recurrent warfare, and the lack of upward mobility in Israeli society.

"Until very recently, the average age of the Knesset," he told me, "increased by one year during each year of its existence."

What makes it all bearable is to live in Jerusalem. "If I couldn't live in Jerusalem, I wouldn't live in Israel!" is a remark I heard a dozen times.

A deep attachment to the place, some feeling that it is truly important, begins to deepen in the soul, and then you know that Jerusalem will stand in the door some spring morning, with her golden stones and flowers, her intimate friendship with God and Allah, her vivifying beauty and melancholy ruin, and call your name.

I went out to one of the villages that had lost much of its land to a new neighborhood. It was Friday, and the *muezzin* was singing of Isaac and Abraham from the minaret. Around me a rampart of apartment houses closed off the view.

"The Jews live like bees," said an old man. "They have no land with their house. But maybe we have changed their minds about land, because they are always trying to take ours."

He pointed to several detached houses on a hill: "Captured by the Jews," he said, using the universal term in Jerusalem for land that has been confiscated.

"They came there in 1967 and told the owners: Go away from this place! This land has been taken!

"This was once a peaceful green valley, with green fields and orchards and strong young people. Now the young people leave to go to Jordan and America, and the village is old men who are laborers for the Jews. We are living in a hard time."

Jerusalem's litany of terror has many passages, Jews dead, Arabs dead—Passover 1920, May 1921, August 1929, the 1936 Arab rebellion. The bombing of the Semiramis Hotel, the Jewish market—again and again, the blood sacrifice.

Two events especially have seared themselves in the city's memory so deeply they are neither mentioned nor forgotten.

At four o'clock on the morning of April 9, 1948, 132 Jewish terrorists from the Irgun and Stern Gang fell upon the peaceful, sleeping Arab village of Deir Yasin, west of Jerusalem. For eight hours, terrible murder occurred until more than 200 men, women, and children lay dead, 15 houses dynamited. The corpses were piled in a nearby quarry and burned, and that pillar of black smoke has darkened the Jerusalem air ever since.

Today a hospital for the mentally ill covers the site; many think that use appropriate. Irgun leaders like Menachem Begin (who was not present at Deir Yasin) have denied the accusation of atrocity; the deaths were a result of what he considered, then and now, a legitimate military action.

Five days later, on Wednesday, April 14, thousands of enraged Arabs ambushed the weekly convoy taking supplies and personnel to the Jewish university and hospital on Mount Scopus, which had been cut off from Jewish Jerusalem by Arab irregulars. On the road to Scopus, near the Orient House Hotel, dynamite stopped the convoy at 9 a.m. An intense battle went on until dark, while the British did little or nothing to intervene. There were left 78 dead in the smoking hulks of armored cars and buses—doctors, nurses, scholars—a dreadful waste.

Why remember such things? Are they not too horrible to remember, when the memory brings no redemption, no salvation, no forgiveness? It is not stones you see in Jerusalem, the most permanent of all of man's artifacts; it is the living and fragile web of memory, as enduring as hatred, as deep as love. Memories there are millennia old; they reach to the root of human life and nature, and man stands naked before them, fully revealed as animal and angel.

Toward evening, there were few lights in old East Jerusalem. The shops had shuttered in another strike following more violence in the West Bank. The city was quiet and somber. Prayers were going up to heaven from mosque, church, and synagogue— seeking the justice of Allah, the salvation of Christ, the coming redemption of the Messiah.

So it goes this year in Jerusalem— the Arab despondent in his Palestine, the Christian uncertain in his Holy Land, the Jew triumphant in the Land of Israel, yet all summoning will and courage to survive this history, to preserve the ancient commitment to the most revered of man's cities, which like a vast sundial of golden stone counts down the years to the final one when all bargains are sealed and promises kept.

In that final time, then will every man take the hand of his brother in love and understanding and forgiveness; then will love bloom like a million spring flowers on the desert slopes of Kidron; then will mankind come into its inheritance of peace—peace forever, peace everlasting, peace without end.

So they say. ☐

Saudi Women

BY MARIANNE ALIREZA   PHOTOGRAPHS BY JODI COBB

■ *In her first piece for National Geographic, author Marianne Alireza gave readers a rare glimpse of life behind the veil in one of the Muslim world's most conservative societies. Her report is based on firsthand experience, which began when she met a young Saudi studying in her native California, married him, moved to Arabia in 1945 and started a family. The couple divorced in 1958, but her 13 years in a harem gave Alireza lasting ties to the Saudis—and an insider's view of Arabian women.*

Marianne Alireza, "Women of Saudi Arabia," photos by Jodi Cobb, Oct. 1987, pp. 423-453

"Say to the believing women, that they cast down their eyes . . . and reveal not their adornment . . . and let them cast their veils over their bosoms."

KORAN, SURA XXIV:31

"SHUF, SHUF," sang Ibtissam Lutfy, giving me a start because the words mean "See, see," and she is blind. We had been talking about Arabia in the1940s, when I went to live there as the American wife of a young Saudi. That was a time when Arabian women, bound by tradition, veiled, cloaked, segregated, often illiterate, had little say in their lives.

For city women like us, just about the only activity (besides living communally within the extended family) consisted of leaving our harem quarters to visit other women in theirs. Family men or male servants did the shopping. Older women ran the household, with younger women having few such duties. Yet despite this hierarchy of age, everyone belonged—even I—even before I learned to share and care as a small part of the big whole. "We love you as we love our son," were the first words I heard from my mother-in-law, Asma, and my extended family sailed me through my first Christmas with a roast turkey and gifts placed under the tree Mother had had flown in from Cairo. With wonderful sensitivity they helped me celebrate my religious feast. Outside the walls we had little, but what we did inside the walls was live together.

"Yes, those were narrow days," Ibtissam said. "But there are no more narrow days for me—and, besides, things have changed. We women have stretched our boundaries to the limit!" Now in her mid-30s, she overcame these same taboos to become a professional singer, something men didn't do 20 years ago, let alone a young girl.

Veiled to all men outside her family, a young Bedouin woman wears the classic face covering of her people.

Divided by sex and custom, a Saudi family spends Thursday evening relaxing by the Red Sea. Men often observe Friday, the Muslim holy day, at the mosque while women pray at home.

Impulsively, Ibtissam invited photographer Jodi Cobb and me to a wedding in her home city of Jiddah—but telephoned next day to cancel because her father would not permit more photographs of her.

Before we left Saudi Arabia, many other women from all strata of society would make similar apologies. In the sense that nearly three-quarters of a million girls go to school in the kingdom and thousands of women have earned university degrees and play a role in the progress of the nation, lives are indeed broader. But this is still a country where the man's word is usually final, where even six-year-old girls cover their heads.

Today, as if overnight on history's clock, Saudi Arabia has a new face from development, modernization, industrialization; its people adapt to change while simultaneously being educated; and there's a new reality

whose meaning and direction can still not be fully assessed, particularly as concerns women, as concerns Islam.

Islam is the one thing not changed. It is the state, the moral and civil code; it is all matters big and small, ever imbued with an awareness of God's will and word. Now, though, the big and small changes unloosed over the Saudis have created a need to rethink how God's will and word apply in their world of today and to invent ingenious ways to make it all fit together.

Sunni Islam as it is practiced in Saudi Arabia has no hierarchy of priesthood, not even a formal clergy, but there is no shortage of definitive religious directives for the faithful. These emanate from a powerful body of Islamic scholars called the *ulama*, who cling tenaciously to strict puritanical tenets and moral codes and whose minds are set in archaic and traditional beliefs, particularly regarding the decency and morality of women.

Public-morality committees, the regional Societies for the Preservation of Virtue and the Prevention of Vice, ensure strict compliance with religious requirements and what passes for religious requirements. Salaried morals police patrol the public domain making sure that businesses close at prayer times, that women are properly covered and observe the off-limits signs on, say, popular disco-music cassette shops, where mingling might provide a breeding ground for assignations.

Men, of course, go right on doing what they do, so the import for them is nowhere near what it is for women, who certainly seek no diminution of their role as Islamic women but may nonetheless perceive that role differently—especially as they learn to read and understand for themselves the legitimate rights given to them by Islam in the seventh century A.D.

In Islam the woman has a fully independent legal personality. She can

inherit and own property, can divorce in certain situations, and has the same religious duties as a man: "O mankind, We have created you male and female, and appointed you races and tribes, that you may know one another. Surely the noblest among you in the sight of God is the most god fearing of you" (Koran, Sura XLIX:13).

Man-created traditions and practices often denied women the rights due them, and years ago, while living the restrictive life, I often blurted to my mother-in-law, "But how can you accept this, why do you allow it to be?" She answered always, "It is our way." Well, the way has changed. And yet . . . .

For local color, Fridays on Jiddah's corniche along the Red Sea is hard to beat. Miles of sun-protected picnic areas and playgrounds line the shore where hundreds of Jiddawis *en famille* gather in their own private public spot—men, women, and children together—a notable difference from the days of men with men in public and women with women in homes.

But it is understood that being in public does not mean going public. Women's head coverings (not always over faces) stay on, and cloaks, though billowed by sea breezes, are kept firmly in place with ease and grace while ladies serve food, play with children, swing on the swings, or make the rounds on a Ferris wheel. But never mind, it's the outing that counts, so credit the government for planning and providing, and credit the change in mentality it represents.

In Riyadh we met a citified *Badawiyah*, Umm (mother of) Abdallah, who lives in an apartment and has a hospital technician daughter and a pharmacist son, but keeps her makeshift stall in the Bedouin market selling everything from gold, turquoise, and silver to ragtag notions and remnants of old Bedouin clothes.

We sat there on the ground with her and friends, partaking of dates and Arabic coffee served from a coffeepot that was identical in shape to the traditional brass one, but it was a thermos made of plastic. Other signs of the

Newlyweds—and distant cousins—Salma and Khalid Sadiq celebrate their wedding in Jiddah. Despite a quiet trend toward love matches, most Saudi marriages are alliances between families.

times are traditional *madass* (men's sandals) available now in the fine leathers of Italian shoemakers and the ultimate in veils and cloaks bearing logos and labels of famed Paris couturiers.

Umm Abdallah loved adorning herself for photographs with every possible piece of silver, but her fun and ours stopped when a male passerby shouted a protest and announced he was going for the police.

"May you be blinded and boiled in oil," Umm Abdallah shouted after him, but she scurried to hide all camera gear in Bedouin baskets, under old clothes, in an old trunk. That time the police did not come.

Women such as Umm Abdallah are only partly out of the old time. The real changes lie in the generation or so after them. Today's educated women might still wear the veil, might still be the wives and mothers they have always been, but they have become other things too.

In their ranks are teachers, computer technicians, social workers, laboratory technicians, physical-fitness instructors, physicists, engineers, bankers, filmmakers. All these when the first public schools for girls weren't approved by the government until 1960!

"Thank God things have changed for us!" This not from the younger nurses at a hospital dispensary but from a widowed mother of seven (the oldest a boy of 15) just now learning to read and write in the government program for adult illiterates, having to juggle time seeing to her children, working required hours, attending class.

At King Abd al-Aziz University Hospital in Jiddah I asked Sabah Abu Znadah, coordinator of training and development, how she had gotten into nursing.

"Do you want a flowery answer

Official Saudi censors blot out forbidden sights in foreign periodicals and conceal all references to pork and alcohol.

or do you want the truth?" she fired back with a smile. In truth she wanted to be a physician, but she missed the college's deadline for applications. Nursing was next best. "So I went for it," she said, "and now I'll fight for it."

Most Saudi professionals we interviewed "went for it" in one way or another. Some came from traditional families whose men objected to their working—"not," said Sabah, "because they were not open-minded men or too strict, but out of fear that society would look down on them."

Many had uneducated mothers pushing daughters to achieve what they never had; others had family support all the way. "My father always told us to get an education first, because the more like us, the more others will follow," said Fatmah Yamani, chief of personnel at the university hospital. One of her colleagues said that her father is now proud of her in her profession, but initially objected so strongly that he sent her to Jordan, where she found the "too free life" uncomfortable, so she returned to sit idly at home until her father gave up and gave in.

However they made it, women who have achieved avoid doing anything that could stem the tide of advancement. They proceed quietly on their merits, wanting no backlash spoiling things for them and for the women who will come after them.

Although most work in all-female facilities, some doctors, nurses, administrators, radio announcers, and journalists do work with men. Long skirts, long sleeves, and head scarves are customary for women on the job.

"There is no problem," said one hospital worker. "We are well accepted, get the same pay, and men here want more women in jobs, appreciating our efforts and respecting the levels of education that put us here."

"There *are* objections around the country though," said another. "Someone wrote the newspapers asking how their girls could work next to men. Then everyone waited to see what would happen and *nothing* happened. Someone must make the first step."

Unveiled women may not be seen by their male professors, so courses are conducted via closed-circuit television, each student having her own desk set. If, as the professor speaks, the student has a question, she has only to pick up her own telephone by the TV and have direct-line access to the lecturer.

Today's apparel could be anything imaginable because everything imaginable is available, but veil and cloak lend anonymity and appearances are deceiving. Underneath might be a high-society lady in haute couture, a high schooler togged in blue jeans and a T-shirt, a villager in colorful cotton, or an old-time lady in her old-time dress. Anything goes, but the outer layer—with slight variations, perhaps—remains the same.

Maha Bukhari, educated in the United States, teaches aerobics at a women's welfare center.

It is a shock to see sedate cloaked figures peeling to leotards in a fitness center to do routines popular the world over. Some to whom the concept is new have tried to remain modest and decorous in their wraps while pedaling bikes or walking treadmills, until the machinery demonstrates its nasty tendency to gobble loose flaps of material and long veils attached to quite long hair.

Remembering the strict segregation of the past, I am still amazed at mixed society in public. Married couples can be seen shopping together, dining tête-à-tête in public in a hotel or restaurant, but still cherished and jealously guarded is their personal privacy. Increased one-on-one sharing as husband and wife, as parents, may be due to a certain fragmentation of the extended family, with the added factor that some wives are now as educated as their spouses.

Marriage is something for which many now wait longer than before, wanting an education first. This is not to say that pressures to marry are not still there. "Our Girls and the Right Path" was the subject of a seminar in Jiddah in 1986 where Saudi scholar and Professor of Islamic Culture Ahmad Jamal indicated that marriage is a woman's primary obligation and takes precedence over the pursuit of learning. Unless, that is, a hus-

band agrees informally or by legal prenuptial writ to her continuing studies after marriage.

Just getting married poses problems for some because of prohibitively high dowries and excessive outlays for celebrations. One sheik representing ten tribes attempted to set dowry limits in his region when they reached 160,000 Saudi riyals ($42,000). He proposed maximums of 10,000 riyals plus some jewelry and a gold watch for a virgin, and 5,000 for a divorcée or a widow. One news report in 1986 listed the nationwide average as 100,000 riyals.

A Muslim can have four wives legally at a time if—a big if—he can give each wife equal material goods and equal time. So monogamy is by far the norm, although divorce rates are on the rise. With a man allowed to divorce his wife without stating reasons, there can be instances where the divorcée faces dire problems. Women can divorce too, given certain reasons outlined in the Koran, but instituting such action in a male-dominated society can be as difficult as trying to counteract any unfair conditions unilaterally imposed on a woman and children by an uncooperative or vengeful husband.

An iron fist dominates a passerby in Jiddah, where it decorates a traffic circle. Even here, in the most worldly of Saudi cities, a woman cannot board an airplane or stay overnight in a hotel without written permission from a male relative. And her modesty is guarded by *muttawwiun*—morals police armed with camel prods, who publically shame anyone offending their sense of propriety.

With all that women *can* do, there are things even today that they cannot do, such as board airline flights without written permission from a male family member or check into any of the kingdom's hotels without a letter in hand from a male relative or official sponsor permitting them to do so, and this also applies to foreign women.

One distinguished gentleman friend regards the travel restriction as a source of shame and embarrassment when he or one of his five brothers must sign for their beloved mother when she leaves on a jaunt.

"When our father died," he said, "she single-handedly raised us, did for us, taught us, shaped us into what we are today, and after all this *we* have to sign for *her*. How demeaning!" ☐

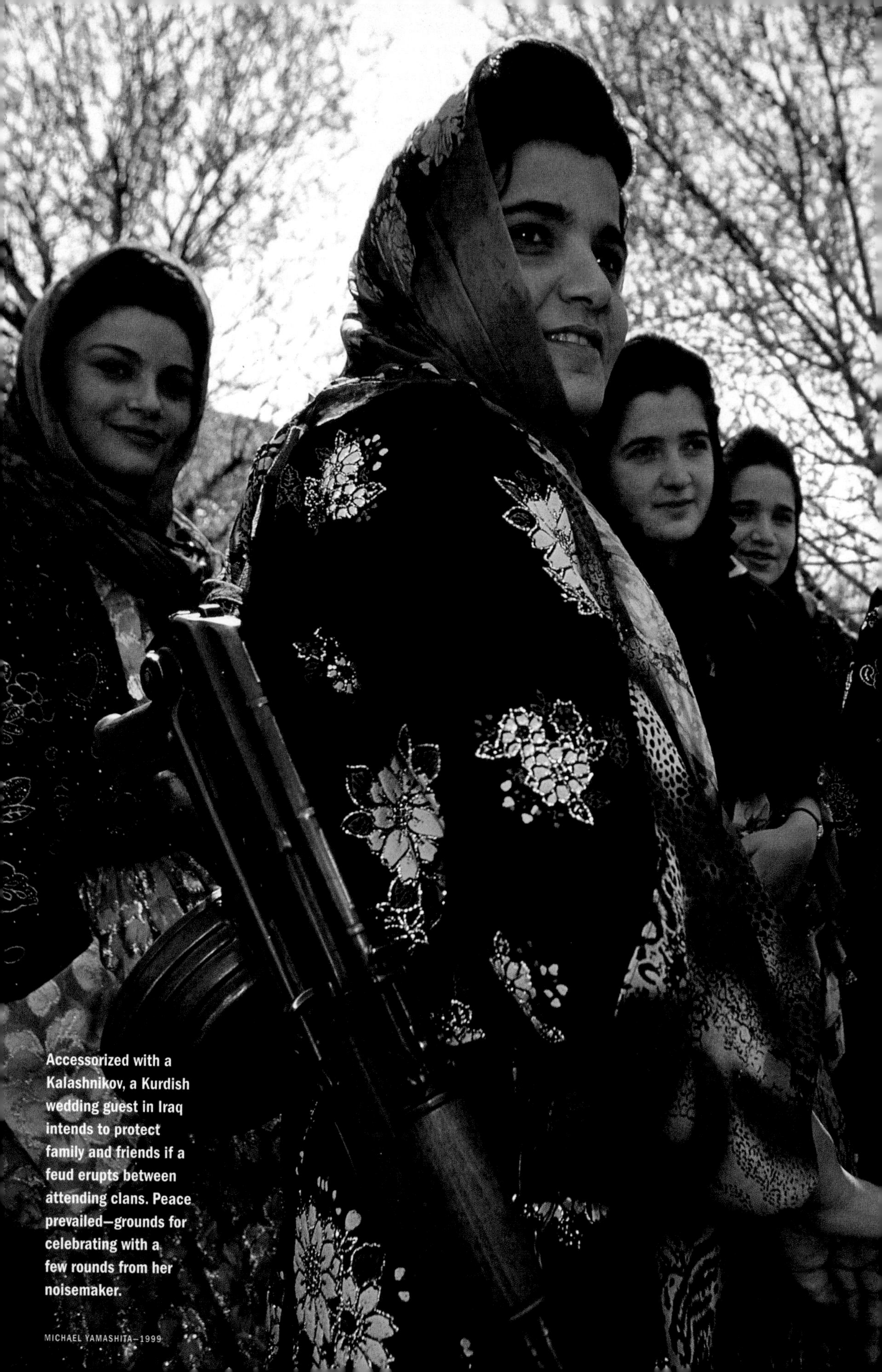

Accessorized with a Kalashnikov, a Kurdish wedding guest in Iraq intends to protect family and friends if a feud erupts between attending clans. Peace prevailed—grounds for celebrating with a few rounds from her noisemaker.

MICHAEL YAMASHITA—1999

PART FOUR

SEEDS OF CONFLICT

1991-2002

Will it be Islam versus the West, or something in between? Fighting a quiet war on ignorance, *National Geographic* explores the chasms and mountaintops of the Muslim world today.

Escaping the strict codes of their homelands, Persian Gulf Arabs eye a dancer at a club on Pyramids Road in Cairo, Egypt. "I've seen Saudis stick thousands of dollars in a dancer's garter," says photographer Reza.

Kneeling in the train station in Alexandria, Egypt, Muslims fulfill a duty to stop five times a day and pray in the direction of Mecca—no matter where they happen to be.

STUART FRANKLIN—1999

Expectations building as they stream along Ibrahim Street, Muslim pilgrims on the *hajj* arrive in Mecca, Saudi Arabia. Heeding the call, Muslims come from every corner of the globe to walk in the footsteps of Abraham, Hagar, Ishmael, and Muhammad—and to worship Allah, the One.

شارع جبل الكعبة
Jabal Al Kaabah St.

طريق أم القرى
Qura Road

جـ
dah

Baring feet and little else, the women of a Muslim family cool themselves on the beach north of Latakia, Syria's busiest Mediterranean port and its window on Europe and beyond.

ED KASHI—1996

Who Are the Palestinians?

BY TAD SZULC   PHOTOGRAPHS BY JOANNA B. PINNEO

■ *For more than 50 years the Arabs of Palestine—the vast majority of them Muslims—have been coping with life on the move. The founding of a Jewish homeland, Israel, in the region of their birth sparked what is essentially one long, intermittent war of survival. In 1948 and 1967, this war drove more than a million Palestinians from their homes. Many have lived as refugees ever since, either in foreign lands or in the Israeli-occupied West Bank and Gaza Strip, where poverty, humiliation, and despair fuel extremist movements that mix violence with radical Islam. In this groundbreaking story, veteran correspondent Tad Szulc asks a very essential question.*

Tad Szulc, "Who Are the Palestinians," photos by Joanna B. Pinneo, June 1992, pp. 84-113

P alestine, the region that once stretched from the shores of the Mediterranean eastward beyond the Jordan River, exists as a nation only in the imagination of six million Palestinians scattered throughout the Middle East, North Africa, Europe, and the Americas. Nearly two million chafe under military control in the Israeli-occupied Gaza Strip and West Bank. Another 750,000 Israeli Arabs who live inside Israel consider themselves Palestinian, but they try to walk the line between Israeli citizenship and their Arab heritage.

During months of traveling among the Palestinians, I found that the old stereotype—of the scruffy rebel in a checkered Arab *kaffiyeh*, with a gun in one hand and a Koran in the other—fits a few well-organized extremists but does not accurately describe most Palestinians. They are an immensely varied and sophisticated people, with the highest rate of literacy—along with the Lebanese—in the Arab world. Many are solidly middle-class. They are Christians as well as Muslims. Among the Palestinians, in short, I discovered an array of successes, surprises, and tragedies.

In the Gaza Strip, I meet Ahmad Abu Nasir, who fled his home in Jaffa, Palestine (now Yafo), in 1948, settling in a refugee camp not far from the Mediterranean, where he once worked as a fisherman. Now 69, he still lives in Gaza, in a two-room shack with no running water. "This is where I raised my family," he tells me, "and this is where I'll die. I'll never see my home again." But another exiled Palestinian, Hasib Sabbagh, who fled his home in that same crucial year, made his way to Lebanon, where he had earlier earned an engineering degree from the American University of Beirut. In exile, he went on to a spectacular career in construction. Today

In Jordan's Baqaa refugee camp, ten-year-old Khulud Ghunaym draws and dreams about living in Jerusalem, although she has never been there.

he is one of the wealthiest Palestinians, contributes generously to hospitals and schools around the world, and has homes in seven countries.

Like Sabbagh, many Palestinians put a premium on family, hard work, and education. "Just as with the Jews, adversity leads Palestinians to education and knowledge as a way to salvation," says Hanna Siniora, the editor in chief of an Arabic newspaper in East Jerusalem and an adviser at the Middle East peace talks.

Indeed, Palestinians and Israelis are often more striking for their similarities than for their differences. Both peoples trace their origins to the same Semitic roots, both come from a pastoral tradition, both have languished in diaspora, both have endured persecution, humiliation, and torture. By all normal standards, they should get along famously. But both groups have resorted to violence in pursuit of their dream, an independent homeland.

Between the White Mosque and the Mediterranean sprawls Gaza Beach refugee camp, where 50,000 people crowd into small concrete dwellings.

In the Israeli-controlled West Bank, the visitor senses that violence is brewing just beneath the surface of things. Residents of Dheisheh, a refugee camp near Bethlehem, come and go under the gaze of soldiers manning machine guns in watchtowers, and military jeeps kick up dust in the unpaved streets. There's hardly a tree or shrub in sight; the alleys are open sewers; and youths mill about, looking sullen. There's no spring in their step. Little wonder: Most of the working-age people in this camp are unemployed, and almost everyone else is very young. Some 60 percent of the population is under 18. They have known nothing but camp life. They live under frequent curfews, their homes are subject to unannounced searches or even bulldozing, their free speech is limited, they can be arrested and held without trial, they cannot travel without proper permits, they rarely get to see their families in Jordan or elsewhere, and many have friends and relatives in jail.

But it must also be said that the troubles stem, at least in part, from the

Palestinians' *intifada*. Some Palestinians, armed with knives, have killed Israelis in the cities, and others have fired upon Jewish settlers in the occupied territories. Among the most militant Palestinians are followers of the fundamentalist Islamic group Hamas. Palestinian kids throw rocks and gasoline bombs at patrols in a show of defiance. And the Israelis answer all this with further violence and repression.

"The children become radicalized early," a Palestinian friend tells me as we walk around Dheisheh. "They never have a chance to play. When they go to school, they have to confront the army on the way." I almost trip over an unexploded tear-gas grenade. "They're all over the place, so be careful."

Dheisheh, like 27 other camps in the occupied territories, has been active in the intifada. Since 1987, when it began, close to 900 Palestinians and some 85 Israelis have been killed throughout the region. At any one time, as many as 12,000 Palestinians are imprisoned.

As night falls, I set out into the alleys with Joanna [photographer Joanna Pinneo] and some Palestinian friends. The youths of Dheisheh begin to gather, ready to taunt Israeli soldiers on patrol. Huddled against the plaster walls in a side street, suddenly the youths look sinister in the failing light, and I try hard to convince myself that they are the same friendly boys I saw kicking soccer balls in the neighborhood earlier.

We turn the corner and come face-to-face with an Israeli Army patrol, four soldiers in helmets, protective visors over their faces, M16 rifles clutched in their hands. They advance slowly, their helmets swiveling this way and that, ever watchful. The patrol stops. I greet the leader in English, explaining that I am an American journalist here for the night.

The Israeli corporal raises his visor, revealing the fresh face of an 18-year-old. In an instant he looks lost and defenseless despite his formidable weaponry. He tells me pleasantly that he cannot give his name —Israeli Army regulations—but he reveals that he went to high school in

Torching tires and trash, Palestinians in the West Bank town of Ramallah try to provoke a confrontation with Israeli soldiers.

New Jersey. He leaves me with some advice. "Be careful around here," he says, clamping down his visor and motioning for the night patrol to resume.

In that moment, the reality sinks in. This is a war between children, all scared of one another but determined to show their mettle.

"Kids talk about who was arrested," says Saeb Erakat, a Palestinian professor of political science. "Teenagers talk about how many times they were in jail and how good they were with the Israeli interrogators."

The troubles even reach down to scar younger children. One day I see a picture of a Palestinian child, no more than seven or eight years old, his leg ripped by a stray bullet, his tiny mouth twisting in pain. Another day I meet a mother in Gaza who talks about her eight-year-old daughter, hit in the head by a rubber bullet four years ago. The child has since been unable to speak, the mother tells me.

Erakat describes a game his kids invented, based on their lives in the occupied town of Jericho. "They block my way with a piece of furniture. I must give them a kiss to get by." He offers a sad smile: "They call it checkpoint."

The conflict leaves scars on both sides, of course. I arrange to meet privately with a 22-year-old Israeli lieutenant who speaks about his army duty in the territories.

"You can walk up to someone, punch them in the face, and they'll just stand there. You can see the hatred, but they can't do anything," says Myron, who asks that his real identity be concealed. For several hours the stories pour out of Myron, as if the talking is therapeutic. As an army officer, Myron says, "you feel that you're strong, you're in control. You can walk into a house at two o'clock in the morning, take someone out, and arrest them. The only thing you can do is prove to him you're stronger. Slap him once, slap him twice. He gets the idea."

Most of the soldiers aren't looking for trouble and try to avoid it, Myron says, but they become hardened and jumpy in the territories, where nothing happens for long spells, then everything explodes in a single incident.

"They have perfected throwing stones," says Myron, referring to the Palestinian youths. "They know exactly when to throw the stone so it hits the windshield of the car, and if the car is going fast enough, it will kill the driver."

As in all wars, soldiers make mistakes. Myron recalls how a colleague's life was threatened and how the colleague responded. "He saw a guy aiming a gun at them in the middle of the street. What do you do? You shoot." Only when the soldiers got closer did they see they had shot a 13-year-old. "The gun wasn't a gun; it was a broomstick painted black. You're still killing a child. But what are you going to do? The kid wants you to think it's a gun. He is playing around with you.

"I hate it. In a war you can be idealistic and fight for a cause. But here we're fighting children and women. I believe the Palestinians are sick of the intifada too. The same way we're sick of it, they're sick of it."

On another day I hear almost the same lament from the other side. "We're tired. We're frustrated," says Khalil Mahshi, a Palestinian who serves as principal of a Quaker boys school in Ramallah, a city of 24,000 in the West Bank. "We want to go back to normal life, which means we want to get rid of the occupation. There's a whole generation of young people without a future."

Ramallah, which used to be predominantly Christian and claims to have the best-educated citizens in the Palestinian world, now sees many of its brightest citizens emigrating, many of them to the United States.

Those remaining seem depressed about the future, as I learn during a visit with a middle-class family in a traditional Arab neighborhood in East Jerusalem. I sense a growing rift between the father, who seems moderate and somewhat optimistic, and his son, who is willing to take risks in confronting the Israelis.

The father is a soft-spoken man in his 50s whose clan has lived in the same neighborhood through four generations, not far from where King David established his capital in the tenth century B.C. after battling the Philistines, among the forefathers of the Palestinians, for lands to the south.

A bit wistfully, the father recalls how Jews and Arabs once coexisted easily, doing business with one another, helping out as neighbors do from time to time. "Now we don't visit each other or even say hello," he says, pointing to the Jewish side of the street. The man, a clerk who wishes to keep his identity secret, wants no trouble from Palestinian extremists, who often harass those expressing sympathy for Israelis.

When I ask for his view of the intifada, the older man turns to a slender 16-year-old sitting quietly beside us on the enclosed porch. "Ask my son," the father says. "He can answer."

The youth, whom I will call Samir, is articulate and well educated, having attended private school in Jerusalem. But his smile vanishes when I ask about his future plans.

"I have no future here," he tells me. "I can't go to any university. My education is going lower and lower because of the situation in the schools, where classes have been canceled or interrupted because of strikes and civil disturbances. And you can't find jobs. We feel lonely all the time because we have nothing to do or see. I need to go to another country."

Samir believes the intifada is working, wearing down the resolve of the Israeli military and pushing them to talk peace. "We think the intifada is the only hope," he says. "There's nothing else that can help us."

Although Samir used to be afraid of throwing rocks at Israeli soldiers, now he isn't. "You don't think you're going to be caught. You think you are on the good side. It's now routine," he tells me.

"What happens when you get caught?"

Samir lowers his voice and tells me about a classmate who was sent to an Israeli prison. "He was beaten and left without food for nine days. He had to give 18 names of his friends who were with him. Some are in prison now for a month, and they are under torture. One of them is my cousin."

His reports of torture are confirmed by human-rights organizations, which have criticized the Israeli Army's treatment of Palestinians in detention, and by a report from the U.S. State Department describing how prisoners are slapped around and subjected to "'hooding;' deprivation of food, sleep, and sanitary facilities; forced standing; and confinement in a narrow, small space."

Could such a fate befall Samir, this engaging kid whose future would be bright in other circumstances? As I leave him, I wonder if he will ever pursue his dream of writing poetry, learning political science, and traveling. ☐

In that moment, the reality sinks in. This is a war between children, all scared of one another but determined to show their mettle.

When Richard Mackenzie and photographer Steve McCurry visited Afghanistan for this October 1993 article, they found a nation in a state of anarchy. Afghan factions that had united to drive out the Soviet army in 1989—ranging from tribal warlords to thousands of foreign mujahidin *who had rallied to the defense of Islam—were fighting fiercely over who would rule an Afghanistan laid to waste by two decades of war. Then, as now, it was the Afghan people who suffered most.*

Richard Mackenzie, "Afghanistan's Uneasy Peace," photos by Steve McCurry, Oct. 1993, pp. 58-89

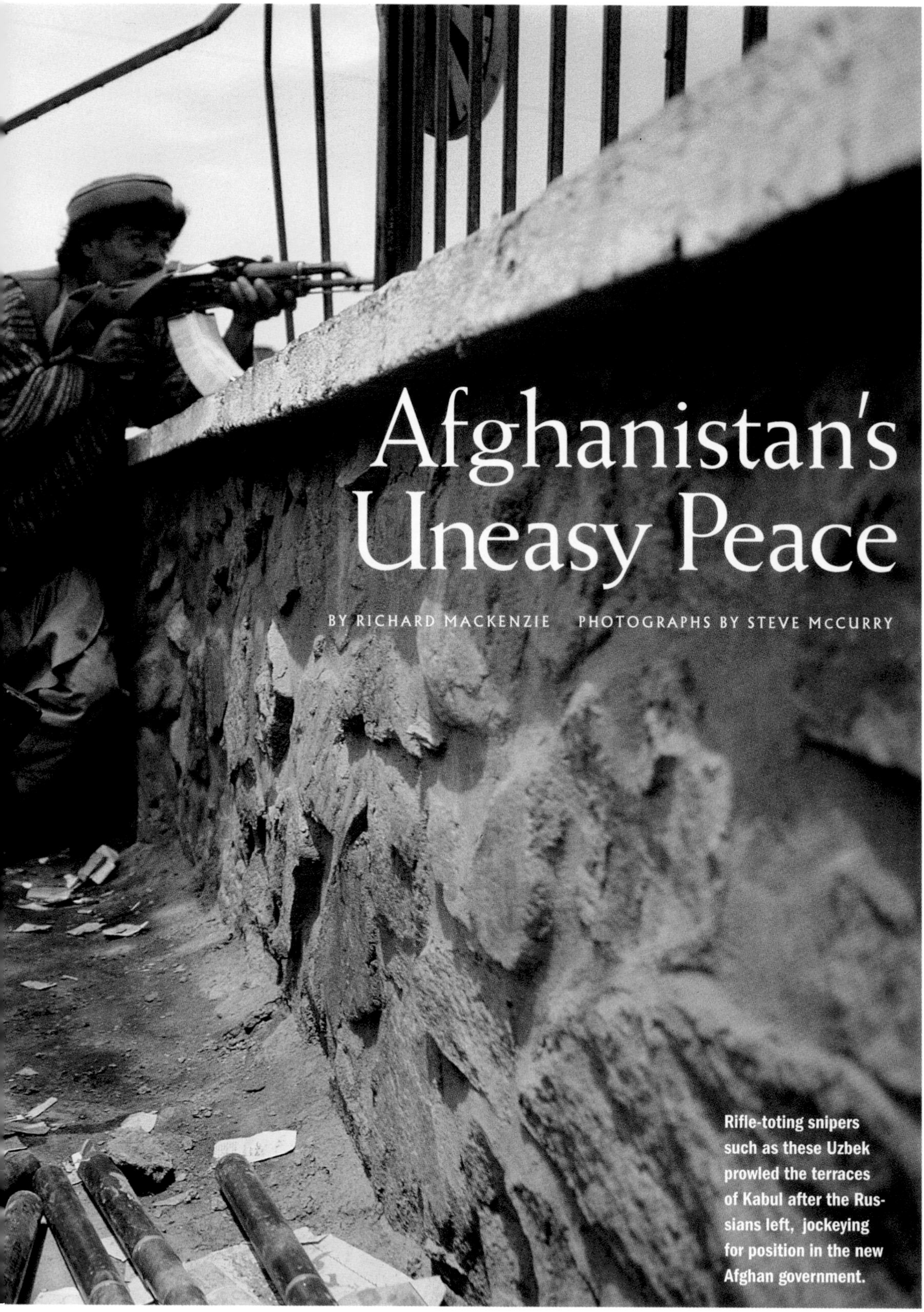

Afghanistan's Uneasy Peace

BY RICHARD MACKENZIE   PHOTOGRAPHS BY STEVE MCCURRY

Rifle-toting snipers
such as these Uzbek
prowled the terraces
of Kabul after the Rus-
sians left, jockeying
for position in the new
Afghan government.

The driver grasps the wheel of the rattling old Russian-built taxi, accelerates, and steers wildly around potholes and what few pedestrians are left on the streets of Kabul. We are driving through the capital of Afghanistan, where rival gangs of *mujahidin*, or Islamic guerrillas, are fighting for control. For a decade the resistance confounded the Soviet military, forcing the invaders in 1989 to withdraw from the country. Now in the spring of 1992 the guerrillas are turning their weapons on one another.

Gunfire sounds up ahead toward big, grassy Pashtunistan Square. The pounding of heavy arms echoes through tall pines around the park in the once grand Shar-i-Nau neighborhood. Tanks blast the marbled presidential palace. Smoke rises from the smoldering, deserted barracks of the presidential guard.

In the backseat of the careening cab, my friend Ramazan frowns. "This is ridiculous," says the wizened, bankrupt, 45-year-old restaurant owner. "This is no place to be. We can't tell one mujahidin group from another. Half the gunmen are just street thugs. We are going to die."

We would not be out here at all if I had not gotten a call saying the house I am renting has been looted. We are on our way to check the damage. This is only my second week back in Afghanistan. Since 1985 I have made a half dozen trips here as a journalist, traveling in the mountains with the guerrillas, whose fierce determination I have come to respect. Now, days after the collapse of the communist regime, it sickens me to see Kabul, the ultimate goal of the mujahidin, reduced to anarchy at their own hands.

In the hours before the mujahidin closed in, it seemed as if every worker and shopkeeper and barrow merchant in this city of 1.5 million tried to flee to the suburbs. They packed into buses or clung to the back of pickup trucks in human pyramids. Those who couldn't ride ran. Cars full of soldiers from the Afghan Army, some stripped down to their T-shirts, joined the galloping masses. At one secret-police center, I watched men I assumed to be agents back up a truck, fill it with rugs and office furniture, and drive off in a cloud of dust.

Now we pass empty bazaars, long lines of dilapidated little shops with their shutters drawn and locked, and empty, impersonal government buildings. We turn onto a dusty, unpaved side street just wide enough for the taxi. After we bounce 50 yards or so, four men with rifles and a rocket-propelled grenade launcher step out to block our way.

"Halt," says one with wild eyes and matted hair. "Get over here. A boy is dying."

The gunmen hustle us toward a teenager lying on the ground in front of an empty fruit-and-vegetable stand, its striped, blue-and-white awning torn and snapping in the wind. The boy's left leg has been blown apart just below the knee by a rocket explosion. His lower leg hangs by shreds of flesh. The bone glares white in the blood. Quickly I take off my leather belt and cinch it tightly around his thigh to stop the bleeding. Together we lift him into the back of the taxi. His face is ghostly. His eyes roll back. He tries to speak but makes only a gurgling sound.

Clinging to slim hope, a desperate mother searching for a son missing in action waits outside the presidential palace; a sympathetic guard tries to arrange a meeting for her with officials. The formal authority of President Burhanuddin Rabbani, in the portrait, didn't translate into order in the streets. He was driven from power in 1996 by the Taliban.

We head off toward the hospital of the International Committee of the Red Cross, the only medical facility in the city still operating at full strength. There we hand the boy to orderlies, who rush him to a triage area. And that is the last we ever see of him.

In the confusion we have not learned the boy's name. We have no way of asking whether he will live or die. I look for him later in the corridors of men, women, and children with bullet wounds, gaping shrapnel holes, and limbs mangled by land mines. But it is hopeless. He has been swallowed up by the chaos.

Add him to the list of war casualties. A million Afghans killed. Two million driven from villages. More than five million made refugees in Pakistan and Iran. In all, half the nation's people are dead, disabled, or uprooted.

"The war mutilated our homeland," says Muhammad Eshaq, historian and former *mujahid*. "It destroyed everything. You cannot set off dynamite inside a house and not expect the windows to be broken."

In contrast to the desperation of Kabul, I find some signs of hope in the rugged Panjshir Valley. The roar of the mighty Panjshir, or "five lions," envelops us as we drive our jeep through the narrow, mountainous valley. My companions are an unlikely crew: a former Afghan Army sergeant and three former mujahidin. We are on a journey to find peace, chase ghosts, and exorcise a few demons.

Crowding into the trunk while adult relatives ride up front, boys in Kabul settled in for an open-air taxi ride across town.

The Panjshir, like other waterways in northeastern Afghanistan, cascades from the Hindu Kush, whose peaks tower 15,000 feet or higher. But no other valley matches the strategic importance of the 70-mile-long Panjshir, which points straight down at Kabul like an arrow. For that reason, the Soviets launched nine major offensives in the Panjshir from 1980 to 1986 in a vain effort to destroy the elusive mujahidin.

The guerrillas in our group are former members of an eight-man squad from the Panjshir Battalion of the front led by Ahmad Shah Massoud. Their squad leader, a self-effacing 26-year-old named Nasrullah, is heading home to the village of Hambia halfway up the valley. Nineteen-year-old Ashraf, who looks as though he has stepped from the pages of a Banana Republic fashion spread, is also returning to Hambia. His combat fatigues are always clean and pressed. His boots seem never to gather dust. The third, 29-year-old Faizuddin, has seen the worst. As a teenager he was tortured by the secret police and dragged off to Pul-i-Charkhi prison. Released after 18 months, he returned home to the village of Qalacha in the lower Panjshir

Valley to find that both his elder brothers were dead. One was shot and killed while resisting arrest. The other died when Soviet soldiers tied a mine to his stomach and exploded it.

Only Nasrat, the 30-year-old former Afghan Army sergeant, is not going home. His journey up the Panjshir is an anguished search for his lost brother, who was stationed at Peshghur in a garrison overrun by mujahidin. Nasrat is hoping to find some hint that he is alive, perhaps being held prisoner.

"To this day our mother refuses to believe that he is dead." Nasrat says. "Every week she washes, presses, and folds his clothes along with the rest of the household laundry. I do not think her heart can take it much longer."

Remnants of the war litter the landscape as we drive. The rusty wreckage of one Soviet tank is surrounded by a field of wheat. Another tank lies submerged in the river, its nose and gun pointed up as if gasping for air. There are countless more.

At the end of the first day we reach the house of Nasrullah's parents in Hambia. Inside, Nasrullah and his father, Muhammad Amin, sit cross-legged on long cushions lining the walls of the common room, staring at each other. Nasrullah's mother has made pink-and-white covers to celebrate Id al-Adha, a joyous Islamic festival. For 20 minutes Nasrullah and his father do not speak. They just sit, smiling and absorbing each other by the glow of hurricane lamps.

Sikhs and Hindus run currency-exchange kiosks in Kabul, profiting from Islam's strictures against trading money.

"After all these years my family can be together again," Muhammad Amin says finally. "I have waited for this day for so long. I have prayed for this day. I have dreamed about it. I wondered if it would ever come."

The night is punctuated with visits from friends and neighbors. All simple farmers and all men, they come one after another to hug Nasrullah and sit for half an hour or so to pepper him with questions.

"Have you seen my son?" one asks.

"What are those fools doing in Kabul now?" another asks.

"Did they really release everyone from Pul-i-Charkhi?"

The next morning Ashraf and I go strolling in the hills. Two fat cows plod up a slope ahead of us. For the first time, the lad is not carrying his automatic rifle or the weight of ammunition. He stops and breaks off a piece of an acacia bush, smelling its exquisite fragrance. We talk about what will happen to young men like him, a whole generation of Afghans who have known nothing but war.

"I just want to come back here and work in the fields," Ashraf says.

"I wouldn't care if I never see Kabul again. This is my country."

Ashraf stares off toward Safid Kuh, the "white mountain" on the border with Pakistan that is mantled in snow all year. The valley here is about a mile wide. Bowing poplar trees line the banks of the river. The floor of the valley is covered with square plots of farmland in differing shades of green. A gentle wind comes from the northwest, rippling fields of wheat like ocean waves.

We wander down to the road, where scores of Kuchi, nomads who have crisscrossed Afghanistan for centuries, are driving sheep north for summer grazing. Irrigation canals destroyed in the Soviet attacks again gurgle with fresh water. As the animals sweep by, Ashraf leans over and picks up a newborn lamb and hugs it.

Back at the house Nasrullah bows and kisses his father's hands.

"I will be back soon," he says. "But first I have a promise to keep." With Ashraf and Faizuddin, he has vowed to take Nasrat, the former army sergeant, to look for his brother up in Peshghur.

Late in the afternoon of the second day we drive into Peshghur, a shady outpost where the valley narrows. We enter the town with some trepidation, not knowing what we will find. As we drive past the ruins of the garrison where Nasrat's brother was last seen alive, it becomes obvious that the fighting was gruesome. The former sergeant stares out the window, then starts to tremble. Finally, he slumps forward, sobbing, and buries his face in his hands.

No one in the jeep speaks. Then, from his seat beside Nasrat, Ashraf wraps his arms around his former enemy's shoulders, pulling him to his chest. He holds him, and Nasrat weeps softly for the next 15 minutes.

At what was once a mujahidin base in Barak, Nasrullah takes Nasrat to meet a red-bearded *mullah* who is the keeper of the books of prisoners.

"They have all long since been released," he tells Nasrat and takes him by the arm to a shed beside the house, where Nasrat frantically searches through the lists of those who lived to be prisoners. His brother's name is not there. The mullah offers tea. Nasrat tries but cannot drink. "Go home and pray," the mullah says.

After dinner at a smoky tea shop that night, Faizuddin, the former torture victim, takes Nasrat out for a walk in a grove of trees. A full moon lights the natural park, and the scent of juniper wafts in the air.

"Give it up," Faizuddin says. "Your brother is gone, and you are only tormenting yourself. I know from my own experience that the past must be buried. You must live for the future. The past will kill you."

That night, Faizuddin and Nasrat begin a lasting friendship. What Faizuddin does not tell Nasrat is that he took part in the attack on the Peshghur garrison. □

Muffled footsteps accompany the dawn in dusty Kandahar, historic home of Afghan kings. When the war with the Soviets ended, feuding *mujahidin* groups centered their battles in Kabul, freeing the provinces to begin recovery.

■ *If Iran's 1979 Islamic revolution shook the walls and windows of the modern world, then its aftershocks are still being felt in the political substrate of every Muslim nation. Overthrowing a corrupt regime and replacing it with a government founded on principles set down in the Koran—this is the dream of Islamist political movements from Algeria and Egypt to Pakistan and beyond. In Iran, meanwhile, 20 years later, Fen Montaigne found that the radicals of 1979—and their children—are ready for a change.*

Fen Montaigne, "Iran, Testing the Waters of Reform," photos by Alexandra Avakian, July 1999, pp. 2-33

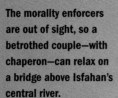

The morality enforcers are out of sight, so a betrothed couple—with chaperon—can relax on a bridge above Isfahan's central river.

Iran after the Revolution

BY FEN MONTAIGNE

PHOTOGRAPHS BY ALEXANDRA AVAKIAN

On a sparkling afternoon in April, three young couples climbed the steep hiking trail that follows the Darakeh River in northern Tehran. The river rushes out of the Elburz Mountains, whose snow-covered peaks form a majestic backdrop to the nondescript sprawl of the capital. At nearly 5,000 feet the area along the Darakeh is one of the few refuges from the dirty air and clamor of Tehran, and on this Friday, an Islamic day of rest, the couples were chatting easily as they strolled under willows and plane trees loaded with brilliant green buds. They passed vending stalls where merchants offered dozens of varieties of nuts and dried fruits or sodas cooled in old bathtubs filled with frigid river water. Men popped corn on propane stoves. Nearby, people paid a few hundred rials (about a dime) to a man whose parakeets told fortunes by strutting along a line of folded papers and pecking out missives that predicted wealth, long lives, and marriage.

Suddenly a stranger in civilian clothes approached one of the young men, Majid Rafiai, barking, "What are you doing? Why are you holding that woman's hand? Are you afraid someone will steal her?" In Iran, displays of affection between the sexes, however innocuous, are frowned on.

The inquisitor was a *basij*, a term often used disparagingly to describe people who, with the blessing of the authorities, act as guardians of public morals. The word originally applied to the members of a loose-knit Islamic militia, many of whom served as suicide fighters in the war with Iraq from 1980 to 1988.

The young people were indignant at the intrusion but held their tongues. Later I sat with them on a carpeted platform above the river, drinking tea and listening as they vented their anger. They said they had voted for the popular new president, Mohammad Khatami—a moderate clergyman, intellectual, and former minister of culture who ran on a platform of greater openness—precisely because they were tired of this kind of meddling from the die-hard defenders of the Islamic regime. "The period of Khatami has come, and the period of those people is finished," said Hossein Youssefian, a 24-year-old university student, as the others nodded in agreement.

Twenty years after Ayatollah Ruhollah Khomeini and his devoted followers overthrew Shah Mohammad Reza Pahlavi—the last in a line of Persian monarchs dating back to Cyrus in 559 B.C.—and installed a religious government, many of Iran's 64 million people are fed up with the scowling clerics who have run their country and their lives. The dissatisfaction boiled to the surface in May 1997, when 70 percent of the electorate chose Khatami as president. Since his election Iran has been undergoing an uneasy transformation, a second revolution in as many decades and one that seeks to soften the overbearing rule of the theocracy.

"When I look at Iranian society, I see a society that has graduated from the school of fundamentalism," says Mohammad Jafar Mahallati, who served as Iranian ambassador to the United Nations under Khomeini and is now a professor in the United States.

As Iran struggles to liberalize its Islamic republic (no one would suggest publicly that the theocracy be scrapped), the big question is how far

On a goodwill mission, President Khatami addresses a gathering of Kurds, whose separatist yearnings have long been repressed by the Iranian government. To its credit, Iran has accepted thousands of Kurdish refugees from its bellicose neighbor, Iraq.

Khatami's geniality and popular support will carry him in his contest with the hard-liners, headed by Ayatollah Ali Khamenei, the "supreme leader" of the republic. What is certain, however, is that Iranians, after two decades of war and revolution, want some freedom and levity back in their lives.

"People are very tired," said Farideh Farhi, a political scientist. "We didn't expect so much austerity. Severity is against our nature. We like fun. We like color."

Although the mood of Iranians has shifted under Khatami, the fundamentalist laws and customs of the Islamic republic remain in place. Under Iran's constitution the real power rests with Khamenei, the orthodox heir to Ayatollah Khomeini, chosen by a council of religious leaders. Khamenei is not nearly as popular as Khatami, nor does he have the following of the charismatic Khomeini, who died in 1989 and is still revered by devout Iranians. Yet Khamenei and his allies control the army, the police, the judiciary, and the Revolutionary Guard, a volunteer unit originally created as a parallel force to the army. They also have a core of powerful supporters, including businessmen and bureaucrats tied to the regime, as well as veterans and war widows who receive government stipends.

Today the struggle between the two sides overshadows everything else, and change comes in fits and starts. Newspapers proliferate, exploring the limits of the allowable, and then are shut down; reform politicians, such as Gholamhossein Karbaschi, Tehran's mayor, are convicted on dubious corruption charges; five critics of the regime are mysteriously killed, and the government announces that rogue agents of the Intelligence Ministry have been arrested for the slayings.

As the larger struggle has unfolded in Iran, many citizens have watched quietly, hoping Khatami and the reformers will prevail.

"We are a very complicated people," said Shahla Lahiji, a publisher and advocate of women's rights who lives in Tehran. Lahiji is a handsome woman with pale skin, prominent cheekbones, and a deep, infectious laugh. "We always live two lives—one outside the home and one inside. Obedience was always for the outside. Disobedience was for the inside. Outside we don't trust anyone. It is the reason for our survival. We had all these invasions, but we still have our language, and we still have our land. We obey the invaders, then change them."

Interest in the West has been heightened by the close contact between Iran and its diaspora. An estimated one million Iranians, many of whom fled after the revolution, now live in the U.S., Canada, and Europe. I saw the effect of these expatriates at a wedding one evening in a middle-class neighborhood in Tehran.

A dark-eyed beauty of 22 named Toktam, wearing a bare-shouldered, Western-style wedding dress, was marrying 31-year-old Hossein, who runs a rental-car agency. Her family had lived for years in San Jose, California, and the ceremony, attended by several dozen guests, was a blend of American and Persian traditions. A *mullah* read the vows to the couple as older women in chadors looked on. But before the ceremony the mullah had to avert his eyes from female guests who were dancing provocatively in sexy gowns.

For sheer brazenness, none of the women could match Toktam's 18-year-old sister, Azadeh, who had long dark hair and black eyes. Azadeh, whose name means "freedom" in Persian, spent the first 12 years of her life in northern California. She wore a tight, royal blue dress that spectacularly violated the Islamic dictum against showing curves. Dancing around the room, she showed a lack of inhibition that seemed, well, un-Persian. She told me she chafed under the restrictions of the Islamic government and had been a rebel at her all-girls school in Tehran.

"I don't like it here . . . I can't wait to go back to America," said Azadeh. "You can't walk down the street without someone bothering you. How can you be a teenager here? You're always 50 or over . . . I'm really trying to take the best of American culture, like being honest and direct, and mix it with the best of Iranian culture, like the way families are so close, and become a better person. In the authoritarian atmosphere of Iran, Azadeh was a fresh breeze of freedom and irreverence.

Young women like Azadeh demonstrate that patience with the sexually discriminatory laws of the Islamic republic is dwindling. Women's rights advocates say inequities still exist in Iranian family law, citing statutes that allow a man to have several wives and to divorce more easily than a woman and that give fathers preference in custody battles. Despite the constraints, women are more integrated into Iranian society today than they were under the Shah, mostly because higher education is more accessible.

Iranian women are, in fact, among the most educated and accomplished in the Muslim world. Before the revolution 35 percent of women were literate; now the

Seven years after censors found fault with his last film, Bahram Beyzaie, in green, is shooting again; he credits President Khatami. Even with restricted content, Iranian films draw critical acclaim.

rate stands at 74 percent. In the shah's time about a third of university students were women; now women make up fully half of new admissions. Better education is paying off professionally: Today one in three Iranian physicians is a woman.

Shireen Ebadi, a lawyer and former judge, whom I met in her office in central Tehran, explained this seemingly paradoxical progress. "Before the revolution many traditional women would not go to university or work. But because the revolution made these places so accessible, conservative families let their daughters go to university and into the workplace." But this had an unintended consequence. "With the revolution, many women came out of the kitchen. Women who emerge into society cannot be oppressed anymore." Iranian women have indeed begun testing the limits of freedom. Women are still required by law to observe the *hejab*, the Islamic dress code, by covering their hair and the curves of their bodies. But

in Tehran and other cities it is now common to see young women showing hair under their scarves and wearing makeup.

The high hopes Iranians had for Khatami have been tempered by time and the slow pace of change. But two years ago his candidacy stirred passions that caught the fundamentalist regime utterly by surprise. One of four presidential candidates approved by a religious council, Khatami delivered a restrained, often populist message that caught on like a prairie fire. He emphasized respecting people's privacy and guaranteeing their "civil rights and freedoms." His gentle demeanor, as much as his words, won over the Iranian people.

"Everybody was depressed," said Shahla Lahiji, the Tehran publisher. "It seemed that laughing was forbidden. Khatami had a huge open smile. He showed he cared about people." His election also showed that the yearning for change cuts across Iranian society: women, resentful of inequities and restrictions; journalists, intellectuals, and artists, chafing under government censorship; workers and businessmen, weary of the economic stagnation brought on by the government's mishandling of the economy; and, most of all, the young. In Iran 40 million people are younger than 25 years old. Comprising two-thirds of the population, they are the baby boom that followed the 1979 Islamic revolution. Many of them have no memory of either Ayatollah Khomeini or the birth of the Islamic republic.

Men and women mix openly on the slopes of Shemshak, a ski resort in the Elburz Mountains. At the less liberal Dizin resort morality enforcers insist that the two sexes ski on separate slopes.

The war against Iraq is still a presence in Iran: Thousands of city streets are named after martyred soldiers, martyrs' cemeteries with flapping green-and-red flags (green is the color of Islam and red signifies the martyrs' blood) exist in virtually every village, and gigantic murals of well-known martyrs are painted on billboards throughout the country. Every year in observance of the martyrdom of Imam Husayn, Iran marks Muharram, a month of mourning in which people march through towns and cities, flaying themselves with chains and reciting tales of the nobility of his sacrifice.

I was in Isfahan on Ashura—the tenth day of the month, marking the moment of Husayn's death—when the ceremonies became a pep rally to cheer conservative political forces and attack the United States. The focus of Ashura in Isfahan is Imam Khomeini Square, a quadrangle flanked by several great monuments of Persian architecture. Among them is the Imam Mosque, completed in 1638, which rises above the low-slung skyline of Isfahan, its cerulean dome and beige trim matching the desert sky and sand.

Thousands of mourners filed through the square, including members of the Revolutionary Guard. Barefoot, many of them wearing the red-and-green bandannas signifying their desire to make the ultimate sacrifice for Islam, the mourners trotted en masse past the reviewing stand, chanting and pounding their chests. Standing just a few feet from these die-hard defenders of the republic, feeling the concussive thump of hundreds of fists on chests, I felt a wave of awe—and fear—run through me.

The speaker, referring to the American and Western culture that was creeping back into Iran, praised the demonstrators and declared, "These are fighters for Islam! Yesterday they were at the war front fighting the enemy. Today they are fighting a cultural invasion!" The bearded men ran in rows through the square. "We are going to blind those who love the United States," they chanted.

The zealotry was an unnerving reminder of the Iran that President Khatami seeks to moderate. As the men filed out of the square, I hurried after them, wanting to find out if their personal opinions were as fierce as their public slogans.

"Whenever relations between a wolf and a sheep become good, then we can have good relations with the United States," Hamid Reza Salimian, a 30-year-old computer technician, said, as his cohorts nodded in assent and pressed in on me. One man warned me not to twist what they were saying; others heaped scorn on the U.S. government. Quietly my translator urged me to leave, and we squeezed through the marchers and disappeared into Imam Khomeini Square.

On May 23, 1998, the first anniversary of Mohammad Khatami's election, the soft-spoken president and tens of thousands of his supporters—most of them young, many of them women—took part in a rally unlike any seen in Tehran in the two decades of the ayatollahs' rule. This time no one burned Uncle Sam in effigy. Instead the marchers flowed down Vali-ye-Asr street under the shade of the plane trees calling for an end to the religious regime's stranglehold on power.

"The enemy of our society is prejudice and monopoly," shouted a line of young women in long black *chadors*. Demonstrators carried banners reading "Freedom of the Press," "The Military Should Be Reformed," "Freedom of Thought Is Everybody's Right." Onlookers stood on balconies and in shop doorways, many of them nodding or smiling in approval. As I hustled alongside the rows of marchers, listening to the chanting and taking in the expressions of hope and excitement on the demonstrators' faces, I was reminded of the pro-democracy, anti-communist marches I'd seen in Moscow in the waning years of the Soviet Union.

The marchers converged on the Friday Prayer pavilion at Tehran University, a place where Iran's revolutionary leaders have traditionally spit fire and led chants of "Death to America." Khatami, dressed in a light gray robe, black loafers, and the black turban that marks him as a descendant of the Prophet Muhammad, faced a crowd that spilled out from under the pavilion and onto nearby sidewalks and streets. For more than five minutes his supporters whistled and cheered and pumped their fists in the air. At last Khatami succeeded in quieting them.

"The future of religion is that it has to cope with freedom; otherwise it has no future," he told the crowd. "If religion confronts freedom, then religion will suffer."

As he continued speaking, a small group began chanting "Death to America!" They were soon drowned out by louder chants of "Death to Monopoly!" For a moment Khatami stood quietly, the late afternoon sun filtering in golden shafts onto the speaker's platform. Then he uttered a remark that silenced everybody. "I prefer," said the President of Iran, "to talk about life, not death." □

■ *Flash point between India and Pakistan, Hindu and Muslim, Kashmir may be—after Afghanistan—the biggest political powder keg in Central and South Asia. Though predominantly Muslim, this scenic mountain region remained a province of India when Pakistan was created in 1947; the two nations have been fighting over it ever since. On the ground Indian troops battle Islamic insurgents backed by Pakistan, while the two governments, each armed with nuclear weapons, engage in a bitter test of wills.*

Lewis M. Simons, "Kashmir: Trapped in Conflict," photos by Steve McCurry, Sept. 1999, pp. 2-28

Artillery thunder shakes the Karakoram Range as Pakistani soldiers trade fire with Indian opponents across the Siachen glacier.

Kashmir: Trapped in Conflict

BY LEWIS M. SIMONS   PHOTOGRAPHS BY STEVE MCCURRY

The neighborhood fight over Kashmir has been going on since 1947, when the British partitioned predominantly Hindu India to create Pakistan as a homeland for South Asia's Muslims. Jammu and Kashmir—a princely state with a primarily Muslim population ruled by a Hindu *maharaja*, Hari Singh—floundered. The maharaja wanted independence for the state, but he didn't know how to get it. At the 11th hour he signed an agreement of accession to India, but by that time Pakistani-backed tribal fighters had invaded Kashmir.

The leaders of India and Pakistan were desperate to acquire Kashmir to bolster their respective visions of nationhood. India's Jawaharlal Nehru, the secularist, wanted to demonstrate that an Islamic population could coexist with the Hindu majority; Mohammed Ali Jinnah, the Muslim nationalist, insisted that Pakistan would be incomplete without the Muslim enclave. Almost immediately the two countries went to war, tearing Kashmir apart. Ebbing and flowing, that war has, in essence, never ended. Today there are some 400,000 Indian troops in Kashmir and about half as many Pakistani soldiers.

Beneath the surface of this South Asian geopolitical game board are the aspirations of a people who consider themselves Kashmiris—neither Indian nor Pakistani—but who live divided by an artificial line. Hardly a day goes by without local newspapers in both countries reporting new violence—from artillery shelling across the line of control (LOC), from cross-border incursions of Muslim guerrillas backed by Pakistan, from indigenous Kashmiri Muslim militants who have been fighting Indian security forces for independence since 1989. These confrontations have blended together in a single cauldron of blood.

Casualty figures from fighting in and over Kashmir since 1947 are notoriously unreliable. In the past ten years—the period of the Kash-

Slumped in grief, a Muslim cleric leads funeral prayers for his son—militant leader Shariq Bakshi—killed by Indian security troops. Some call Kashmir's insurgents *mujahidin*, holy warriors for Islam. Others call them criminals, whose victims—of kidnapping, extortion, and rape—are often other Kashmiris.

miri Muslim militancy—an estimated 30,000 to 40,000 Kashmiri civilians and militants and Indian and Pakistani soldiers have died. Indian police place the toll at 24,000; Kashmiri Muslims say it's more like 80,000. Both India and Pakistan now have nuclear weapons, and because Kashmir is the flint against which either could strike a nuclear spark, fatalities of this magnitude could become mere footnotes.

Why these two countries would remain at each other's throat for so long, at such cost in life and fortune, over a remote patch of land comes down to the great truism of real estate: location. Kashmir perches like a raja's jeweled turban in the Himalaya at the very top of the great subcontinental landmass. There it is a gateway—or a barrier—between the two protagonists as well as between them and China and Afghanistan. Kashmir also sits astride Pakistan's major rivers, the Indus, the Jhelum, and the Chenab.

This land exerts a powerful emotional pull as well. Millions of sweltering,

plains-dwelling Indians and Pakistanis dream of its green mountains, its blue rivers and lakes, its fertile farmlands and cool, dry climate. Kashmir is their Maui, Aspen, and Palm Springs all rolled into one. Hindi-language musicals from Mumbai's (Bombay's) "Bollywood" movie studios still court success at the box office with scenes of lovers romping through flower-strewn Kashmiri meadows and snowy hillsides.

When Kashmiris speak of Kashmir, more often than not they're thinking of "the valley," the Vale of Kashmir, which lies wholly under Indian control. Only a fraction of what India rules as Jammu and Kashmir state, the valley is ringed by the high peaks of the Himalaya and the ridges of the Pir Panjal. It is a lush green heartland of thick pine and fir forests, with fields of rare saffron crocuses and terraces of rice bordering mulberry groves and orchards heavy with apples, pears, plums, and walnuts. Centered on the city of Srinagar, the valley is the prize.

In the 1970s when I was a foreign correspondent based in India, I would take my family up to Kashmir in summer to escape the New Delhi furnace. On Dal Lake in Srinagar, then, as now, Kashmir's summer capital, we'd rent a houseboat of polished wood, carved with the fanciful patterns of an Oriental carpet. Like latter-day colonials, my wife and I would sip gin-and-tonic sundowners on the rear deck while our two little girls paddled around in a dainty *shikara*, a kind of gondola, with a boatman who'd be delivering groceries.

We'd stroll through twisting medieval streets, among half-timber and plaster structures, more like old Europe than old India. We'd be accosted by honey-tongued souvenir *wallahs*, offering sets of walnut stacking tables, papier-mâché boxes, magnificent hand-knotted wool and silk rugs, and feathery shawls of wool harvested from the Kashmir goat. Kashmir was, if not quite paradise, certainly a delight.

All that is no more. In the summer of 1995 Muslim insurgents from the Indian side seized six Westerners. One, an American, managed to escape. A Norwegian was later found beheaded, and the remaining four are assumed dead. The next summer another local Muslim group killed six Indian tourists on Dal Lake.

The Muslim insurgency traces back to 1987, when Indian officials rigged local elections to install their choice as chief minister, inflaming widespread resentment. In 1989 dissent exploded into a full-blown separatist movement, as some young Kashmiri Muslims, traditionally docile, took up the gun and began killing Indian soldiers and members of a Kashmiri Hindu community known as Pandits. The Muslim rebels imposed harsh Islamic regulations throughout Kashmir, which included burning down government schools, banning women from going out of their homes with their faces or hair uncovered, and closing movie halls and wineshops, many owned by Pandits.

Estimates vary, but a decade ago Pandits numbered from 150,000 to 300,000 out of the eight million inhabitants of the state of Jammu and Kashmir, a small but disproportionately well-educated and successful minority. They have since been persecuted so ferociously by some of their Muslim neighbors and by infiltrating guerrillas that as few as 5,000 remain in their homes.

Ashok Kumar, once a farmer, now unemployed, was a willing Pandit spokesman. I sat with him on the packed-earth floor of his allotted 14-by-

9-foot room, which he shares with his wife and two children, in a long row of roughly made, single-story brick tenements in a refugee camp. He said he had been in despair since 1990, when he fled his home northwest of Srinagar near the border with Pakistan.

"One day my Muslim neighbors came to our houses and began screaming: 'Indian dogs, leave here or die.' A few days later they raped a woman. Then they set fire to my house, and we ran for our lives. I had owned my own orchard; now I'm a beggar. The Muslims are determined to eradicate the last of this microscopic community. Why is the world deaf?"

Pakistan's leaders deny giving the rebellion material aid, but a Muslim leader I spoke with in Rawalpindi confirmed that money originating in Saudi Arabia and Iran is funneled through Pakistan to the militants in Kashmir. The money is also used to pay Islamic fighters—among them Pakistanis, out-of-work Taliban zealots from Afghanistan, and other soldiers of fortune from as far away as Libya and Chechnya—who infiltrate the Indian-held side on the pretext of waging *jihad*, holy war.

Not surprisingly, given their recent history, Kashmiri Muslims yearn for independence. Even without the turmoil of recent decades their desire would be understandable, for they were once a self-contained people, evolved mainly from Central Asia and Persia, with characteristically fair skin, light eyes and hair, their own interpretation of Islam, a distinct language, architecture, and style of dressing.

The few Indians who take Kashmiri separatism seriously are those who know the most about the place and its people. A senior Indian administrator in Srinagar, who spoke candidly only when I agreed not to use his name, put it this way: "The truth is that the Kashmiri does have a case. He says, 'Give me my rightful place in the sun, give me my dignity, my religious sensibilities, my cultural identity. Don't impose yourselves on me.' That's legitimate. But the militants are chasing up a blind alley when they go in search of *azadi* (independence). We will never grant them independence. Never. India is a hard state."

India feels obliged to show Pakistan its intention to bend Kashmir to its will. After years of street battles Indian troops had weakened the separatist militants to the extent that touches of daily life had recovered. Schools were open. Lal Chowk market in central Srinagar was packed with jostling women, some hidden inside voluminous *burkas* in deference to the militants, others having reverted to the more liberating Kashmiri-style robes and headdresses. Butchers casually waved flies from hanging mutton joints, and most goods were in ample supply. At a fruit stall a woman accepted an apple slice proffered by the vendor and gave it to her small son. Averting her luminous green eyes as I asked her how life was these days, she replied without hesitation, "Oh, there's no question that things are better. We're able to walk about without worry and to shop for our daily needs."

On Sundays families arrive by the busload at the splendid Mogul gardens near Dal Lake to indulge their fondness for picnics. Photographers encourage couples to pose in richly colored period costumes, and vendors entice children with balloons and ears of roasted corn. A young couple, she in a loose, pumpkin-color robe, he in a sky blue safari suit, were sitting near a trickling stream, eating ice cream cones. "This is the first time we've come to the gardens in some years," said the man, licking at his droopy mustache. "But just because you can go out for a few hours hardly means that life is normal, which is what the government says." Then, showing me a pale scar running from his left ear to the corner of his mouth, he said, "This is what the soldiers did to me." He'd been caught in the cross fire between Indian troops and some militants, but he blamed only the soldiers.

As if to illustrate his point, plainclothes security men appeared shortly before dusk and, casually swinging machine guns, began ushering stragglers out of the gardens. Movie theaters in the city were still closed, banned by the militants, as were liquor shops and bars. Most tourist hotels, and a good many abandoned Pandit-owned houses, were being used as troop billets, their balconies hung with laundered uniforms, their entrances sandbagged. There was little call for hotel space. At the Palace Hotel overlooking Dal Lake, once the maharaja's residence and now under reconstruction, I was the only guest most nights. Rebuilding the palace was an act of faith. "*Inshallah*—God willing—tourists will begin coming back to Kashmir, perhaps next year," a lonely clerk at the front desk said one evening. Then, hesitantly, "Don't you think so?"

It seemed unlikely. It has taken India nearly a decade to limit the revolt, and in doing so soldiers raped, tortured, illegally detained, and robbed thousands of Kashmiris, according to international human rights organizations. The Indian Army has weakened the militants, but people are by no means ready to forgive, nor to forget the dream of independence. And so Kashmir remains an armed camp, in which not even the simplest farmer is free to come and go.

Although India and Pakistan seem incapable of coming to a resolution, it's not for want of talking. As I was witnessing the shelling across the LOC near Uri, political leaders were attending a South Asia regional conference in Sri Lanka—discussing Kashmir. The outcome: There would be another round of talks.

In much the way that Tibetans have been forcibly surrounded by the dominant Han culture of China, Kashmiris are being subsumed by India and used by Pakistan. In both places, as in other parts of the world where larger powers determine the fate of smaller ones, the land matters more than the people. With no other country willing to intervene on behalf of the Kashmiris, it is evident that they have no way out. ☐

The devout gather under the carved wood windows of Srinagar's largest mosque, Jamia Masjid. Since the 14th century the city's Muslim faithful have come here to pray.

■ *Much has been said and written about the suffering of the Iraqi people since the Persian Gulf War—the devastation wrought by economic and political sanctions levied against Saddam Hussein's regime in Baghdad. Passing through Iraq on the trail of Marco Polo for another* Geographic *story, staff writer Mike Edwards was welcomed by the Iraqi government—to a point—and invited to see for himself.*

Mike Edwards, "Eyewitness Iraq," photos by Michael Yamashita, Nov. 1999, pp. 2-27

Eyewitness Iraq

BY MIKE EDWARDS

PHOTOGRAPHS BY MICHAEL YAMASHITA

Ornate exception to the fraying city around it, Baghdad's Kadhimain Mosque awaits the faithful for dawn prayers.

The director general of antiquities apologized for yawning. It was
1:30 p.m. in his office near the Iraq Museum in Baghdad. "I got up
at three this morning," Muayad Said Damerji explained. "That's
when the electricity came on in my neighborhood."

Bombed in the 1991 Persian Gulf war, Iraq's power plants still wheeze
along at half their former capacity. So for six hours every day, every Baghdad neighborhood takes a turn without electricity.

"This is a quiet time in archaeology," Damerji said. "We get to do our
own projects now." He rose early to write a little more of what surely will be
a massive text, the history of architecture in Mesopotamia, the land between
the Tigris and Euphrates Rivers, where Western civilization took root.

United Nations sanctions, which include a trade embargo in effect since Iraq's invasion of Kuwait in 1990, keep away the foreign teams—American, German, Italian, French, Japanese—that used to stream into his office to propose excavations in Iraq's fabulous ruins. It is still possible to ascend the ziggurat of Ur and puzzle over the cuneiform scribed there or to stroll in Babylon and imagine the splendor of the hanging gardens. I did those things, but I was all but alone, for tourism is dead, dead.

And to enter the Iraq Museum is like entering a succession of looted tombs. In those halls had been gathered treasures from all the epochs of Iraq; an entire room was devoted to gold ornaments from the eighth-century B.C. Assyrian capital, Nimrud. The display cases are empty now; all the objects that could be moved have been packed and stored.

It is a melancholy refrain, the closing of the museum. The display cases were emptied twice in the 1980s, when bombs and Scud missiles rained on Baghdad during the eight-year war with Iran. In the gulf war, bombs exploded only 20 yards from the museum. "Face-to-face!" exclaimed curator Nedhal Ameen. The apparent target was a telephone center a block away. Vibrations shattered glass. Two Babylonian figures toppled. "What can we do with America?" Nedhal sighed. Then, brightening: "You come again someday; maybe you can see everything, *inshallah*."

All Mesopotamian empires endured paroxysms of war and destruction; the gulf war is one more chapter. With photographer Michael Yamashita, I spent almost six weeks gauging the echoes of that war. We found southern Iraq bristling with the guns of President Saddam Hussein's army. The people, mostly followers of Islam's Shiite branch, rose in 1991 against Saddam, long their oppressor. Shiite guerrillas still mount raids against his troops.

We saw plenty of guns in the north too, but they were in the hands of some three million Kurds, the largest minority in this mainly Arab nation. In their off-and-on war with the Iraqi Army the Kurds also suffered terribly; Saddam even used poison gas, killing 5,000 Kurds in a single town. But in 1991, threatened by a new Kurdish revolt, the army retreated from the mountains of the Kurdish homeland, and today the Kurds run their own affairs.

Both the Shiites and the Kurds receive a modest measure of protection from U.S. and British warplanes patrolling no-fly zones to keep Iraqi aircraft from flying there. Iraqi gunners sometimes fire at the planes or track them with radar. The planes retaliate against military targets, though straying missiles have hit civilian neighborhoods.

That has happened, for example, in the city of Mosul, within the northern no-fly zone. One day there I asked a priest—720,000 Christians live in Iraq—if air-raid sirens made people afraid. His answer described a numbed populace: "They have lived with war for so many years they don't care. Nearly every family has lost someone. Life is very cheap here." In the Iranian war an estimated 500,000 Iraqi soldiers were killed or wounded; Operation Desert Storm inflicted between 60,000 and 100,000 casualties more.

When photographer Mike Yamashita and I set out, we expected to spend only a couple of weeks in Iraq. We were following the route of Marco Polo, who may have passed through the area in 1271 on his way to China. Perhaps the Iraqi government allowed us to stay longer in hope that we'd report extensively on the suffering of Iraqis under the UN sanctions. Since no airline flies into Iraq—another manifestation of the sanctions—we set

Under a sheltering sky patrolled by United States and British planes, Iraqi Kurds relax on Little Zab River in the north. Attempts by U.S. leaders to use the Kurdish zone as a base for unseating Saddam Hussein have failed.

off from Amman, capital of Jordan, in a hired van. Ten hours later, beside the Euphrates, the bare desert gave way to palm groves, and in another hour we were among Baghdad's modern, sand-colored buildings.

War, what war? I asked myself at first.

Although Baghdad was bombed in 1991 and again in December 1998, most of the debris has been cleared. Rebuilt bridges span the Tigris.

In place of a toppled communications tower the government raised a spire with a revolving restaurant. As I dined there one night, about 125 yards up, Baghdad—home of five million people—spread out as a great disk. The slowly turning windows brought into view the stylish apartment and office buildings that oil paid for in the 1970s and 1980s, then rows of large homes bathed by street lamps. Next came a swath of darkness—a neighborhood whose turn had come to do without electricity. (Imagine your air conditioner shutting off in summer when the temperature is 120°F.) The restaurant moved, and I beheld an enormous domed edifice, brilliantly lit, surrounded by a high wall. This is one of Saddam's new palaces; by some counts he has more than a hundred palaces and mansions. Iraqis say Saddam and his family occupy only a few; evidently the others exist to gratify his ego.

Timeless pleasures of a playground divert families visiting the ruins of Samarra, a ninth-century capital of the Abbasid dynasty, rulers of Iraq for 500 years. An enormous spiral minaret commands the site.

I wasn't the first journalist to ask Mohammed Fatnan, my government guide—known in the trade as a "minder"—about these Arabian Nights creations. Touchy subject. "Why do the Western media make propaganda about the palaces?" he shot back. "The royal family of Saudi Arabia has palaces. Why don't the Western media write about them?"

Mohammed's main job was to keep an eye on me and tell me what I could and couldn't do (no interviewing soldiers, for instance). He was 32, with a short beard. His salary was about 10,000 dinars a month—handsome pay before Iraq's economy sank under the weight of the embargo and two costly wars. Now a single dollar buys 1,200 dinars. So he lived in the Ministry of Culture and Information press center, sleeping on a couch. Yet if Saddam's palace profligacy angered him, he never showed it.

Though money is scarce in Iraq, no one should be starving, even though the country in normal times produced only 30 percent of its food. Poor families receive flour, rice, tea, sugar, cooking oil, even soap. These began to be imported in 1997 under the UN's "oil-for-food" program. To relieve suffering, the UN Security Council eased the sanctions, permitting Iraq to sell oil to get money for food, medicine, school supplies, farm equipment, and spare parts for essential industries. Iraq decides what to buy, but the UN keeps the checkbook and must approve all purchases. At present Iraq can sell 5.2 billion dollars' worth of oil in a six-month period. Some money goes to persons who suffered losses in Kuwait; two-thirds is reserved for humanitarian goods.

The oil-for-food program has boosted rations from 1,300 to 2,000 calories a day; that's close to the average intake of many Western nations. Nevertheless, says the UN, perhaps 20 percent of Iraqi children are malnourished, missing protein, vitamins, and minerals.

Journalists are often taken to the 320-bed Saddam Children's Hospital—one of numerous institutions bearing the president's name—to hear reports such as Dr. Mazin Shimar offered. "In this hospital we have two or three deaths a day," he said. "It used to be one a week." The Ministry of Health claims that more than a million children under five have died as a result of the embargo.

Such figures have helped win support in the U.S. for Iraq's campaign to end sanctions. "The death and suffering . . . seems to us morally intolerable," the United States Catholic Conference has declared. Antiwar activists have condemned the sanctions as "genocidal."

"I'm sure that Saddam Hussein decided 'we have to show a lot of deaths,'" says Richard Garfield, a public health specialist at Columbia University in New York. "It happened that they had a lot of deaths. But their information was so poor they didn't really know how many." Using demographic and other studies, Garfield has estimated the number of excess deaths of children under five from the start of sanctions in 1990 until March 1998. His most likely figure: about 227,000. He believes the number of deaths per thousand children more than doubled from 38 in 1990 to 87 in 1998. "It is a remarkable statement of how bad conditions are," he said. A UN survey puts the number of deaths even higher, 131 per thousand, during the past five years. The causes of death include malnutrition, a decline in immunizations, and polluted water. Water systems are in bad shape; mains leak, pumps don't work. And both water and sewage systems are handicapped by the power outages.

Many observers put some of the blame for deaths on Saddam. He delayed more than a year before agreeing to the oil-for-food program proffered by the UN. His government paid scant attention to repairing water systems; most of the new pumps ordered under the program were sitting in government warehouses during my visit. More than 275 million dollars' worth of medical equipment had gathered dust for months. Some highly placed UN diplomats suspect that Saddam was more interested in making propaganda about the deaths than in breaking bottlenecks.

Sanctions were conceived as a means of forcing Saddam to give up the weapons of mass destruction—chemical, biological, nuclear—that he was believed to possess or to be making. U.S. officials say Saddam intended to use such weaponry to dominate his oil-rich neighbors around the Persian Gulf. But after the 1998 bombing of Iraq, Saddam refused to let the UN weapons inspectors into the country. So, for now, the sanctions saga has no end.

All the same, the U.S. is convinced that the embargo applies pressure on Saddam. And besides, a State Department official says, "If he were handling his money instead of the UN, he'd go right back to making weapons."

To a 25-year-old woman named Rana, whom I met one day in Baghdad, sanctions were just one more source of grief. "We are a broken generation," she said. "My generation opened our eyes on war, the war with Iran. We all saw men coming home without an arm or a leg. We have only small dreams, and we are losing even those. Why does the embargo have to continue? Haven't we suffered enough?" Half a dozen infernos blazed around the city Kirkuk, burning waste gas from one of Iraq's major oil fields. Iraq has more petroleum reserves than any other nation except Saudi Arabia.

Reminded of that wealth, an engineer told me one day: "Once we hoped that by the end of this century Iraq would be an advanced country, that it would move up from the Third World group. We could contribute something to the world in any field—science, the arts—because we have the background. We have 7,000 years of history. We introduced mathematics;

we watched the stars and made a calendar." And invented the wheel. And writing.

Oil indeed could have made Iraq a modern nation. Oil could have bought anything. But it did not buy peace. Instead it paid for weapons. And when Saddam threatened the West's main oil suppliers in the Persian Gulf, Iraq found itself a defeated state and a pariah.

In some future time archaeologists will scour the record of Iraq at the end of the 20th century, as they have scoured the records of King Sargon, who founded the first Mesopotamian Empire, and Hammurapi of Babylon, the giver of laws. And when listing the achievements of Saddam, they will write: He built a lot of palaces. □

The Outcast

BY ANDREW COCKBURN   PHOTOGRAPHS BY REZA

■ *Libya was a deeply conservative Muslim society in 1969, when a brazen young Army captain named Muammar Qaddafi seized power in a bloodless coup. Reviled by the West in the years since, Libya's maverick Leader has nonetheless transformed his country by steering the Islam of his subjects toward a pragmatic socialism based on modern values and practices. As Libya, like most Muslim countries, has undergone an Islamic resurgence, Qaddafi has resisted, jailing activists and labeling Afghan-trained* mujahidin *heretics.*

Andrew Cockburn, "Libya: An End to Isolation," photos by Reza, Nov. 2000, pp. 2-31

Housam, a guide from the Libyan Ministry of Information, had run only 20 yards from his hotel room to mine, but he was perspiring. "Come quickly," he said, "the Leader is waiting for you in Banghazi. There is a plane ready." We raced downstairs. The government driver, allegedly on standby for just this occasion, had characteristically disappeared. Cursing, Housam led me in a sprint to his own car, and we roared off down the corniche that runs along the Mediterranean seafront of Tripoli, Libya's capital city. We were heading away from the city's main commercial airport.

After a few miles we suddenly peeled off the highway and sped through a gate onto an airfield where a dozen huge Russian-built Ilyushin-76 military transport planes were parked. We climbed a ladder into the vast cargo bay of one of the planes. Waiting inside were Fuad, Muammar Qaddafi's English interpreter, and a youth named Ibrahim toting two large cardboard boxes tied with string. I asked what was in the boxes. "Correspondence for the Leader," replied Fuad, lighting a cigarette. So this was how Muammar Qaddafi gets his mail.

"Do you notice how they're trying to get that light in the cockpit to go out?" remarked Fuad. "There is a problem with this plane." A nervous-looking pilot appeared at the door moments later and concurred that the plane was not safe. We climbed down, got back in our car, and drove into town. "*Kul takhira fi'khira*," said Fuad cheerfully, "sometimes it is better to delay," a common Libyan phrase that I was beginning to know well.

This was a voyage of exploration. For years Libya has been a country largely unknown to the outside world. Even the few outsiders who

Long hidden behind the face and rhetoric of ruler Muammar Qaddafi, oil-rich Libya is slowly emerging from seclusion, seeking to rejoin the outside world.

managed to make their way here usually found it impossible to penetrate beneath the surface. Casual contact between ordinary Libyans and foreigners was discouraged as Qaddafi, who came to power in 1969, gradually imposed his own brand of revolutionary theory on the country. As embassies closed and foreign companies pulled out throughout the 1970s and '80s, there was an ever diminishing number of visitors from the Western world.

Still, Libya is hardly a country where travel for outsiders is routine, a truth rendered evident by my journey to meet the Leader. No sooner had we returned after the abortive trip to the military airport than Housam reappeared. "There's another plane," he gasped. "Come quick."

This time we drove to the main civilian airport, where we were ushered onto a modern jetliner, part of the Libyan Arab Airlines fleet. Ibrahim reappeared with the boxes containing the Leader's mail. Later I was told that our plane had been diverted from its scheduled afternoon flight to Malta, leaving would-be passengers steaming in the terminal.

Qaddafi makes his feelings about fundamentalist Islam quite clear . . . Islamic activists have been rounded up and jailed by the score.

We took off, soaring east over green fields dotted with farmhouses along the fertile strip that edges the coast. Far to the south I could see the yellow fringe that marks the beginning of the great sandy waste of the Libyan desert, stretching far into Africa. We were headed for Al Bayda, a sleepy town in the mercifully cool Cyrenaic uplands east of Banghazi.

Late that night I was driven down dark and empty back roads to Qaddafi's temporary residence, a marble-floored villa set in spacious grounds. Just before we pulled up, I noticed an open canvas shelter with a brightly colored checkerboard pattern—a familiar image from pictures of Qaddafi, dressed in extravagant cloaks and turbans, greeting visitors "in his tent." We bypassed the tent, and I was ushered into the mansion to a formal drawing room furnished with white velvet chairs and decorated with framed pictures of Qaddafi's wife and children.

Qaddafi himself finally entered the room, leaning on an aluminum crutch that clicked rhythmically on the marble floor. He had broken his leg some months before, the injury variously ascribed to an assassination attempt, an accident on the football field, a fall in the bathroom, or a fall while climbing out the bathroom window—a confusion indicative of the miasma of rumor that surrounds Qaddafi. (A close friend of the Libyan leader insisted to me that the fall in the bathroom was the correct version of the story.)

Clad in a faded sport shirt, khaki slacks, and worn leather slippers, Qaddafi presented a very different picture from the flamboyant figure in extravagant dress long familiar to the outside world. He looked tired. In the past 12 hours he had talked with three African presidents and the Italian foreign minister, worked on plans for a summit conference, and given a stern lecture to the city fathers of Al Bayda regarding unchecked development in the picturesque Green Mountains around the city. "We are a backward country," Qaddafi said matter-of-factly. "People don't understand that we are damaging the land, damaging the environment."

The Leader had also spent a few hours reading a book on mergers and acquisitions in pursuit of his present project to unite Africa. "I work 25 hours a day—but reading is part of the work, and I am a slow reader. Often I have to read things several times to understand." He sighed. The effect was disarming, as were his frequent chuckles and word-play jokes.

The fact that the isolation is beginning to lift might not be immediately evident to visitors who switch on the TV in their Tripoli hotel rooms and find only a single local channel of unremitting tedium, heavy on the Leader's speeches and the historical iniquities of various foreign invaders over the centuries. Yet the rooftops of Tripoli and Banghazi are studded with satellite dishes beaming in dozens of channels from around the world.

"It used to be almost an act of conspiracy to approach a foreigner," remarked Yousuf, an entrepreneur in the tourist industry, as we chatted openly in a coffee shop. "You just wouldn't dare. But things are changing, much more relaxed. We have many problems, but at least now we can talk."

Hitham, an air-conditioning engineer who works at a health spa in Al Ujaylat, close to the Tunisian frontier, certainly qualifies as an informed observer on the subject of repression, for he is an Iraqi—one of the vast diaspora of professionals who have left the ruined state of Saddam Hussein in search of a better life.

Sitting outside the health spa, the Iraqi appeared far more cautious than the affable Yousuf about talking with a visitor from the West. But finally he broke his silence to draw an implicit comparison with his home country: "I came here as a stranger, but nobody asks me, even at midnight, 'Where are you going?' When I go to Banghazi, Surt, or Al Bayda, nobody, no police, asks me, 'Who are you, what are you doing?'"

R oaming Libya, I certainly found few impediments, beyond the semi-functional telephone system and a baroque bureaucracy, placed in the way of contact with ordinary Libyans, naturally friendly and prone to shaking hands with perfect strangers in the course of an elevator ride.

Accompanying new attitudes toward open communication is a theme that resonates throughout the Arab world—acceptance of modern values that conflict with the tenets of traditional Islam. Before the revolution Libya was a deeply conservative Muslim society—the majority of the population shocked by the decadent habits spread by foreign occupation and the oil boom. Women in public places were almost invariably invisible behind the all-encompassing traditional white *furushiya*, and the number of female university graduates amounted to just 35. Today, the furushiya has all but disappeared, and the number of women graduating from universities exceeds that of men.

Qaddafi, famous for his interest in promoting women, has also seen to it that they find their place in traditionally male occupations. One blisteringly hot summer afternoon in Tripoli, I sat on a dais overlooking a barracks square. Beside me sat a row of senior officials in sport shirts and slacks (only the minister of the interior was wearing a suit). We were on hand for the graduation ceremony of the Libyan Women's Police Officers' Academy, class of 1999. As a verse from the Koran echoed from loudspeakers around the barracks square, the green-uniformed ranks of teenage girls in front of me hefted their automatic rifles and snapped smartly to attention. Green flags fluttered in the breeze, and the white-uniformed girls' military band struck up the national anthem:

I with my beliefs and my weapons will sacrifice myself
For my nation as the light of the truth shines in my hand. . . .

Once the last strains had died away, academy commandant Col. Mohammed Amiel stepped up to the microphone. "My daughters, now you participate in serving our country. Our task is to maintain public security, and that can only come with revolutionary action. You have to be aware of the Leader's support in getting you here. We salute our Leader!" he shouted. A high-pitched chorus of revolutionary slogans arose from rows of the graduates' younger siblings in the bleachers beside the dais.

Away down the coastal road, on the dark beach beyond the seawall, groups of young people huddled on blankets, passing soft drink cans to each other in a manner that suggested they contained something stronger than Pepsi—alcohol does not appear to be in as short supply these days as it was 30 years ago. Nor are the penalties for violating prohibition that severe, at least in comparison with other "dry" Muslim countries like Saudi Arabia or Iran.

"A first offender gets a year's suspended sentence and a fine," stated Shawki, who, as a veteran judge, is in a position to know. "Heroin is the big

A serene view of al-Shaab Mosque from a hotel on Tripoli's harbor diverts foreign businessmen, whose days are spent chasing deals in the investment-hungry country.

problem now, especially among students and young people," he continued, echoing a striking confession made by Qaddafi himself in 1996: "We have lost our youths."

I asked him about *sharia*, the Muslim code of justice, that applies in Libya. "According to sharia, the penalty for theft is the amputation of a hand," he answered. "That's the law here, but the doctors refuse." What about whipping an unmarried couple when the woman gets pregnant, also a standard sentence? Shawki's grizzled face grew serious. "It is very rare; usually the families pressure them to marry. But yes, it does happen. In fact the last case was about three months ago, in Sabha."

I thought of this grim practice strolling one evening on Gargaresh Street in southwest Tripoli; upscale boutiques and fast-food restaurants make this a favored haunt of the younger set. A ponytailed young man in an Italian designer shirt was revving the engine of his Korean car in evident hopes of attracting the attention of two girls climbing into an Isuzu. Getting no reaction, he turned up the volume of his tape player, booming out the latest local hit over the noise of the traffic. They drove off. A few minutes later I saw both cars cruising by, nose to tail. The young man's hopes may have been raised by the stretch pants and T-shirt worn by one of the women, but her companion's hair was concealed under a head scarf, a *hijab*, in conformance with the dress code many Muslims believe is mandated by the Koran. I suddenly realized how many hijab I was seeing around me—on women driving cars, running government departments, working as doctors and lawyers.

"The government has tried to resist, but Islamic influence is seeping in; it's a real change," remarked a friend later. "Look at this." He flipped open an old book to a picture of a crowded Tripoli street, taken in the 1970s. "You don't see a single hijab on any of the women."

Qaddafi himself makes his feelings about fundamentalist Islam quite clear. Those who fought in Afghanistan and now seek to impose their views on Arab countries, including Libya, he refers to contemptuously as *zanadiq*—heretics. His attitude extends beyond forceful language. Islamic activists have been rounded up and jailed by the score. An armed fundamentalist uprising in the east of the country in 1996 was harshly and summarily repressed.

Yet traditional attitudes, particularly with regard to the rights of women, persist in society at large—to the Leader's irritation. When the General People's Congress, Libya's version of a parliament, voted to withdraw the requirement for a husband to get his wife's permission before marrying a second spouse, he erupted in fury, both at the Congress and at women for not using their right to speak out. "Your education is a waste of time. You are like furniture," he told a meeting of women shown on Libyan TV (which sometimes has its moments). "From now on, any law or measure connected with half of society that is decided in the absence of women is null and void," he declared, tearing up a text of the amended law and storming out of the meeting hall.

Office high-rises climb above a cramped urban core, adding one more stratum of buildings to 2,600-year-old Tripoli, Libya's capital.

In his collection of stories and essays, *Escape to Hell and Other Stories,* Qaddafi conveys his deep distaste for cities and other manifestations of what he sees as the barren materialism of Western urban culture: "Life in the city is merely a wormlike biological existence where man lives and dies meaninglessly." However, as he told me in the house in Al Bayda, *jahannam*—Arabic for "hell"—is also the name of an area in the desert close to Surt and to his birthplace. He still spends time there. "The desert climate gives me a chance to think. When there is a lot of work, I escape to hell." He laughed, displaying an author's pride at the play on words.

Conscious of the widespread perception in the West that the old rabble-rouser has changed his spots, abandoning his youthful plans to transform society, I inquired if he was still a revolutionary. He gave a chuckle and an emphatic "yes," and then observed that although he is "really satisfied with what we have done in 30 years," there is "still room for improvement." Eventually he moved slowly off to bed, to rest up for the new and uncertain days that are dawning over Libya. ☐

■ With more Muslims—181 million—than any other nation on Earth, Indonesia is a powerful force in the modern umma, or body of Muslim believers. As Indonesia's staggering economic and social problems have compounded over the past decade, Islamic political movements have gathered momentum. And beyond Jakarta, extremists of various ethnic and religious backgrounds have incited murder and mayhem. Traveling to the eastern fringe of Indonesia's 6,000 inhabited islands for National Geographic, Tracy Dahlby found himself in the middle of a religious war.

Tracy Dahlby, "Indonesia: Living Dangerously," photos by Alexandra Boulat, Mar. 2001, pp. 74-103

Safe under an adult arm, a youngster whirls above a carnival in Yogyakarta on the Indonesian island of Java.

Indonesia
on Edge

BY TRACY DAHLBY   PHOTOGRAPHS BY ALEXANDRA BOULAT

Night fell fast over the harbor at Bitung on the far northeastern tip of Sulawesi, and the refugee camp, an old rattan factory, was hot and steamy as a terrarium. A group of shell-shocked Christians, gathered in the glare of a hanging bulb, were telling how they'd lost their homes on Ternate in the nearby Moluccas.

"The Muslims burned our houses!" said a retired army sergeant. "They destroyed our churches!" the village English teacher chimed in. "We were massacred!"

Such commotion was new to this sweet-smelling hillside town of neat homes and manicured yards but part of a larger malady racing through the watery gut of eastern Indonesia. For decades the area, also called the Spice

Islands, had touted its mixed communities of Muslims and Christians as models of interfaith neighborliness. Then, in January 1999, it plunged into primeval war, and now thousands were dead, a half million uprooted, and nobody could say exactly why.

The ex-army man, Anton Letsoin, said that Ternate's troubles began when a letter on faked church stationery was circulated among the island's Muslims. Convinced that a "cadre of Christ" was forming up to attack them, they rallied at the local mosque. There, a witness said he overheard his neighbors raise a chilling cry: "Seek out the *Obets*"—slang for Christians—"and destroy!"

Who had manufactured the letter? The refugees blamed local political schemers, rogue military units, or maybe gangsters from Jakarta, who sought profit by sowing discord. Nobody wanted to believe it was religion. "We were living in peace," cried the teacher. "We never experienced religious hatred before!"

This is the mystery of Indonesia today. Three years after a crashing economy ended the 32-year rule of Indonesia's former president Suharto (who, like many Indonesians, uses one name), the world's fourth most populous nation boils with such comprehensive religious and ethnic strife that even Indonesians have a hard time explaining it. That's not surprising, considering their anchor-shaped archipelago sweeps 3,200 miles end to end and contains 6,000 inhabited islands and 225 million people, who are, in turn, divided by religion (Muslim, Christian, Hindu, and Buddhist), ethnicity (some 300 groups and as many distinct languages), and water (four-fifths of the country's total area).

It is easy to forget that Indonesians now live in a time of great promise. The collapse of Suharto's corrupt, crony-encrusted regime in 1998 made way for the republic's first democratically elected government in over 40 years and a chance to rebuild its badly corroded

Shy glances and bold strumming accompany young Muslim students visiting Kebon Raya, a botanical garden in Bogor. More than 180 million Indonesians—88 percent—are Muslim, making this the most populous Islamic country in the world.

political and economic institutions. But the same surge of popular will that shoved Suharto aside also ended the steely controls he used to cap social unrest. Now the lid is off, said a Western diplomat in Jakarta, and "there is extraordinary trauma and a clashing of mental tectonic plates" that could pull the country apart.

At 181 million, Indonesia has the largest population of Muslims in the world, making it inevitable that its road to the future run through the country's Islamic identity. I began to appreciate what such numbers mean when I visited Kediri, a dusty crossroads city in East Java's volcano-ringed farming belt, and watched tens of thousands of the faithful stream into a narrow, maze-like lane to attend the annual convention of Nahdlatul Ulama, Indonesia's biggest Muslim organization.

A leaden sky was spitting rain the temperature of bath water when I squeezed into the slow-moving throng. Never much for crowds, I had decided to call it quits when a muscular young man in wraparound sunglasses appeared at my right elbow.

"Hello, Mister!" he said—the universal greeting for foreigners. His name was Yudha. "I'm a victim of foreign corporate reorganization!" he said, adding that unrest in nearby Surabaya, Java's industrial second city, had prompted his European employer to pull out.

Numerous Indonesians facing hard times had found their anchor in Islam. "Something to hang on to," said a Muslim friend in Jakarta, "and a backlash against Western influence," which was washing through the culture and widely blamed for encouraging antisocial behavior.

Like many Muslims I met, Yudha was a thoughtful, generous person, and with him in the lead, we reached "convention central" in no time, a big white tent in a soggy field, where Abdurrahman Wahid, the country's first democratically selected president and a former Nahdlatul Ulama chairman, was speaking.

Waves of polite laughter rippled through the crowd, and Wahid's constituents seemed delighted with his promises to bind the country together with renewed respect for cultural diversity and human rights. Yet many Indonesians saw his inability to stem terrorism as encouraging the forces of disintegration.

When I spoke with Gus Maksum Djauhari, who heads a local Islamic boarding school, he assured me there was no cause for alarm. "God willing, we can now have unity in diversity," he said, limning Indonesia's founding motto, "with a big sense of national pride." With Wahid at the helm, he said, government could finally rally the teachings of Islam as "a potent force for character building."

But the mingling of mosque and state worries many moderate Muslims, who, though still probably in the majority (reliable numbers are hard to come by), are wary of the inroads of Islamic fundamentalism. Wardah Hafidz, a leading advocate for the urban poor, told me that a growing number of female office workers had adopted the *jilbab*, or Islamic head scarf, which she saw as a symbol of how women in particular were caught in the middle. "They want to act in society," she said, "but are made to feel they're not good Muslims if they do."

The line between Islam as a fashion statement and as a deeply held belief can be a blurry one, but according to Mochtar Buchori, a member of the

Dewan Perwakilan Rakyat, Indonesia's parliament, the fundamentalist drift raises a question that few people are willing to talk about openly. "What kind of Islam are we going to have as the mainstream?" said Buchori. "If we're heading for a hard-line Islamic civilization, this country is really going to disintegrate."

I got a glimpse of what such chaos might be like in the old trading port of Makassar at the southwestern tip of Sulawesi the night I boarded a passenger ship called the Bukit Siguntang, bound for the remote Banda Islands. Under floodlights police armed with automatic weapons prodded travelers up the packed gangway or pulled them aside to search their luggage for guns or knives. Security was tight because the ship would first stop in Ambon, the city in the southern Moluccas where the worst of the fighting between Christians and Muslims had taken place.

Not thrilled about traveling such treacherous waters, I was nonetheless determined to see the Bandas because of their central role in shaping early Indonesia. In the 17th century this tiny subset of the Spice Islands was the center of European efforts to monopolize the trade in nutmeg, prized in pre-refrigeration Europe for preserving meats and wrongly thought to ward off plague. Most intriguing was an obscure 1667 treaty that capped off a "spice war" with a novel arrangement: England would swap its piece of the Bandas for an isolated Dutch trading post, the island where I live—Manhattan.

So to prove to myself that even in middle age curiosity can trump raw fear (and because airports were closed), I elbowed my way on board. There I made an unsettling discovery: My friend Norman Wibowo and I would be sharing the ride with 600 members of a militant Islamic group called the Laskar Jihad. Reports I had seen in which the Jihad allegedly had vowed to defend Muslims in Ambon by cleansing the area of Christians flickered through my mind. Since all *bule*—white people—were automatically "Christian" hereabouts, and Norman was in fact one, I was now truly worried.

The dim companionway was clogged with the Jihad, young men with prayer caps and scraggly chin whiskers, looking hollow-eyed and severe.

Locked in my tiny cabin, I entertained unmanly thoughts of jumping ship. But in the morning light, as I picked my way along the corridor, the Jihad looked like kids away from home for the first time, awkward, a little malnourished, and slightly less dangerous than teenagers waiting in line for a rock concert.

From the bridge the Banda Sea, broad and inky blue, combed along in luminous sunshine, but a dispute was brewing on board. Chief Officer Andre Pontoh said Jihad leaders had accused him of a grave error—posting the wrong times for the five daily prayers when devout Muslims are required to bend toward Mecca. They were wrong—the veteran seaman had carefully calculated the schedule according to the ship's position. That didn't matter. On a recent trip a minor dispute had sparked a shipboard riot, and angry young men had lined up at the bridge windows to jeer at Christian crew members and run fingers across their throats.

"That man saved us!" said Pontoh, nodding at an avuncular gentleman in a baseball cap whose name was Abdurrachman Khoe. A frequent passenger and a Muslim leader in Ambon, Khoe had used the ship's public address system to calm the rioters.

Locked in my tiny cabin, I entertained unmanly thoughts of jumping ship.

What do the Laskar Jihad intend to do in Ambon? I asked him. Although physical attacks on Muslim villages and mosques in the Christian-dominated city had escalated, Khoe assured me they were bent not on vengeance but on a purely social mission to aid downtrodden Muslims.

That last point was debatable, but it was true that the Moluccas were now so tense that *habis,* slang for annihilation, awaited Muslims caught in Christian strongholds and vice versa. The flood of refugees fleeing the turmoil had further complicated travel in a country that is largely water. All the ships were overcrowded and worked to the point of breakdown, but, said Pontoh, "If we don't sell tickets, people burn our ticket offices down!"

Yet I marveled at how most of the ship's passengers went quietly about their routines, taking the risks in stride. That afternoon Pontoh and I visited the cabin of a pearl trader, a snaggletoothed man in a check-

A stained and wrinkled image of paradise fills the wall behind a solitary diner in Larantuka, a port on Flores. Similarly tattered, Indonesia's union may yet survive—if its diverse peoples find equitable ways to share the burdens and opportunities of rebuilding their society.

ered sarong who presided over a box of plastic baggies bulging with pearls from the Arafura Sea.

"*Bagus*—Excellent," he said, holding aloft a lustrous black pearl the size of a pea. As a boy I'd read tales of wild, seagoing corsairs and smugglers of tropical islands, and for a moment I was caught up in the romance until the door opened. In shot a pair of heads, two rough-looking characters who surveyed the scene with sharklike smiles. The trader slammed the door in their faces and locked it.

"So I don't get murdered," he said.

The next day at noon we sailed into Banadaira, the Bandas' main harbor, gliding under the towering green cone of its sentinel volcano. I was relieved to finally be there but disheartened that the rage sweeping other parts of Indonesia had found this remote spot too, as Tanya Alwi, an environmental activist, was quick to point out. Tanya, whose family ran the local hotel, said an argument between a village headman, a Christian, and a teenager, a Muslim, had unspooled, and 28 Christian homes went up in flame in a single night.

"One thug said to me, 'Be grateful we purified your island,'" said Tanya, with a mirthless giggle. A Muslim *hajja*, who had made several pilgrimages to Mecca, Tanya abhorred the violence. And it hadn't been good for business: I was the first guest to stay at her Dutch colonial-style hotel in two years.

That evening Tanya and I sat on the battlements of Benteng Belgica, a Dutch fort built in the high days of the nutmeg trade, as the orange-white sunset blazed around us. "I'll swap you a building lot over there," she said, pointing toward the glimmering volcano, "for your apartment in Manhattan!" I appreciated her effort to lighten the mood by recapitulating local history, but I declined. The Bandas were absolutely gorgeous but too rough a neighborhood for your average New Yorker. □

Two Warlords

BY EDWARD GIRARDET

■ *Veteran Afghan correspondent Ed Girardet was on assignment for* National Geographic *in early September 2001 when he crossed paths with two Arab television journalists on their way to meet Ahmad Shah Massoud, commander of the Northern Alliance. Several days later, as they were interviewing Massoud, the two detonated a bomb in their camera, killing him. Two days later came the attack on the World Trade Center and the Pentagon. Probably related, the two attacks lead back to Osama bin Laden, whom Girardet encountered several times in Afghanistan. His impressions of the two men—Massoud and bin Laden—appear in this excerpt.*

Edward Girardet, "Eyewitness Afghanistan,"
Dec. 2001, pp. 130-137

It was midafternoon when we pulled into the parched, dust-blown settlement of Khvajeh Baha od Din in northern Afghanistan. Once a bleak caravansary for nomads and traders, Khvajeh Baha od Din in early September served as the bustling rear supply base for the forces of Afghanistan's leading anti-Taliban commander, Ahmad Shah Massoud. I had returned to Afghanistan to explore the impact of 23 straight years of war on the country and its people, traveling with an old friend, Mohammad Shuaib, my interpreter and guide. We drove up to a guesthouse with a courtyard and neatly planted flowers, operated by the foreign ministry of Massoud's Northern Alliance. Asim Suhail, a young official wearing pressed jeans and shirt and tie with a blazer, looked up from his computer. As with all electrical appliances in a country debilitated by years of war and neglect, it only worked when the diesel generator was running. It also had to be covered constantly with a muslin cloth because of the ever penetrating dust. Asim immediately called for tea, studied our letters of recommendation, and smiled.

"Of course, I know who you are and that you were coming."

There were several other journalists in the compound. A Russian from Prague-based Radio Liberty, an Uzbek from the London-based Institute for War and Peace Reporting, two French reporters, and two Arabs. There was also a group of American women on a fact-finding trip on the status of women in Afghanistan for the Feminist Majority in the United States.

MICHAEL YAMASHITA

With a prayer at sunrise, the late Ahmad Shah Massoud of the Northern Alliance led his men in worship and in war.

I was somewhat surprised to see the Arabs, wearing jeans and T-shirts and surrounded by backpacks with the usual equipment of a television team. One didn't normally find Arab journalists reporting from the 15 percent of the country—mainly the north, with pockets of resistance elsewhere—held by groups opposing the Taliban. Given the large number of Islamic radicals from the Middle East and North Africa supporting the Taliban in Afghanistan, people in the opposition-held areas regarded Arabs with suspicion.

Curious, I asked them where they were from. "Morocco," said the older one, a somewhat severe man in his mid-30s with short hair and wire-rimmed glasses. "We're doing a TV report." When I asked which network, he shrugged: "A Middle Eastern one." He then withdrew to his room next to Shuaib's and mine. Asim later told me that they carried Belgian passports and had come with credentials issued by a London-based Islamic group. For the next three days, we lived side by side but saw little of them.

Shuaib and I had good connections with the Northern Alliance, also known as the United Front, and had radioed ahead requesting a meeting with Massoud. As the first American journalist, in 1981, to have interviewed Massoud, I had come to know him well. An ethnic Tajik from the Panjshir Valley, known as the Lion of Panjshir, he was in his late 40s, with a beard, sharply defined Roman nose, and broad, ready smile. He wore a Palestinian-style scarf and was never without a *pakol*, the floppy woolen cap that had become the trademark of the *mujahidin* (holy warriors) during their resistance against the Soviets in the 1980s.

With the Taliban and their radical Muslim backers, including the reclusive Saudi millionaire Osama bin Laden, seeking to create the world's first "pure" Islamic state by destroying what remains of Afghanistan's 3,500-year-old cultural identity, many Afghans regarded Massoud as the only man capable of someday uniting the various factions against the Taliban as they had once been united against the Soviets.

I wanted to discuss with him the impact of more than two decades of war. I also wanted further insight into what impelled the Taliban, whose support came not only from Afghanistan's Pashtun (also called Pathan) majority but also from an Islamic "foreign legion" of volunteers from Pakistan, the Middle East, and other parts of the Muslim world. These outsiders were believed to constitute about a third of the Taliban's fighting force.

I had interviewed Massoud on numerous occasions since 1981. Sometimes we met by gas lamp in hidden caves or shrapnel-scarred farmhouses among the side valleys of the Panjshir, with Soviet bombs and rockets crashing barely several hundred yards away. With the takeover of Kabul by the mujahidin in 1992, three years after the Soviets pulled out, we met in more comfortable surroundings in safe houses dotted around the city. The rockets still thudded around us, but this time fired by rival factions, including, later, the Taliban. Ironically, it was during the years following the Soviet withdrawal, when Massoud couldn't control mujahidin infighting, that Kabul absorbed the greatest amount of damage, which virtually annihilated the city.

During one of our interviews over green tea and sugared almonds sometime in the mid-1990s, I asked Massoud what he wanted to do when the war finally ended. As usual we conversed in a combination of French and Dari, the Persian dialect spoken by many Afghans. "Read Persian poetry," he said, "and then go somewhere where there are no damn mountains."

Soon after Shuaib and I arrived in Khvajeh Baha od Din, heavy sand clouds began to envelop the mountains from the west—one of the results of a punishing three-year drought that has turned much of northern, central, and western Afghanistan into a dust bowl, with abandoned villages and arid fields. Combined with the terrible effects of seemingly endless war, Afghanistan was on the edge of famine. The UN, Oxfam, and other aid agencies had warned that the country could develop into a catastrophic humanitarian disaster by the onset of winter. Since spring of last year, when the rains had failed yet again, hundreds of thousands of Afghans had fled to towns inside the country or across the border into Pakistan and Iran in search of food and shelter. To survive, many had sold their remaining

Called the Lion of Panjshir for his tenacious defense of Afghanistan's most strategic valley during the Soviet war, Ahmad Shah Massoud led the last major military force opposing the Taliban until September, 2001. He was killed by assassins posing as television journalists.

livestock and belongings, even their daughters in marriage—some as young as eight or nine. Now, with the sand reducing visibility to less than 500 yards, the helicopters could not operate, and Massoud could not fly in from wherever he was. (Massoud's movements were always kept secret until the last moment for security reasons.)

"It could last a day, but it could drag on longer," said Mohammad Kamaludin, head of reconstruction for the Northern Alliance. He had come to Khvajeh Baha od Din in search of money for a slew of projects he had designed. "Everyone is obsessed by the war, but we must rebuild in those areas where there is no fighting," he told me. Numerous roads, irrigation canals, and other essential infrastructure were simply falling into dereliction for lack of maintenance. "If we do nothing now, there will be nothing left," he lamented.

When it was obvious that the dust was not going to clear, Shuaib and I decided to leave. We would catch up with Massoud later. We were impatient to reach the Panjshir to see how things had changed in this 70-mile-long fertile valley once renowned for its mulberry and apricot trees. During the Soviet war many of its towns, villages, and irrigation ducts had been destroyed, rebuilt, destroyed again, and rebuilt again. Parts were also damaged during the more recent fighting between the Northern Alliance and the Taliban—until Massoud blew up the entrance to the valley, making it impossible for the Taliban fighters to enter by road.

REZA

Most, but not all, of the other journalists were also anxious to leave. Before heading off that morning, I spoke with one of the Moroccans as he returned from his morning ablutions, a towel carefully draped over his head to protect him from the sand. "Will you try and go?" I asked. "This dust could persist for days."

No, he answered. "We'll wait for Massoud." Back in Islamabad less than a week later, on September 9, I heard the grim news over the BBC. An assassination attempt had been made against Massoud by two Arabs posing as journalists, the same two Moroccans I had met in Khvajeh Baha od Din. They were said to have packed explosives to their bodies as well as in the camera. One of them triggered the device as Massoud settled down for the interview. The Arabs reportedly died immediately as did Asim, the young foreign ministry official who had greeted us on our arrival. Massoud was dead, came a report. He was alive, came another.

Two days later the world's attention turned to the attacks on the World Trade Center and the Pentagon. It was clear to me that the timing of the attempt on Massoud's life was no coincidence. On September 15, Northern Alliance sources announced that Massoud had died of his wounds, and the next day Massoud was laid to rest as a hero at a funeral attended by thousands of followers in the Panjshir. An extraordinary era of hope and defiance had come to an end. It was also an era that heralded a new and uncertain future for Afghanistan.

This was my 40th-odd trip as a journalist to this Central Asian nation of mountains and deserts since I first began covering Afghanistan's dragging civil war, which erupted in Kabul in the summer of 1978. Three months before the Soviet invasion in December 1979, I had found myself in Kabul reporting what was then a low-key but steadily expanding conflict. Once the Soviets rolled in, I made repeated trips to the region, often traveling clandestinely with the mujahidin.

And once the Soviets came, so eventually did the U.S., with backing for the mujahidin to the tune of three billion dollars—funneled through Pakistan's military intelligence, which favored Pashtun-dominated fundamentalist resistance groups; little went to Tajik or Uzbek commanders such as Massoud. Wittingly or not, the U.S. intervention aimed at ousting the Red Army also helped Arab and other foreign Islamic militants establish themselves in Pakistan, creating a breeding ground for the Taliban's rank and file.

During the latter years of the Soviet occupation it was not uncommon to run into Islamic militants who had come to Afghanistan for what they saw as the only *jihad* (holy war) in the world. Armed with cash, but not necessarily military skill, they proclaimed a deep hatred for the U.S., Israel, and the "decadent" West. Desperately seeking to prove themselves as "soldiers of God," they tended to volunteer for frontline combat against the Soviets, regardless of risk. The Afghans, never without a sense of humor, often ridiculed them for wanting to get killed and being quite *diwana* (the Persian word for "silly" or "crazy") about it, too.

In 1996 the Taliban took control of Kabul and then proceeded to occupy most of the country. Initially the security offered by the Taliban appealed to many Afghans tired of war. After the mujahidin takeover in 1992 warlords and armed gangs had set up roadblocks to "tax" travelers or, quite simply, to rob people at gunpoint. In the name of Allah, the Taliban halted this activity by confiscating weapons and punishing culprits by executing them or chopping off limbs. As the Taliban soon boasted without exaggeration, their authority enabled traders to travel from one end of Afghanistan to the other with a "truckload of gold" without being stopped.

This new sense of law and order, which many Afghans had not known for nearly 20 years, was evident when I visited Kabul in 1997. Driving to the Pakistani border, I came across only a handful of checkpoints, where I was frisked for weapons and my papers were examined. Earlier trips along the same route during the mujahidin era had required a multitude of stops where armed men, sometimes local villagers, placed a "toll" rope across the road and demanded some form of *baksheesh*, or gifts.

By the time I returned last year, I found that bitter resentment had taken hold among Afghans against the Taliban's increasingly totalitarian Islamic policies, particularly in urban areas such as Kabul, Herat, and Jalalabad. Minority groups—Tajik and Uzbek prime among them—complained about discrimination, beatings, and even killings. Aid agencies particularly criticized the regime for its complete disregard for the plight of ordinary civilians and populations at risk; widows, for example, were prevented from working. Only in the tribal Pashtun areas of the southern and eastern parts of Afghanistan did the Taliban appear to retain considerable public support. But even this was beginning to erode. In some eastern provinces

Taking power in 1996, the Taliban soon forbade women from working and from leaving home unescorted and uncovered. Girls no longer attended school, and boys often got no education either; most teachers in Afghanistan were women. Almost 70 percent of Afghans are illiterate.

sporadic but growing armed resistance was emerging against the Taliban leadership, based in the southern city of Kandahar. Some of the Pashtun commanders had joined the Taliban opposition, giving the Northern Alliance a broader—but still not inclusive—representation of Afghanistan's ethnic and tribal groups.

Ever since Arabs first began converging on Afghanistan in support of the anti-Soviet jihad, many Afghans had been offended by the way the Taliban's foreign Muslims, men like Osama bin Laden, treated them as ignorant provincials who did not understand what "true" Islam was all about. They had also chafed at edicts designed to curtail the country's deep-rooted sense of culture and tradition, including a profound love for music and poetry—edicts banning everything from kite flying and music cassettes to women walking with loud shoes.

I first met bin Laden in February 1989, during the week in which the Soviets pulled out of Afghanistan. He was operating in the eastern mountains with a group of volunteers, mainly Arabs with a few Afghans. The factions that had united to push out the Soviets had already trained their guns on each other in a bid to gain control of the countryside; others were trying to dislodge the communist regime that still held Kabul, despite the Soviet withdrawal. Traveling with Afghan mujahidin, I was scouting for a television documentary among the frontline positions manned by Arabs on the outskirts of Jalalabad.

A tall, bearded man flanked by armed men, stepped up to me demanding—in good English, with a slight American accent—to know who I was and what I, a *kafir* (infidel), was doing in Afghanistan. For the next 45 minutes we had a heated debate about the war, religion, and foreigners. Haughty, self-righteous, and utterly sure of himself, he proceeded to lambaste the West for its feebleness and lack of moral conviction. When I pointed out that Western journalists and aid workers had been present in Afghanistan since the early days of the war, a time when no Arabs were to be seen, he spat dismissively. Finally he announced

MICHAEL YAMASHITA

that if I returned, he would kill me. A week later I did return, with mujahidin and a film crew, as communist troops on the other side of the ridge were pounding the position with mortar bombs.

On seeing me again as I pulled up at his trenches, the tall Arab screamed at me. The next thing I knew, Arabs and Afghans—both supposedly fighting on the same side against the communists—had raised their guns at each other. One of the Arab militants cocked his AK-47, thrusting it into the back of the cameraman. "We will kill you. We will kill you all," he shrieked. At this point the Afghan commander I was with intervened, pleading that such anger was not good for Islam. Cautiously, we pulled back. It was several years before I learned that the tall man who threatened to kill me was Osama bin Laden. □

INDEX

STAFF FOR THIS BOOK

EDITORIAL
DON BELT Editor in Chief
PETER MILLER Senior Editor
MEGHAN ST. JOHN Assistant Editor
CATHLEEN S. LINEBERRY Assistant Editor
LESLEY B. ROGERS Director of Research
ANNE MARIE HOUPPERT Indexer
ALEX NOVAK Project Manager

DESIGN
CONNIE PHELPS
Design Director,
National Geographic Magazine
MARIANNE KOSZORUS
Design Director,
National Geographic Book Division
BOB GRAY Art Director
JENNIFER CHRISTIANSEN Designer

ILLUSTRATIONS
SUSAN WELCHMAN Illustrations Editor
SARA WICKWARE Illustrations Assistant
MAURA MULVIHILL Image Collection
BETTY BEHNKE Image Collection
BILL BONNER Image Collection
CARL MEHLER Director of Maps

PRODUCTION
GARY COLBERT Production Manager
CHRIS BROWN Manufacturing Manager

TROOPS OUTSIDE FARAH, AFGHANISTAN SALUTE THE
1931-32 CITROËN-HAARDT TRANS-ASIATIC EXPEDITION
AS IT THUNDERS ALONG A ROUTE FROM THE MEDITER-
RANEAN TO THE YELLOW SEA. NATIONAL GEOGRAPHIC'S
MAYNARD OWEN WILLIAMS WAS THE ONLY JOURNALIST
INVITED TO JOIN THE EXPEDITION.
PHOTOGRAPH BY MAYNARD OWEN WILLIAMS—1931

PUBLISHED BY THE NATIONAL GEOGRAPHIC SOCIETY

JOHN M. FAHEY, JR.
President and Chief Executive Officer

GILBERT M. GROSVENOR
Chairman of the Board

WILLIAM L. ALLEN
Editor in Chief, National Geographic Magazine

NINA D. HOFFMAN
President, Books and School Publishing

KEVIN MULROY
Editor in Chief, National Geographic Book Division

DON BELT

A native of South Carolina, National Geographic *Senior Editor Don Belt has traveled the world to report for the magazine's readers on subjects as diverse as Sweden, Siberia's Lake Baikal, Baja California, the Russian Arctic, and Georgia's Chattooga River. In the past decade he has concentrated on the Middle East, traveling to the region more than a dozen times while authoring articles on Lawrence of Arabia, Petra, the Golan Heights, Israel's Galilee region, and other subjects from the Muslim world. He has served as the magazine's Middle East specialist since 1994. With his wife,* National Geographic *photographer Annie Griffiths Belt, and his children, Lily and Charlie, Belt makes his home near a soccer field in northern Virginia.*

One of the world's largest nonprofit scientific and educational organizations, the National Geographic Society was founded in 1888 "for the increase and diffusion of geographic knowledge." Fulfilling this mission, the Society educates and inspires millions every day through its magazines, books, television programs, videos, maps and atlases, research grants, the National Geographic Bee, teacher workshops, and innovative classroom materials. The Society is supported through membership dues, charitable gifts, and income from the sale of its educational products. This support is vital to National Geographic's mission to increase global understanding and promote conservation of our planet through exploration, research, and education.

For more information, please call 1-800-NGS LINE (647-5463) or write to the following address:

National Geographic Society
1145 17th Street N.W.
Washington, D.C. 20036-4688 U.S.A.

Visit the Society's Web site at **www.nationalgeographic.com**.

ISBN 0-7922-6894-6

Library of Congress Cataloging-in-Publication Data applied for.